FOR USE WITH ACCPAC SIMPLY ACCOUNTING VERSION

TEACH YOURSELF

ACCPAC® Simply Accounting
for
Windows®

M. PURBHOO   D. PURBHOO

Addison Wesley Publishers

Don Mills, Ontario • Reading, Massachusetts
Menlo Park, California • New York • Wokingham, England
Amsterdam • Bonn • Sydney • Tokyo
Madrid • San Juan

PROJECT EDITOR: Heather Rignanesi
COPY EDITOR: Jennifer Dennison
COVER DESIGN: Anthony Leung
LAYOUT: Anthony Leung

Canadian Cataloguing in Publication Data

Purbhoo, Mary, 1949-

Teach yourself ACCPAC Simply Accounting for Windows

Includes computer disks.
Includes index.
ISBN 0-201-60198-2 (set)   ISBN 0-201-60196-6
ISBN 0-201-60197-4 (5.25" disk)
ISBN 0-201-60203-2 (3.5" disk)

1. ACCPAC Simply Accounting (Computer program).
2. Accounting - Computer program.
3. Windows (Computer programs). I. Purbhoo, D. (Dhirajlal).   II. Title.

HF5679.P87 1992   657'.0285'5369
C92-093468-4

Acknowledgements

We want to thank Mary Watson at Computer Associates for continuing to provide her usual professional and caring support for our work. In working with her over the years on our various projects, we have always valued her guidance and friendship.

Freda Lofts, Business Consultant from the Board of Education for the City of Toronto, and Phil Maturi, Department Head at the City Adult Learning Centre, have been very helpful by encouraging and arranging workshops for teachers. We appreciate their assistance in promoting our work.

We appreciate the contribution that Jennifer Dennison has made to this book. Her patient editing of the manuscript has resulted in a better book.

We also want to acknowledge present and former staff at Addison-Wesley - Andrea Aris, Beth Bruder, Roberta Dick, Paula Goepfert, Jackie Gross, Carolyn Hanover, Susan Howell, Cindy Kantor, Melanie Pequeux, Heather Rignanesi and Ron Doleman, our mentor. Over the past five years they have shown complete confidence in our work, and have given us both support and friendship. Extra credit goes to Anthony Leung whose conscientious and professional design work have helped to keep the entire project on schedule. Our acknowledgements would be incomplete without recognizing the secretarial, marketing and administrative staff. They too have helped to create the warm and caring working environment for us at Addison Wesley.

And finally, we want to thank our children - Kevin for letting us have just enough computer time to finish this project and Adrienne for always being there. This book is dedicated to them.

Preface

Teach Yourself ACCPAC Simply Accounting for Windows has been written to help you learn this latest version of the popular accounting software from Computer Associates. It includes the Goods and Services Tax (GST) and Employer Health Tax (EHT) for Ontario, and follows the same approach as our other workbooks.

The twelve accounting applications in the Workbook cover all six ledgers of the ACCPAC Simply Accounting program: General, Payables, Receivables, Payroll, Inventory, and Project (Jobcost). Each journal and jobcosting is introduced in a separate application, with a detailed demonstration of keystrokes and matching screens for each new type of sample transaction. These applications have been set up in advance so that you can begin to work with the software immediately.

The eighth application, Chapter 9 (Artistic Interiors), is a comprehensive introduction to setting up a computerized accounting system using ACCPAC Simply Accounting. Again, detailed instructions are given. The authors walk you through each step as you learn to convert, design and implement a complete accounting system. Input forms are provided in Appendix A to assist with the organizing and entering of the accounting data. Additional applications dealing with advanced level topics have also been set up in advance.

The final application, Chapter 14 (Pacific Chalet) offers another opportunity to convert a manual accounting system to a computerized one. This time you are asked to enter accounting transactions using descriptive and realistic source documents to give you the "feel". of actual company transactions.

At the end of most application you will find one or more case problems. These are provided to supplement and extend the principles covered in the applications.

A number of appendices have been included for reference or further study. Appendix A includes a complete set of input forms to use for setting up a company's computerized accounting system. The systems and control approach is further illustrated in Appendix B, where there is a discussion on how ACCPAC Simply Accounting reports can be integrated with other software for analysis and decision making. A section for correcting errors after posting is provided in Appendix C.

Using This Book

The accounting applications in this Workbook were prepared using the **Version 1.0A** of the ACCPAC Simply Accounting software published by Computer Associates International, Inc. If you are using a subsequent version of the software, you may find some changes in screens and keystrokes. It is important to refer to your user's guide, readme files, update notices and bulletins when you work with your later version of the software.

To take advantage of the keystrokes and screens provided in this workbook you should be using an IBM personal computer or compatible with a hard disk system and single or dual floppy drives, or a network system. Windows must be installed. You will need a copy of the licensed ACCPAC Simply Accounting software or access to that software through a network environment. Each user must have a formatted data disk or a pseudo data disk on a network system, with the correct attributes and permissions for each user. For network systems, the author's recommend that users work with the facilitator, site-administrator or superuser of the system under consideration.

In addition, users should have access to a standard accounting text, which they can consult when they need to review accounting principles. The Workbook does provide the user with some accounting principles and procedures, but it is not intended to replace the broadness and depth of all the principles covered in most standard accounting texts. Copies of the ACCPAC Simply Accounting User's Guide, should be available to consult with when computer and software assistance is needed.

The Workbook is as simple and straightforward as we could make it, but users will still need some familiarity with computers before they work through it. They should know how to turn on the computer and printer. They should also know how to load, retrieve, save, finish and backup files. Their lives will be easier still if they have acquired some of the fundamentals of troubleshooting.

Note on Date Restrictions

Educational Versions of the ACCPAC Simply Accounting software restrict the using date. You will not be able to go beyond a given date, usually the year preceding the actual calendar year. All applications in this book therefore do not go beyond December 31, 1991 so that users of both educational and non-educational versions will be able to complete the applications.

Contents

Preface
Using This Book

PART ONE

Getting Started

CHAPTER ONE

Getting Started

OBJECTIVES

Upon completion of this chapter, you will be able to:

1. *install* the ACCPAC Simply Accounting program under Windows;
2. *access* the ACCPAC Simply Accounting program;
3. *access* the data files for a business;
4. *save* your work;
5. *finish* your session;
6. *back up* your session.

Files and Abbreviations

The applications in this workbook were prepared using version 1.0A of the ACCPAC Simply Accounting software package produced by Computer Associates International, Inc. Subsequent versions of the software may have changes in screens or keystrokes. Income tax tables change regularly; the most recent ones will be used in later versions of the software. If you are using the **educational version** of the software, you will not be able to go beyond a certain date when entering accounting transactions.

The instructions in this workbook have been written for a stand-alone IBM-PC or compatible computer, with a hard disk drive and single or dual floppy disk drives. Windows should be correctly installed on your hard disk. Your printers are installed and accessible through the Windows program. Refer to your DOS and Windows manuals for assistance with these procedures.

NOTES:
The Pacific Chalet file is not set up in advance for you. You must establish that file on your own.

This workbook reflects the authors' approach to working with ACCPAC Simply Accounting. There are alternative approaches to setting up company accounts and to working with the software. Refer to your ACCPAC Simply Accounting, MS-DOS, PC-DOS and Windows manuals for further details.

APPLICATION FILES

Company	Filename	Chapter
Pilot Plumbing	pilot.asc	3
Carousel Café	carousel.asc	4
Wallstreet Wizard Inc.	wizard.asc	5
Celine's Cleaners	celine.asc	6
Classic Clothes	classic.asc	7
Careful Carpenters	careful.asc	8
Melody Music Centre	melody.asc	9
Artistic Interiors	art-oct.asc	10
	art-nov.asc	10
	art-dec.asc	10
	art-adj.asc	10
Manga Corporation	manga.asc	11
Carefree Carpets	carefree.asc	12
Frame-Around Manufacturing Co.	frame.asc	13
Pacific Chalet	pacific.asc	14

The applications increase in complexity, with each one introducing new ledgers, as shown in the following chart.

APPLICATION	GL	AP	AR	PAY	INV	JC	
			LEDGER USED				EXPORT
Pilot Plumbing	*						
Carousel Café	*	*					
Wallstreet Wizard Inc.	*	*	*				
Celine's Cleaners	*	*		*			
Classic Clothes	*	*	*		*		
Careful Carpenters	*						
Melody Music Centre	*	*	*	*	*	*	*
Artistic Interiors	*	*	*	*	*		
Manga Corporation	*						
Carefree Carpets	*						
Frame-Around Mfg. Co.	*						
Pacific Chalet	*	*	*	*			

Ledgers:

GL = General Ledger
AP = Accounts Payable
AR = Accounts Receivable
PAY = Payroll
INV = Inventory
JC = Jobcost (Project)

Export: Integrating accounting reports with word processing or spreadsheet applications (Appendix B)

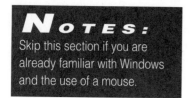
Some Windows and Mouse Basics

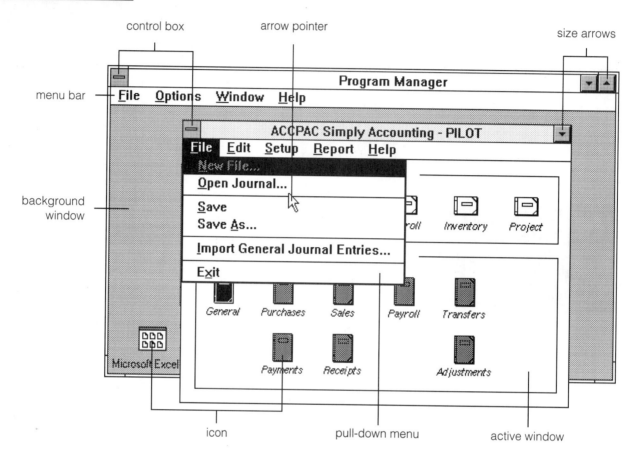

control box   arrow pointer   size arrows

menu bar

background window

icon   pull-down menu   active window

The **mouse** is used to move the cursor. When you move the mouse, an **arrow** or **pointer** moves to indicate the cursor placement. If you click (press) the left mouse button, the cursor will move to the location of the arrow (if this is a legitimate location for the cursor to be at the time). That is, you use the mouse to **click on** (point to and click) a screen location, item on a list, command or icon.

The arrow or pointer changes shape, depending upon what actions you may perform. When you are moving the mouse, it appears as an arrow or pointer. When you are in a field that can accept text, it appears as a long I **bar**. Clicking will change it to a flashing vertical line in a text field. When the computer is processing information and you are unable to perform any action, you will see an **hourglass**. This is your signal to wait.

An **icon** is a picture form of your program, file name or item.

The **menu bar** is the line of options at the top of each window. Each menu contains one or more commands or selections (the **pull-down menu**) and can be accessed by clicking on the menu name. Each window may have different menu selections, and the options in the pull-down menu may differ. To choose an option from the menu, click on the menu name and hold the mouse button down while moving down the options until the one you want is highlighted. Release the mouse button to activate the selection. If an option is dimmed, you will be unable to highlight or select it.

The **control box** ⊟ is situated in the upper left-hand corner of each window. It has its own pull-down menu, including the Close command. This box is used to close windows.

Size arrows are located in the upper right corner of the window. They can be used to make the window larger ▲ or to reduce the window to an icon at the bottom of the screen ▼. If the window is full screen size, it can be reduced with the ⬍ button. The size of a window can also be changed by dragging the side you want to move with the mouse. When the pointer changes to a two-sided arrow, the window size can be changed by dragging. The window size arrows are not needed for the applications in this workbook.

Dragging refers to the method of moving the mouse while holding the button down. As you drag through the options in a menu, each one will be successively highlighted or darkened. Dragging through text will highlight it. Point to the beginning of the text to be highlighted. Then click and hold the mouse button down while moving through the entire area that you want to highlight. Release the mouse button at the end of the area you want to highlight. You can highlight a single character or the entire contents of a field. The text will remain highlighted and can be edited by typing new text. It can be deleted by pressing the Back Space or the Delete key. Clicking on a different location will remove the highlighting.

When a window contains more information than can be displayed on the screen at once, the window will contain a scroll arrow in any corner or direction next to the hidden information (bottom or right sides of the window). Click on the arrow and hold the mouse button down to scroll the screen in the direction of the arrow you are on.

The **active window** is the one you are currently working in. If you click on an area outside the active window, on a background window, that one will become the one in the foreground. To return to your previous window, click on any part of it that is showing.

To **double-click** means to press the left mouse button twice quickly. This action can be used as a short-cut for opening and closing windows. Double-clicking on an icon or file name will open it. Double-clicking on the control box will close the window. For the sake of consistency, the menu approach to opening and closing will be used throughout this workbook.

NOTES:
Skip this section if your ACCPAC Simply Accounting program is already installed.

Installing ACCPAC Simply Accounting

Start the Windows program.

Choose Run from the pull-down menu under **File** in the Program Manager window. (This is the main opening window, which always appears first.) The following window appears:

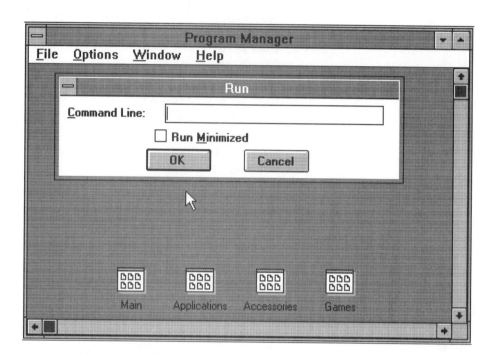

NOTES:
Your windows may look different from those shown in this chapter if you have different software applications loaded.

Insert your ACCPAC Simply Accounting program disk in your floppy disk drive A:

Type: `a:\install`   (If you are using drive B:, type `b:\install`)

Point to **OK** and click (**Click on OK**). The following screen appears:

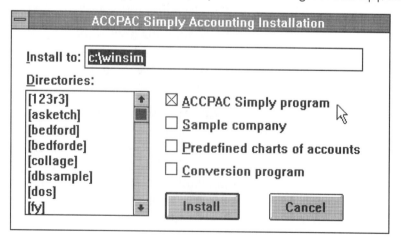

The default location for the program is your hard disk drive C: in a directory called WINSIM, which will be created by the Install program. You should accept this location unless you have partitioned your hard disk and you prefer another drive (e.g., d:\winsim). Enter the changes you need to reflect your own computer setup.

The ACCPAC program disk allows you to install some or all of the following:

- **ACCPAC Simply Program:** the ACCPAC Simply Accounting program that you will need to perform the accounting transactions for your company. Leave this box checked.

- **Predefined charts of accounts:** starter files that you will use to create company records for the Artistic Interiors and Pacific Chalet applications in this workbook or to create your own company files. Click on the box beside this entry to indicate that you want to install these files. These files will be stored in a subdirectory under WINSIM called SAMDATA. The install program creates this subdirectory for you automatically.

- **Sample Company:** a complete set of company records for the company described in the user's manual (Universal Construction). They will be placed in the subdirectory called SAMDATA if you install them. They are not needed to complete the applications in this workbook, so you do not need to check this box.

- **Conversion Program:** a program that can be used to convert accounting records that were created using previous non-Windows versions of the ACCPAC Bedford Integrated Accounting program into a form that can be used with the Simply Accounting Windows version. You do not need this program to complete the applications in this workbook, so you do not need to check this box.

Check the boxes for the files you wish to store on your hard disk now. You can add the rest later if you need them.

Point to **Install** and click (**Click on Install**) to begin the installation. Please wait. It will take some time to finish.

The Install program creates the following:

- WINSIM\, the main directory that contains the accounting program, the help file and two subdirectories;

- WINSIM\SAMDATA\, the subdirectory described above, containing the starter files and sample company;

- WINSIM\DATA\, the subdirectory that is initially empty but will be used to store data files for the applications;

- icons for the ACCPAC document in the Program Manager window and for the Simply Accounting program (and the Conversion program if it is installed).

After the installation is complete, you may see a brief Read file with recent announcements of program changes. Please read this information. After you have read the file, **choose Close** from the pull-down menu under ⊟ .

Backing Up Your Data Disk

HARD DRIVE

Before you begin the applications, you should make a backup copy of the data disk to work with. This way you will have the original for future use if you need to begin again.

Insert the data disk accompanying this workbook in your floppy disk drive a:.

If you are keeping your working copy of the data files on the hard disk under the WINSIM\DATA\ subdirectory created for this purpose, at the DOS prompt (>):

Type: `xcopy a:\*.* c:\winsim\data\*.*`

Substitute the appropriate drives and path for a: and c: above if your setup is different.

DUAL FLOPPY DRIVES

If you have floppy drives on your computer and you want to keep your data on a floppy, place the original in drive a: and a blank formatted disk in drive b:. At the DOS prompt (>):

Type: `xcopy a:\*.* b:\*.*`

This command will copy all the files from the original disk in drive a: to the working copy in drive b:. Label the newly created disk "Working copy - applications data disk."

Store your original data disk in a safe place.

NOTES:
The xcopy command is used instead of the copy command because the data files include a number of journals that are initially empty files. The copy command will not copy these empty files. You will not be able to access the data for an application unless all files are present in the same directory.

If you wanted to copy the files for one application at a time you could do so. The following instructions would copy only the files for Pilot Plumbing into your hard disk subdirectory.

With the original data disk in drive a:

Type: `xcopy a:\pilot.* c:\winsim\data\pilot.*`

Substitute the appropriate file path to suit your computer setup if necessary.

When copying other applications, substitute the filenames to replace "pilot" as indicated in the chart given on page 3.

Loading or Accessing Data Files

Start Windows from your opening menu or from DOS.

From the Program Manager window,

Click on the ACCPAC icon, holding the mouse down to see its pop-up menu.

Choose Restore from the menu to access the ACCPAC Simply Accounting Program icon.

Click on the Simply Accounting Program icon to highlight it as shown:

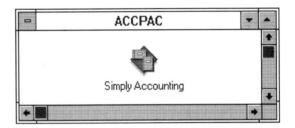

Choose Open from the pull-down menu under **File** to display the following screen:

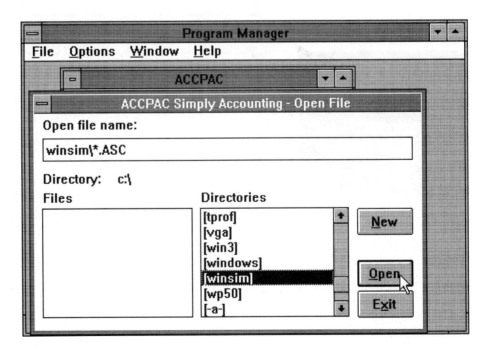

Your current directory is showing in the middle of the window. The screen above shows that C: is the active drive, and it lists the directories in C: The WINSIM directory is highlighted, ready to be opened. The highlighted directory is also listed in the Open file name field.

Click on Open to open the WINSIM directory. The DATA subdirectory is highlighted ready to be opened, as shown:

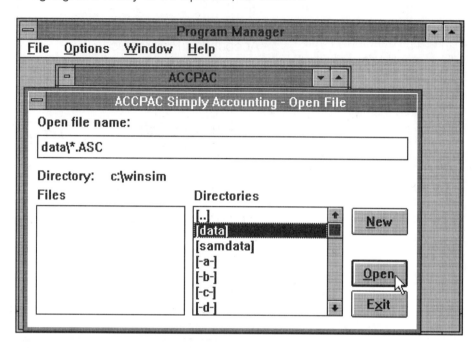

If your path is different, change directories when necessary by clicking on the directory (in the Directories box) in which your data files are located. If you have your data on a floppy, you would click on **[-a-]** or **[-b-]**. For hard disk drive storage, you would choose **[-c-]** (or another letter). **Click on Open** to open the directory.

You may need to open successive directories to reach your data location. For example, from C: you may have to follow the path of opening [..] to list the directories in the hard disk, then [winsim] to access the winsim directory, and then [data] to open the data subdirectory. Your path will then show as c:\winsim\data\.

The ACCPAC Simply Accounting files will be listed in the Files box as shown:

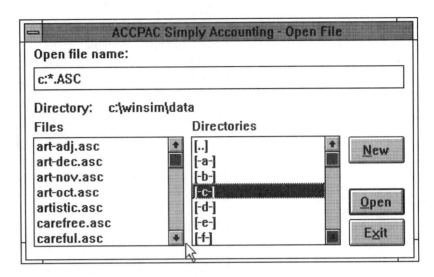

Click on the scroll arrow to move down the list of files.

Click on pilot.asc to highlight this file name. The filename **pilot.asc** will now appear in the Open file name field as shown:

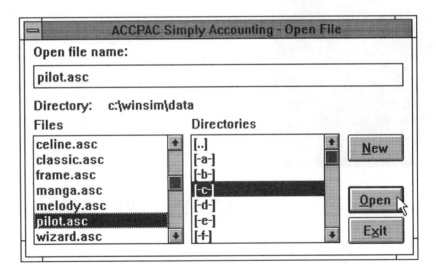

Click on Open to see the following screen prompting you to accept or change the using date:

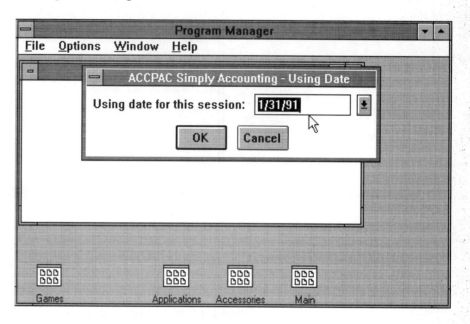

For other applications, substitute the appropriate filename for pilot.asc above.

Another approach to opening a data file is to type in the full path and name for the file you want to open in the Open file name field. For example,

Type: `c:\winsim\data\pilot.asc` if you are using a hard disk, or `b:\pilot.asc` if you are storing your data on a floppy disk.

Substitute the appropriate drive and path or directory for your own setup.

Saving Your Work

At any time while working in ACCPAC Simply Accounting, you can save your work.

Choose Save from the pull-down menu under **File**.

On a regular basis, you should also save a backup copy of your files.

Choose Save As from the pull-down menu under **File**.

When prompted for a filename, use a filename and location that is different from your working copy. For example,

Type: `a:\bakpilot.asc`

Substitute the name and path that is appropriate for your setup.

It is a good practice to keep backup copies on a separate disk from your working copy so that if your working disk is damaged, you can continue your work without starting over.

If you are replacing a previous backup copy with the same name, you will be asked to confirm that you want to replace the previous copy.

Click on Yes to confirm the replacement, or **click on No** to change the filename.

Finishing a Session

Choose Close from the pull-down menu under the control box ⊟ to close the journal input form or display window you are working in.

You will return to the main Ledger/Journal company window.

Choose Close from the pull-down menu under the control box ⊟ to close the Ledger/Journal company window.

Your work will be saved automatically again when you complete this step.

You should now be in the ACCPAC window.

Choose Close from the pull-down menu under ⊟ to close the ACCPAC window.

Choose Close from the pull-down menu under ⊟ to close the Program Manager window.

Click on OK to finish your Windows session and return to a DOS prompt or menu window.

You may now turn off your computer.

CHAPTER TWO
The Goods and Services Tax

OBJECTIVES

Upon completion of this chapter, you will be able to:
1. *understand* the terms relevant to the federal Goods and Services Tax;
2. *understand* the different methods of calculating the GST.

General Accounting Information

Definition of GST

The Goods and Services Tax is a compulsory tax, levied by the federal government on most goods and services in Canada. It replaces the old federal sales tax (regular and construction), which was applied mainly at the wholesale level to manufacturing and construction goods. The present Goods and Services Tax rate of seven percent applies at all levels. Retailers pay the GST to wholesalers and other vendors, but are allowed to deduct it from GST collected from customers. They remit GST owing to the Receiver General of Canada or claim a refund on a monthly or quarterly basis.

Provinces may or may not include GST in the price on which they calculate Provincial Sales Tax (PST). Provincial tax rates vary from province to province.

GST Registration

A business with annual sales exceeding $30 000 **must** register to apply the Goods and Services Tax. Registration is optional for those businesses whose annual sales are less than $30 000. Registration allows a business to recover any GST paid on purchases made.

Zero-Rated Goods and Services

Zero-rated goods and services are those on which the tax rate is zero. These goods include basic groceries, prescribed medical instruments and devices, prescribed drugs, exported goods and services, agricultural products, and fish products. A business selling only zero-rated goods and services is not able to collect GST from customers, but it can still claim a refund for GST paid for any purchases made for selling these zero-rated goods and services.

Tax-Exempted Goods and Services

Tax-exempted goods and services are those on which tax is not collected. These goods and services include health care, dental care, day care services and rents on residences. Most educational and financial services are also included in this group. These businesses are not able to claim refunds for GST they paid for any purchases made for selling tax-exempted goods and services.

Bank and Financial Institution Services

Most bank products and services are not taxable. Exceptions include safety deposit box rentals, custodial and safekeeping services, personalized cheques, fees for self-administered registered savings plans, payroll services, rentals of night depository, rentals of credit card imprinters and reconciliation of cheques.

Collecting the GST

The business must collect and remit the GST at regular intervals for those goods and services sold that are not zero-rated or tax exempt. The business has the option of filing returns monthly or quarterly.

Paying the GST

The business must pay the GST for purchases made specifically for business purposes unless the goods or services purchased are zero-rated or tax exempt. The business can use the GST paid as an input tax credit by subtracting the amount of GST paid from the amount of GST collected and remitting GST owing or claiming a refund. Purchases for personal use do not qualify as input tax credits.

Administering the GST

The federal government has approved two methods of administering the GST: the regular method and the quick method.

The Regular Method

The regular method of administering the GST requires the business to keep track of all GST paid for goods and services purchased from vendors and of all GST collected for goods and services sold to customers. It then deducts the GST paid from the GST collected and files for a refund or remits the balance owing to the Receiver General on a monthly or quarterly basis.

Accounting Examples Using the Regular Method (without PST):

SALES INVOICE:

Sold goods on account to customer for $200 plus GST collected, $14. Invoice total, $214.

Date	Particulars	Ref.	Debit	Credit
xx/xx	Accounts Receivable		214.00	
	GST Charged on Sales			14.00
	Revenue from Sales			200.00

PURCHASE INVOICE:

Purchased supplies on account from vendor for $300 plus GST paid, $21. Invoice total, $321.

Date	Particulars	Ref.	Debit	Credit
xx/xx	Supplies		300.00	
	GST Paid on Purchases		21.00	
	Accounts Payable			321.00

The Quick Method

NOTES:
Certain businesses may be allowed to use the streamlined accounting method, another simplified method for calculating GST. This method is not used in the applications in this workbook.

Some small businesses selling both taxable and zero-rated goods may opt to remit a flat tax payment ranging from one (1) percent to five (5) percent of their sales. This simplified system is available to manufacturers and retailers with sales up to a maximum of $200,000 and to grocery and convenience stores with sales up to $500,000. The GST is calculated by multiplying the total sales for the filing period (monthly or quarterly) by the flat tax rate for the type of business under consideration. A business is still able to deduct any GST paid on **capital expenditures** from the GST liability calculated using the flat tax rate.

The quick method decribed above is not available to legal, accounting or financial consulting businesses. Businesses allowed by Revenue Canada to use the quick method may change methods from year to year.

Accounting Examples Using the Quick Method (without PST):

CASH SALES OVER THE COUNTER:

Cash register tapes in a café for one week total $3 200 including GST collected for goods and services.

Date	Particulars	Ref.	Debit	Credit
xx/xx	Cash in Bank		3 200.00	
	Revenue from Services			3 200.00

PURCHASE INVOICES:

1. Food Inventory
   Purchased basic groceries for café services from vendor for $1 000 on account. Basic groceries are zero-rated goods.

Date	Particulars	Ref.	Debit	Credit
xx/xx	Food Inventory		1 000.00	
	Accounts Payable			1 000.00

2. Non-Capital Expenditures
   Purchased gasoline, oil and repair services for delivery van from vendor on account for $428, including $28 GST.

Date	Particulars	Ref.	Debit	Credit
xx/xx	Van Maintenance		428.00	
	Accounts Payable			428.00

3. Capital Expenditures
   Purchased pizza oven for café from vendor on account for $2 000 plus GST paid, $140. Invoice total, $2 140.

Date	Particulars	Ref.	Debit	Credit
xx/xx	Cafeteria Equipment		2 000.00	
	GST Paid on Capital Goods		140.00	
	Accounts Payable			2 140.00

Calculating the GST Refund or Remittance

The following examples are for a retailer who is filing quarterly and has maximum sales of $200 000.

1. The Regular Method

Quarterly Total Sales	$ 50 000.00	
GST Charged on Sales		$3 500.00
Less: GST Paid on Purchases		
Cash Register	$ 1 000.00	70.00
Inventory	24 871.42	1 741.00
Supplies	500.00	35.00
Payroll Services	200.00	14.00
Store Lease	3 000.00	210.00
GST Remittance		$1 430.00

2. The Quick Method

Quarterly Total Sales	$ 50 000.00	
Multiply by 3%		$1 500.00
Less: GST Paid on Capital Goods		
Cash Register	$ 1 000.00	70.00
GST Remittance		$1 430.00

GST Remittances and Refunds

GST Collected on Sales	>	GST Paid on Purchases	=	GST Owing	
GST Collected on Sales	<	GST Paid on Purchases	=	GST Refund	

The business must file a statement periodically that summarizes the amount of GST it has collected and the amount of GST it has paid. The business may file monthly, quarterly or yearly with quarterly instalments. It is to the advantage of a business, from a cash flow perspective, to file monthly if it is usually eligible for refunds.

Accounting Examples for Remittances and Refunds:

1. Quarterly Remittances

The example below shows how the GST accounts are cleared at the end of three months and a liability is set up to remit GST owing to the Receiver General of Canada.

Date	Particulars	Ref.	Debit	Credit
03/31	GST Charged on Sales		2 500.00	
	GST Paid on Purchases			700.00
	A/P - Receiver General			1 800.00
03/31	A/P - Receiver General		1 800.00	
	Cash in Bank			1 800.00

2. Quarterly Refunds

The example below shows how the GST accounts are cleared at the end of three months and a current asset is set up for a GST refund from the Receiver General of Canada.

Date	Particulars	Ref.	Debit	Credit
03/31	GST Charged on Sales		1 500.00	
	A/R - Receiver General		500.00	
	GST Paid on Purchases			2 000.00
04/15	Cash in Bank		500.00	
	A/R - Receiver General			500.00

NOTES:

The rules concerning the Goods and Services Tax may change periodically. Always refer to current GST guidelines if you encounter difficulties.

Applications

CHAPTER THREE
Pilot Plumbing

OBJECTIVES

Upon completion of this chapter, you will be able to:

1. *access* the ACCPAC Simply Accounting program;
2. *access* the data files for the business;
3. *open* the General Journal;
4. *enter* transactions in the General Journal;
5. *edit* and *review* General Journal transactions;
6. *post* transactions;
7. *display* General Ledger and General Journal reports;
8. *print* General Ledger and General Journal reports;
9. *advance* the using date;
10. *finish* an accounting session.

Company Information

Company Profile

Pilot Plumbing is a small plumbing business owned and operated by Larissa Koontz in the city of Calgary, her home town. After completing a plumbing program at a technical college in Lethbridge and apprenticing with a large plumbing firm, Ms. Koontz decided she would like to work independently. She started her business alone four years ago, and the demand for her excellent work has grown steadily. She now regularly hires two students to assist her during the busy summer months. Most of Pilot Plumbing's revenue comes from home renovation projects obtained through Koontz's contacts with contractors she met at college. In between these projects, Koontz provides maintenance and emergency repair services to a number of homes, apartment buildings and restaurants.

Ms. Koontz decided to use the ACCPAC Simply Accounting software after seeing it demonstrated at a "Computers for Business" show. On January 31, 1991, she converted all her manual accounting records to the ACCPAC Simply Accounting program, and she is ready to start in February.

The following information summarizes the conversion from the manual to the computerized accounting system:

1. Chart of Accounts;
2. Trial Balance;
3. Accounting Procedures.

PILOT PLUMBING
CHART OF ACCOUNTS

Assets
1080 Cash in Bank
1220 A/R - Carmen's Restaurant
1240 A/R - Willow Apartments
1300 Plumbing Supplies
1350 Plumbing Equipment
1400 Van

Liabilities
2100 Bank Loan
2200 A/P - Hudson's Plumbing
2220 A/P - Creative Bulletins
2240 A/P - Bell Canada
2260 A/P - Shaman's Serv Ctr
2600 GST Charged on Services
2610 GST Paid on Purchases
2630 GST Owing (Refund)

Equity
3100 L. Koontz, Capital
3200 L. Koontz, Drawings

Revenue
4100 Revenue from Plumbing

Expense
5100 Advertising
5120 Bank Charges
5140 General Expense
5160 Telephone Expense
5180 Van Repairs

```
PILOT PLUMBING
TRIAL BALANCE

January 31, 1991

1080    Cash in Bank                   $12 000.00
1220    A/R - Carmen's Restaurant        1 200.00
1240    A/R - Willow Apartments          1 800.00
1300    Plumbing Supplies                  950.00
1350    Plumbing Equipment               3 050.00
1400    Van                             16 000.00
2100    Bank Loan                                      $ 4 000.00
2200    A/P - Hudson's Plumbing                             600.00
2600    GST Charged on Services                             315.00
2610    GST Paid on Purchases              105.00
3100    L. Koontz, Capital                               26 240.00
3200    L. Koontz, Drawings                150.00
4100    Revenue from Plumbing                             4 500.00
5100    Advertising                        100.00
5120    Bank Charges                        20.00
5140    General Expense                     80.00
5160    Telephone Expense                   50.00
5180    Van Repairs                        150.00

                                       $ 35 655.00       $ 35 655.00
```

Accounting Procedures

1. **The Goods and Services Tax (GST): Remittances***
   Larissa has chosen the **regular method** for remittance of the
   Goods and Services Tax (GST). She will record the GST collected
   from customers as a **liability** (credit) in the GST Charged on
   Services account. She records GST that she pays to vendors in
   the GST Paid on Purchases account as a **decrease** (debit) to her
   liability to Revenue Canada. Her GST remittance or refund is
   calculated automatically in the GST Owing (Refund) clearing
   account. You can see this account when you display or print the
   Balance Sheet. She will file her remittances or requests for
   refunds with the Receiver General of Canada on the last day of
   each fiscal quarter.

*For details, please read Chapter 2 on the Goods and Services Tax.

Instructions

1. Using the Chart of Accounts and Trial Balance for Pilot Plumbing, enter the source documents for February using the General Journal in ACCPAC Simply Accounting. The procedures for entering each new type of transaction are outlined step by step in the keystroke section that follows the source documents.

2. After you have completed your entries, print the reports indicated on the printing form below. There are two types of reports, **Primary Reports** and **Secondary Reports**. Primary reports are those that must be compiled before they are displayed or printed. For example, a **Balance Sheet** has to be compiled because the user may choose any specific date for this report. Other primary reports are the **Income Statement**, **Trial Balance** and **Ledger accounts**. Secondary reports are displayed directly from information already stored. Journals and lists form this group of reports.

PRINTING

Primary Reports

☑ Balance Sheet
date: Feb. 13

☑ Income Statement
Period covered:
from: Feb. 1 to : Feb 13

☑ Trial Balance
date: Feb. 13

☑ General Ledger
accounts: 1080   3100
             2600   2610

Period covered:
from: Feb 1 to: Feb 13

Secondary Reports

GENERAL

☑ General Journal

⊘ by posting date: Feb. 1 - 13

Source Documents

USING DATE

Feb. 7   ☑   Sales Invoice #PP-105
Dated: Feb. 2/91
To Carmen's Restaurant, $500 for plumbing repair work, plus Goods and Services Tax (GST) charged $35. Sales Invoice total $535. Terms: net 30 days.

NOTES:
The date you entered for your previous transaction will now appear by default until you close the journal window.

☐   Purchase Invoice #HP-2951
Dated: Feb. 3/91
From Hudson's Plumbing, $200 for plumbing equipment plus GST paid for goods $14. Purchase Invoice total $214. Terms: 2/10 net 30 days.

☐   Purchase Invoice #CB-113
Dated: Feb. 3/91
From Creative Bulletins, $300 for advertising brochures plus GST paid for this service $21. Purchase Invoice total $321. Terms: cash on receipt of invoice.

☐   Cheque Copy #415
Dated: Feb. 4/91
To Creative Bulletins, $321 in full payment of account.

☐   Utility Statement #BC-1416
Dated: Feb. 4/91
From Bell Canada, $60 for telephone services plus GST paid for this service $4.20. Purchase Invoice total $64.20. Terms: cash on receipt of invoice.

☐   Cheque Copy #416
Dated: Feb. 5/91
To Bell Canada, $64.20 in full payment of account.

☐   Bank Debit Memo #CT-3452
Dated: Feb. 7/91
From Canada Trustco, $30 for bank service charges.

NOTES:
☑   Create new account 4120 Revenue from Interest. See Keystokes, Adding a New Account on page 38.

Feb. 13   ☐   Bank Credit Memo #CT-302
Dated: Feb. 9/91
From Canada Trustco, $312 for semi-annual interest on bank account.

❑ Sales Invoice #PP-106
Dated: Feb. 9/91
To Willow Apartments, $1 200 to replace all kitchen faucets plus GST charged $84. Sales Invoice total $1 284. Terms: net 30 days.

❑ Purchase Invoice #HP-3277
Dated: Feb. 10/91
From Hudson's Plumbing, $300 for plumbing supplies plus GST paid for goods $21. Purchase Invoice total $321. Terms: 2/10 net 30 days.

❑ Purchase Invoice #SSC-31
Dated: Feb. 11/91
From Shaman's Service Centre, $70 for van repairs plus GST paid for this service $4.90. Purchase Invoice total $74.90. Terms: cash on receipt of invoice.

❑ Cheque Copy #417
Dated: Feb. 12/91
To Shaman's Service Centre, $74.90 in full payment of account.

❑ Cheque Copy #418
Dated: Feb. 13/91
To Hudson's Plumbing, $450 on account.

❑ Cash Receipt #55
Dated: Feb. 13/91
From Carmen's Restaurant, cheque #32, $800 on account.

Keystrokes

Opening Data Files

Using the instructions for accessing a data file in Chapter 1 on page 9, load the Pilot Plumbing application.

The following screen appears, asking (prompting) you to enter the using date for this work session:

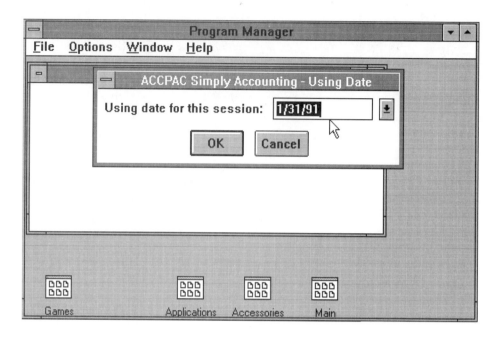

The using date is the date on which you are recording the accounting transactions on the computer. It may or may not be the same as the date on which the transaction actually took place, but obviously it cannot be earlier.

The using date for your session is February 7, 1991. Since this date is not shown by default on the screen, you must change the date. You can enter dates using the following alternative formats. Note that they all use the same order of month, day and then year:

- 02-07-91
- 2-7-91
- 02/07/91
- 2/7/91

For consistency, we will use the first of these date formats (02-07-91) throughout this workbook.

Type: 02-07-91

Click on OK

Your screen shows the following main Ledger/Journal company window:

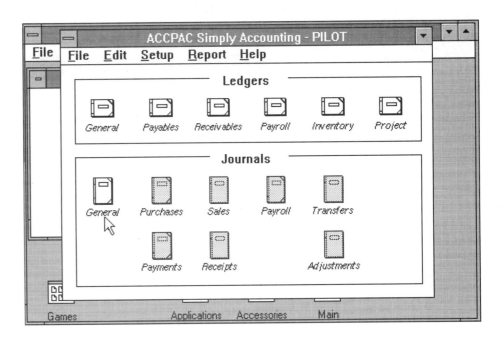

Entering General Journal Transactions

Click on the General Journal icon from the lower portion of the Ledger/Journal company window. Do not confuse this with the General Ledger icon in the upper portion of the window. Clicking will select or highlight the icon as follows:

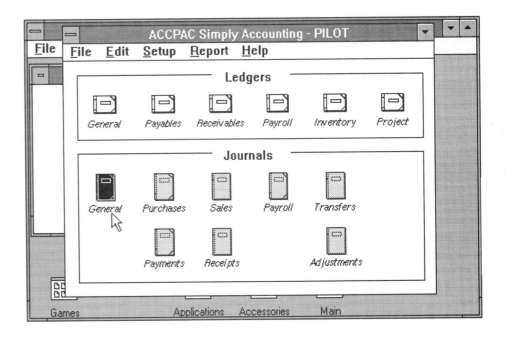

Choose **Open Journal** from the pull-down menu under **File** to open
the General Journal. (You may also open the journal by double-
clicking on its icon.) The General Journal input form shown below
appears on your screen:

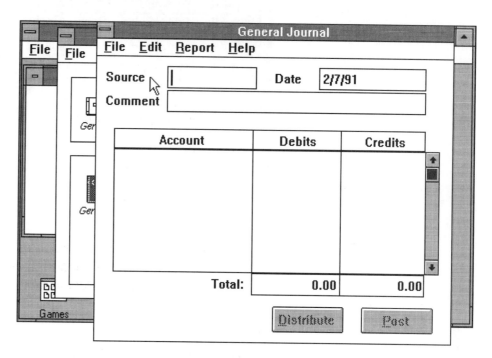

You are now ready to enter the first transaction in the General Journal
input screen. The cursor, a flashing vertical line, is blinking in the
Source field, ready to receive information. The Source field identifies
the reference document from which you obtain the information for a
transaction. In this transaction, the source is the invoice number.

Type: PP-105

Press ⌈Tab⌉

The cursor advances to the next field, the Date field. Here you should
enter the transaction date. The program has entered the using date
by default. It is highlighted, ready to be accepted or changed.
Because the work was completed on February 2, 1991, the using
date of February 7 is incorrect and must be changed.

Type: 02-02-91

Press ⌈Tab⌉

The cursor advances to the Comment field, where you can enter a description of the transaction to make the permanent record more meaningful.

Type: `Plumbing repair work`

Press `Tab`

The cursor moves forward to the Account field. Following usual accounting practice, enter the account to be debited first.

ACCPAC Simply Accounting organizes accounts into categories using the following boundaries for numbering:

- 1000 – 1999 Assets
- 2000 – 2999 Liabilities
- 3000 – 3999 Equity
- 4000 – 4999 Revenue
- 5000 – 5999 Expense

This system makes it easy to remember the first digit of an account. By typing the first digit of an account then pressing `Enter` while the cursor is flashing in an account field, the program will display a list of accounts beginning with that digit.

Type: `1`

Press `Enter`

The following list of accounts appears:

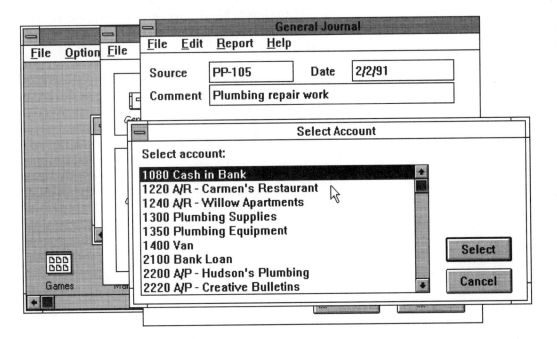

Click on 1220 A/R Carmen's Restaurant to highlight and select it as follows:

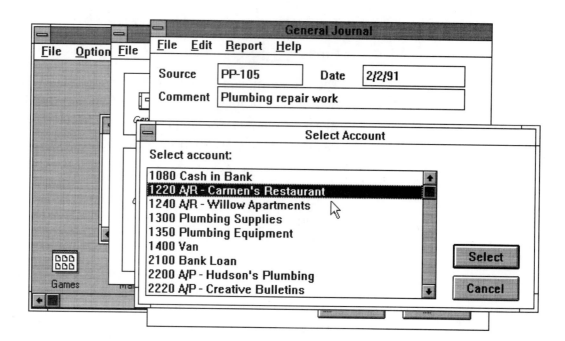

Click on the darkened or highlighted **Select** button. Notice that the account number and name have now been added to your input form so you can easily see if you have selected the correct account. Although the screen may not display the entire account title, you can see the rest of the account title by clicking anywhere on the part that is showing.

Your cursor is now positioned in the Debits column.

Type: 535

Press Tab

Your input form should now appear as follows:

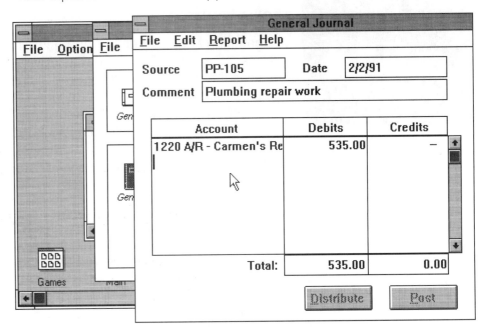

The cursor has advanced to the next line of the Account field so you can enter the first account to be credited for this transaction: the revenue account, *Revenue from Plumbing*. Remember, revenue accounts start with "4".

Type: 4

Press [Enter] to advance your list to the 4000 accounts as shown:

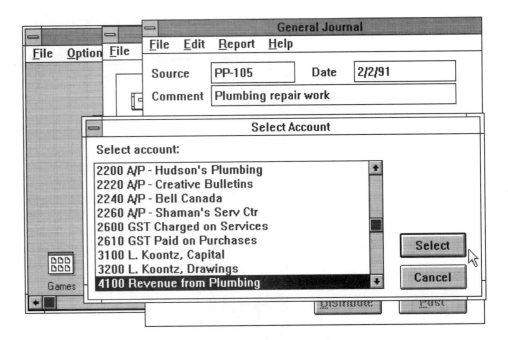

N O T E S :

Instead of using the selection list, you may choose the number from the Chart of Accounts in your workbook, typing it and pressing [Tab] .

Click on 4100 Revenue from Plumbing from the displayed list.

Click on Select

Again, the account number and name have been added to your transaction form. The cursor has advanced to the Credits field, which shows the default amount, $535. This amount is highlighted to indicate that you may edit it. Because this is a compound entry, you must change the amount to remove the GST. The GST must be entered in a separate account, GST Charged on Services.

Type: 500

Press [Tab]

The cursor advances to the next line in the Account field, where you must enter the GST liability account to be credited. Find the account number for *GST Charged on Services* from the list of accounts.

Type: 2

Press [Enter]

Click on 2600 GST Charged on Services from the displayed list.

Click on Select. The cursor advances to the Credits field again, where the remaining balance of $35 is shown by default. Since this amount is correct, you can accept it.

Press [Tab]

The cursor moves to the next line in the Account field. Your completed input form should appear as follows:

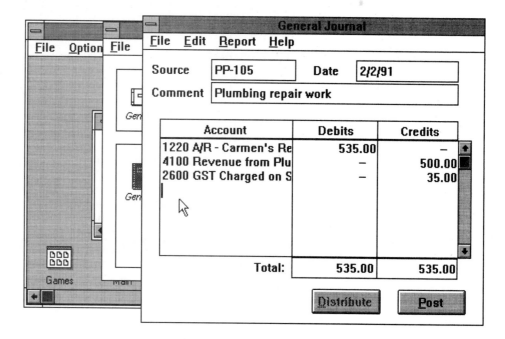

Until the debits and credits of a transaction are equal, you cannot post an entry and the **Post** button will remain dim. It is now darkened to show that the entry is complete, balanced and can be posted. But first you should review the transaction.

Reviewing the General Journal Entry

Choose Display General Journal Entry from the pull-down menu under **Report** as shown:

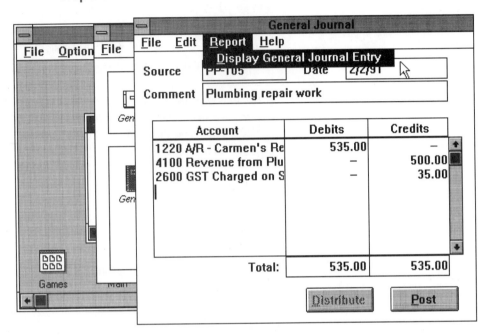

The transaction is displayed as follows:

General Journal Entry				
File **Help**				
2/2/91		Debits	Credits	Proj
1220	A/R - Carmen's Restaurant	535.00	-	
4100	Revenue from Plumbing	-	500.00	
2600	GST Charged on Services	-	35.00	
		535.00	535.00	

NOTES:

Alternatively, you could double click on the control box ⊟ .

If your transaction does not fit completely on the screen, use the scroll arrows to see more of the display. To return to your input form, **Choose** Close from the pull-down menu under ⊟ .

CORRECTING THE GENERAL JOURNAL ENTRY

Press [Tab] to advance to the field that has the error. To move to a previous field, **press** [Shift] and [Tab] together (that is, while holding down [Shift] , press [Tab]). The field will be highlighted, ready for editing. **Type** the correct information and **press** [Tab] to enter it.

You can also use the mouse to point to a field and drag through the incorrect information to highlight it. You can highlight a single number or letter or the entire field. **Type** the correct information and **press** [Tab] to enter it.

To correct an account number, **click on** the incorrect account number (or name) to move the cursor to this field. **Press** [Enter] to display the list of accounts. **Choose** the correct account. **Click on** Select; and **press** [Tab] to advance to the next line and enter the correction.

Posting

Once you are sure that all the information is correct, you are ready to post the transaction.

Click on Post

A new General Journal input form appears for you to enter the next transaction for this using date. Complete the transactions for the February 7 using date using the keystrokes outlined above.

Choose Close from the pull-down menu under ⊟ to close the General Journal and return to the main Ledger/Journal company window.

Advancing the Using Date

When you have finished making all the entries for the February 7 using date, you should save your work.

You may now enter the transactions for February 13.

Choose Advance Using Date from the pull-down menu under **Setup** as shown:

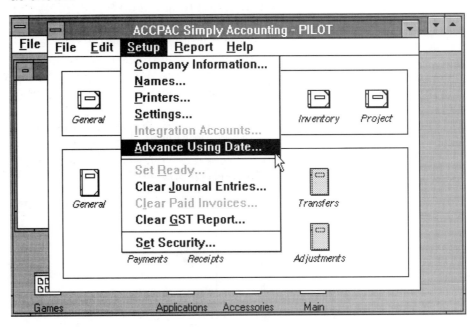

The following dialogue box appears, with the current using date highlighted:

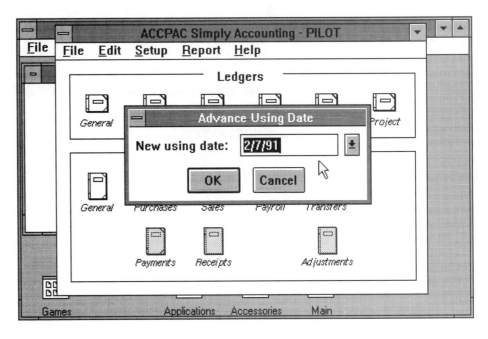

Type: 02-13-91

Click on OK to accept the new date. You may now enter the remaining transactions for this exercise.

Adding a New Account

The bank credit memo on February 9 uses an account that is not listed in your Chart of Accounts. Often a company will need to create new accounts as it expands or changes direction. These future needs are not always foreseen when the accounts are first set up. You must add the account *4120 Revenue from Interest* in order to enter the bank credit memo transaction.

Click on the General Ledger icon on the Ledger/Journal company window to highlight it as follows:

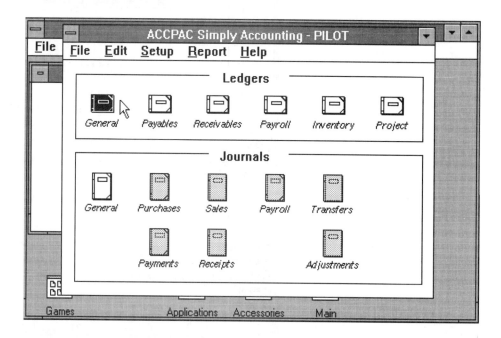

Choose Open Ledger from the pull-down menu under File to open the General Ledger. The account information for the heading Current Assets, the first account in the Chart of Accounts, appears.

Choose **Create** from the pull-down menu under **Edit** to see the following new account information form:

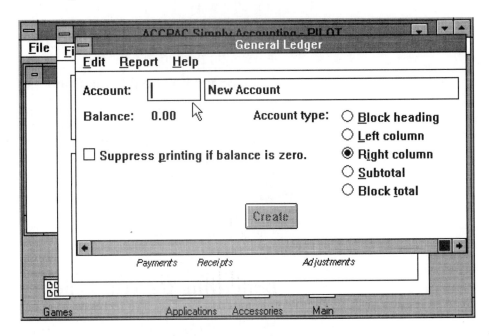

The cursor is in the account number part of the Account field.

Type: 4120

Press Tab

The cursor advances to the name part of the Account field. New Account is highlighted, ready to be changed.

Type: Revenue from Interest

Press Tab

Account type set at "Right column" means that this account's balance will be printed in the right-hand column of the revenue section of the Income Statement. This default setting is correct. The use of different account types will be explained in the Artistic Interiors application, where you will set up the accounting records for a company from scratch.

You should turn on the *Suppress printing if balance is zero* option. This choice means that if the balance in this account is zero, the account will not be included in your financial statements. If you leave this box unchecked, the account will be printed, even if it has a balance of zero. Some accounts, such as Cash in Bank, should always be printed in financial statements.

Click on the box beside the Suppress printing option to turn it on.

Check your work. Make any corrections necessary by highlighting the incorrect information and retyping it. When all of the information is correct, you need to save the new account information.

Click on Create

When you display your Chart of Accounts, you will see that the ACCPAC Simply Accounting program has added the Revenue from Interest account to the list.

Displaying General Reports

Displaying the Balance Sheet

You can display the Balance Sheet at any time except when you are entering a transaction.

Choose Balance Sheet from the pull-down menu under **Report**, as shown:

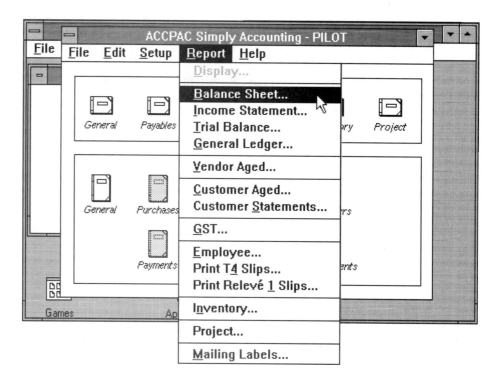

Your screen now includes the following Balance Sheet Options window:

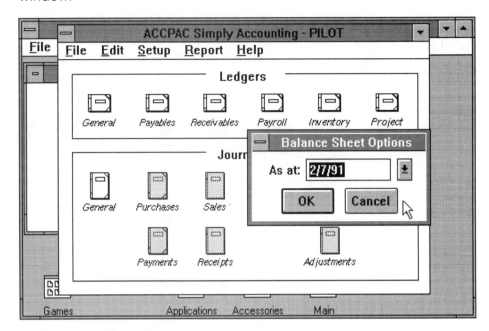

Your most recent using date is displayed by default, highlighted so that you can change it. If you click on the small arrow to the right of the Date (As at) field, you can see some alternative dates for the Balance Sheet. Choose from this list, or type in the date you want using one of the accepted formats given earlier.

Click on OK to display the Balance Sheet.

Choose Close from the pull-down menu under ⊟ when you have finished to return to the screen or window you were last working with.

Displaying the Trial Balance

You can display the Trial Balance at any time while working with the software, except when you are actually entering a transaction.

Choose Trial Balance from the pull-down menu under **Report**. The using date is once again highlighted.

Type the date for which you want the Trial Balance or choose from the options given with the small scroll arrow.

Click on OK to display the Trial Balance.

Choose Close from the pull-down menu under ⊟ to leave the display and return to the previous screen or window.

Displaying the Income Statement

You can view the Income Statement at any time except when you are actually entering a transaction.

Choose Income Statement from the pull-down menu under **Report** to display the following Income Statement Options window with Start and Finish date fields:

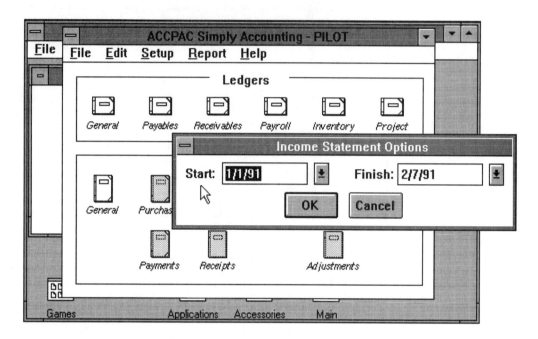

Here you must enter the beginning and ending dates for the period you wish your Income Statement to cover. Again, you may choose one of the dates offered with the scroll arrows or you may type in the dates.

Type the date at which your Income Statement period begins.

Press Tab

Type the date at which your Income Statement period ends.

Click on OK

Close the display window when you are finished.

Displaying General Ledger Reports

You can display the General Ledger at any time unless you are entering a transaction.

Choose General Ledger from the pull-down menu under **Report** to display the following report options:

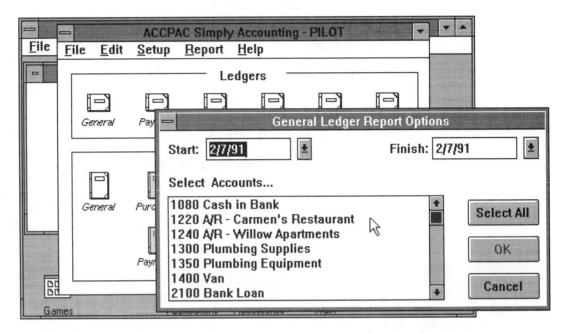

Type the starting date for your General Ledger report, or choose a date from the scroll arrow selections.

Press

Type the ending date for your General Ledger report.

Click on the account you wish to display. Use the scroll arrow to see more accounts if the one you want is not visible. If you want to include all the accounts in the display, click on **Select All.**

Close the display window when you have finished viewing it.

Displaying the Chart of Accounts

You can view the Chart of Accounts only while the General Ledger icon is highlighted or selected in the main Ledger/Journal company window.

Click on the General Ledger icon from the upper ledger part of the main Ledger/Journal company window to highlight it.

Choose Display Chart of Accounts from the pull-down menu under **Report**.

Close the display when you are finished.

Displaying the General Journal

Click on the General Journal icon from the lower journal portion of the Ledger/Journal company window.

Choose Display General Journal from the pull-down menu under **Report** to display the following options:

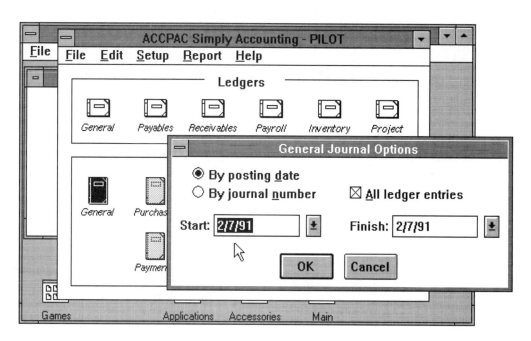

You may display journals either by the posting date of the journal entries or by journal entry number. All reports in this workbook are requested by posting date, the default setting, so leave this option unchanged.

The latest using date is given by default for the period of the report, with the starting date highlighted for editing.

NOTES:

If the box beside **All Ledger entries** is checked, you will display all journal transactions entered in any of the journals. If it is not checked, only transactions entered through the General Journal will be displayed.

Type the beginning date for which you want the journal entries printed.

Type the ending date of the period for your journal report.

Click on OK

Close the display when you are finished.

Printing General Reports

Display the report you wish to print by following the instructions in the previous section on Displaying General Reports.

Choose Printer Setup from the pull-down menu under **File.** Choose the printer that you are using if the one showing is not correct. You can use the scroll arrow to see more printers. Most of the other settings should be correct by default.

Click on OK when the settings are all correct. You will return to the displayed report.

Choose Print from the pull-down menu under **File.**

Wait for the printing information displayed to clear from the screen, then close the displayed report.

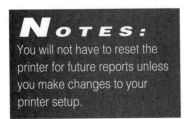

NOTES:
You will not have to reset the printer for future reports unless you make changes to your printer setup.

Finishing a Session

Finish the last transaction you are working on for this session.

Close the transaction window (such as journal input or display) to return to the main Ledger/Journal company window.

Close the Ledger/Journal company window. The ACCPAC Simply Accounting program will automatically save your work when you finish your session and exit properly.

Close the ACCPAC window.

Close the Program Manager window.

Click on OK to confirm your intention to end your Windows session.

You will return to your menu screen or DOS prompt, depending on how your computer is set up.

You may now turn off the computer.

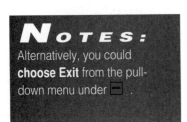

NOTES:
Alternatively, you could **choose Exit** from the pull-down menu under ▢.

Case Problem

On February 28, 1991, Larissa Koontz made a $500 payment towards her bank loan. After a long hard day, she hurriedly entered this transaction in her ACCPAC Simply Accounting files as a debit to the Cash in Bank account (1080) and a credit to the Bank Loan account (2100). After posting the transaction and printing a new Balance Sheet, she wondered whether she had entered the information correctly.

1. Did she enter the transaction correctly? Explain.

2. If the entry was incorrect, how should she void the entry? Describe the procedure involved in correcting the entry.

3. If she had not yet posted the transaction, how would she correct the entry? Explain.

CHAPTER FOUR

Carousel Café

OBJECTIVES

Upon completion of this chapter, you will be able to:

1. *access* the ACCPAC Simply Accounting program;
2. *access* the data files for a business;
3. *open* the General and Payables journals;
4. *enter* vendor-related purchase transactions;
5. *enter* vendor-related payment transactions.
6. *add* a new vendor account;
7. *edit* and *review* transactions in the journals;
8. *post* transactions in each of the journals;
9. *observe* and *understand* integration accounts;
10. *display* and *print* your transactions and reports;
11. *advance* the using date;
12. *finish* an accounting session.

Company Information

Company Profile

After Karel Bloom had worked as a manager for Spartan Restaurants in Saskatoon for five years, his wife's firm transferred her to its Vancouver office. He decided to use this opportunity to start his own restaurant. He chose a rapidly growing business community to locate his cafeteria, **Carousel Café**. Expecting most of his customers to be business people who needed fast service with nutritious and good-tasting food, he decided to concentrate his menu on soups, salads and made-to-order delicatessan sandwiches. He also offered a variety of muffins, Danishes and tarts to cater to the coffee break clientele. All the food was freshly prepared in the restaurant, including the baked goods. Variety was a prime consideration so that customers would want to return regularly.

Mr. Bloom had contracted with Fine Food Wholesalers to provide fresh foods daily and all other food items weekly. Orders were placed weekly when the menus were planned, and the cafeteria was invoiced on a weekly basis. To assist him in operating the business, Bloom hired a full-time manager to help with preparing the menus, placing food orders and handling cash. The manager receives a monthly salary. Bloom also has a full-time chef/baker to prepare the food and two part-time employees to handle the dishwashing and cleaning. These employees receive their wages every two weeks. The cafeteria's payroll is handled by Victoria Trust, which prepares the payroll biweekly.

Mr. Bloom himself is busy looking for opportunities to expand into catering services for business meetings and conferences.

In December 1990 and January 1991, Mr. Bloom bought the equipment and supplies and renovated the café. By February 1, 1991, he was ready to receive his first customers. All of his accounting was to be completed using the ACCPAC Simply Accounting software package. The following information summarizes the accounting records:

1. Chart of Accounts;
2. Trial Balance;
3. Vendor Information;
4. Accounting Procedures.

CAROUSEL CAFÉ
CHART OF ACCOUNTS

Assets
1080 Cash in Bank
1100 Food Inventory
1200 Supplies: Cafeteria
1300 Supplies: Washrooms
1350 Cutlery & Dishes
1550 Cafeteria Equipment
1600 Cash Registers
1700 Delivery Van
1750 Furniture & Fixtures
1800 Land & Buildings

Liabilities
2100 Bank Loan
2200 Accounts Payable
2600 GST Charged on Services
2610 GST Paid on Capital Goods
2620 GST Owing (Refund)
2800 Mortgage Payable

Equity
3100 K. Bloom, Capital
3200 K. Bloom, Drawings

Revenue
4100 Revenue from Services

Expense
5100 Advertising & Promotion
5120 Bank Charges
5140 Cost of Goods Sold
5160 Cleaning Expenses
5180 General Expenses
5200 Hydro Expense
5220 Payroll Services
5240 Repairs & Maintenance
5260 Salary
5280 Telephone Expenses
5300 Van Repairs
5320 Wages

CAROUSEL CAFÉ
TRIAL BALANCE

January 31, 1991

1080 Cash in Bank	$ 18 556.00	
1100 Food Inventory	2 400.00	
1200 Supplies: Cafeteria	300.00	
1300 Supplies: Washrooms	200.00	
1350 Cutlery & Dishes	2 000.00	
1550 Cafeteria Equipment	20 000.00	
1600 Cash Registers	3 000.00	
1700 Delivery Van	12 000.00	
1750 Furniture & Fixtures	15 000.00	
1800 Land & Buildings	150 000.00	
2100 Bank Loan		$ 6 000.00
2200 Accounts Payable		9 028.00
2610 GST Paid on Capital Goods	322.00	
2800 Mortgage Payable		120 000.00
3100 K. Bloom, Capital		88 750.0
	$223 778.00	$223 778.00

CAROUSEL CAFÉ
VENDOR INFORMATION

Vendor Name	Address & Telephone	Invoice Date	Invoice Number	Outstanding Balance
Agora Wholesalers	342 Whistler Rd. Vancouver, British Columbia V9P 3E4 Tel: 345-9821			
B.C. Hydro	87 Energy Ave. Vancouver, British Columbia V6R 1H4 Tel: 896-2345			
B.C. Telephone	976 Signal Rd. Vancouver, British Columbia V9I 2C3 Tel: 784-0981			
Comfort Furniture	91 Mountain Rd. Vancouver, British Columbia V9L 2F5 Tel: 287-7766	Jan. 9/91	CF-231	$1 498.00

Vendor Name	Address & Telephone	Invoice Date	Invoice Number	Outstanding Balance
Commercial Cutlery Ltd.	88 Ontario St. Vancouver, British Columbia V7U 1A2 Tel: 266-9013	Jan. 18/91	CC-101	$ 856.00
Fine Food Wholesalers	33 Brock Ave. Vancouver, British Columbia V9I 1W2 Tel: 284-6393	Jan. 12/91 Jan. 16/91	FF-99 FF-109 Total	$1 400.00 $1 350.00 ———— $2 750.00
Fresh Janitorial Services	91 Grace Rd. Vancouver, British Columbia V9O 3G6 Tel: 987-1234			
Ideal Equipment	181 Brunswick Rd. Vancouver, British Columbia V7U 2D4 Tel: 775-6370	Jan. 21/91	IE-121	$3 424.00
K. Bloom, Owner	n/a			
Provincial Treasurer	39 Legal Ave. Vancouver, British Columbia V5K 4Q1 Tel: 987-1254			
Swift Carpenters	89 Nailing Rd. Vancouver, British Columbia V9I 2C4 Tel: 874-2341			
Total Cleaning Service	39 Quebec Ave. Vancouver, British Columbia V8K 1Y6 Tel: 774-0041	Jan. 28/91	TC-55	$ 500.00
			GRAND TOTAL	$9 028.00

Accounting Procedures

NOTES:

- In some of the source documents that follow, such as purchase invoices (for non-capital expenditures) and cash receipts from cash register tapes, the GST is included in the total amount. Do not record GST separately for these source documents.
- Basic groceries and food items are zero-rated goods and services.
- Most bank and other financial institution services are exempted from GST charges in this application. Bank payroll services are subject to GST charges.
- Provincial sales tax will not be levied in this application. It will be introduced in a later application.

1. **The Goods and Services Tax (GST): Remittances***

   Karel has chosen the **quick method** for remittance of the Goods and Services Tax. All items sold in the café are priced to include the GST, and a sign is posted so that customers are aware that they are paying the GST. At the end of each quarter, a flat tax rate of five (5) percent on Revenue from Services will be calculated and charged to the GST Charged on Services account. Any GST amount paid to vendors on capital expenditures, such as equipment, cash registers, the delivery van, and furniture and fixtures, will be recorded as a reduction (input tax credit) to the GST Paid on Capital Goods liability account. GST paid on supplies and services will not be included as a decrease in the GST liability to the Receiver General under the quick method. Bloom has set up an account, GST Owing (Refund), as a clearing account for remittance of GST to the Receiver General of Canada on the last day of each quarter.

2. **Open-Invoice Accounting for Payables**

   The open-invoice method of accounting for invoices issued to a business allows a business to keep track of each individual invoice and partial payment made against the invoice. This is in contrast to methods that keep track only of the outstanding balance by combining all invoice balances owed to a vendor. ACCPAC Simply Accounting uses the open-invoice method. When an invoice is fully paid, you can either retain the invoice or remove (clear) it.

3. **Purchase of Inventory Items**

   Inventory items purchased are immediately recorded in the Food Inventory asset account. The items in stock are also manually recorded on inventory cards for periodic updating.

4. **Cost of Goods Sold**

   Periodically, the food inventory on hand is counted. The manager then calculates the cost price of the food inventory sold and issues a memo to charge the cost price to the Cost of Goods Sold account and reduce the Food Inventory account.

* For details please read Chapter 2 on the Goods and Services Tax.

Instructions

1. Using the Chart of Accounts, Trial Balance, Vendor Information and Accounting Procedures for Carousel Café, enter the source documents for the month of February using ACCPAC Simply Accounting. The procedures for entering each new type of transaction for this application are outlined step by step in the keystroke section following the source documents.

2. Print the reports indicated on the printing form below after you have completed your entries.

PRINTING

Primary Reports

☐ Balance Sheet
date:

☑ Income Statement
Period covered:
from: Feb. 1 to: Feb. 28

☐ Trial Balance
date:

☑ General Ledger
accounts: 2200 _____
4100 _____

☑ Vendor Aged
○ Summary
⊘ Detail

Period covered:
from: Feb. 1 to: Feb. 28

Secondary Reports

GENERAL

☑ General Journal
⊘ by posting date: Feb. 1-28

ACCOUNTS PAYABLE

☐ Vendor Address List

☑ Purchases Journal
⊘ by posting date: Feb. 1-28

☑ Payments Journal
⊘ by posting date: Feb. 1-28

NOTES:
Remember to turn off the *All ledger entries* option for displaying the General Journal before printing the General Journal. If you do not, you will duplicate the printing of the transactions in the Purchases and the Payments journals.

Source Documents

Feb. 7 ☑ Purchase Invoice #FF-131
Dated: Feb. 2/91
From Fine Food Wholesalers, $800 for basic groceries for café services. Terms: net 30 days.

☑ Cheque Copy #150
Dated: Feb. 2/91
To Comfort Furniture, $1 498 in full payment of account. Reference invoice #CF-231.

☐ Purchase Invoice #SC-19
Dated: Feb. 3/91
From Swift Carpenters, $149.80 to repair damage to counter including GST. Terms: cash on receipt.

☐ Cheque Copy #151
Dated: Feb. 3/91
To Swift Carpenters, $149.80 in full payment of account. Reference invoice #SC-19.

☐ Cheque Copy #152
Dated: Feb. 4/91
To Fine Food Wholesalers, $2 750 in full payment of account. Reference invoices #FF-99 and FF-109.

☐ Purchase Invoice #IE-499*
Dated: Feb. 5/91
From Ideal Equipment, $1 250 for the purchase of freezer plus GST paid $87.50. Purchase Invoice total $1 337.50. Terms: net 30 days.

☐ Purchase Invoice #AW-98
Dated: Feb. 6/91
From Agora Wholesalers, $128.40 for café supplies including GST. Terms: cash on receipt of invoice.

☐ Cheque Copy #153
Dated: Feb. 6/91
To Agora Wholesalers, $128.40 in full payment of account. Reference invoice #AW-98.

* Capital Expenditure

❑ Cash Receipt #1
Dated: Feb. 7/91
From cash register tapes (no.980 - no.1980),
$3 100 including GST collected for food
services. Amount deposited in bank.

Feb. 14

❑ Purchase Invoice #PE-321
Dated: Feb. 8/91
From Pirri's Esso (new vendor), $267.50 for
repairs to delivery van including GST. Terms:
net 30 days.

❑ Bank Debit Memo #VT-1211
Dated: Feb. 9/91
From Victoria Trust, $20 for bank service
charges.

❑ Purchase Invoice #FF-176
Dated: Feb. 10/91
From Fine Food Wholesalers, $750 for basic
groceries for café services. Terms: net 30
days.

❑ Purchase Invoice #FJS-90
Dated: Feb. 11/91
From Fresh Janitorial Services, $107 for
washroom supplies including GST. Terms:
cash on receipt of invoice.

❑ Cheque Copy #154
Dated: Feb. 11/91
To Fresh Janitorial Services, $107 in full
payment of account. Reference invoice #FJS-
90.

❑ Purchase Invoice #CF-311*
Dated: Feb. 12/91
From Comfort Furniture, $750 for new chairs
and tables plus GST paid $52.50. Purchase
Invoice total $802.50. Terms: net 30 days.

❑ Cheque Copy #155
Dated: Feb. 13/91
To Commercial Cutlery, $856 in full payment
of account. Reference invoice #CC-101.

❑ Cheque Copy #156
Dated: Feb. 14/91
To Ideal Equipment, $3 424 in payment of
account. Reference invoice #IE-121.

* Capital Expenditure

❑ Bank Debit Memo #VT-1298
Dated: Feb. 14/91
From Victoria Trust;

Payroll: Staff Wages	$1 800.00
Payroll Services including GST	26.75
Total	$1 826.75

❑ Cash Receipt #2
Dated: Feb. 14/91
From cash register tapes (no.1981 - no.2890), $3 300 including GST collected for food services. Amount deposited in bank.

Feb. 21

❑ Purchase Invoice #FF-197
Dated: Feb. 15/91
From Fine Food Wholesalers, $800 for basic groceries for café services. Terms: net 30 days.

❑ Purchase Invoice #TC-98
Dated: Feb. 16/91
From Total Cleaning Service, $321 for regular café cleaning services including GST. Terms: net 30 days.

❑ Cheque Copy #157
Dated: Feb. 17/91
To Total Cleaning Service, $500 in payment of account. Reference invoice #TC-55.

❑ Purchase Invoice #VS-456
Dated: Feb. 18/91
From Vancouver Sun (new vendor), $96.30 for advertisement including GST. Terms: cash on receipt of invoice.

❑ Cheque Copy #158
Dated: Feb. 18/91
To Vancouver Sun, $96.30 in full payment of account. Reference invoice #VS-456.

❑ Utility Statement #BCH-112
Dated: Feb. 18/91
From B.C. Hydro, $128.40 for hydro service including GST. Terms: cash on receipt of invoice.

NOTES:
❑ Vancouver Sun is located at 34 Harbour Road, Vancouver, British Columbia, V3G 1N4

Tel: 922-0219

❏ Cheque Copy #159
Dated: Feb. 18/91
To B.C. Hydro, $128.40 in full payment of account. Reference invoice #BCH-112.

❏ Memo #1
Dated: Feb. 19/91
From K. Bloom, owner to accountant: For audit and internal control purposes, set up a liability for withdrawal of $175 from the business for personal use.

❏ Cheque Copy #160
Dated: Feb. 19/91
To K. Bloom, owner, $175 in full payment of account. Reference Memo #1.

❏ Highway Offence Ticket #432876
Dated: Feb. 20/91
From Vancouver Police, $30 for illegal parking of delivery van. Enter this liability as a purchase to vendor Provincial Treasurer. Charge to General Expenses account.

❏ Cheque Copy #161
Dated: Feb. 20/91
To Provincial Treasurer, $30 for parking ticket on delivery van. Reference Ticket #432876.

❏ Bank Debit Memo #VT-1421
Dated: Feb. 21/91
From Victoria Trust, $1 200 to reduce mortgage.

❏ Cash Receipt #3
Dated: Feb. 21/91
From cash register tapes (no. 2891 - no. 3980), $3 125 including GST collected for food services. Amount deposited in bank.

Feb. 28 ❏ Purchase Invoice #FF-209
Dated: Feb. 22/91
From Fine Food Wholesalers, $800 basic groceries for café services. Terms: net 30 days.

❑ Purchase Invoice #CC-198
Dated: Feb. 23/91
From Commercial Cutlery, $267.50 for
chinaware including GST. Terms: net 30 days.

❑ Utility Statement #BCT-981
Dated: Feb. 24/91
From B.C. Telephone, $64.20 for telephone
service including GST. Terms: cash on receipt
of invoice.

❑ Cheque Copy #162
Dated: Feb. 24/91
To B.C. Telephone, $64.20 in full payment of
account. Reference invoice #BCT-981.

❑ Bank Debit Memo #VT-1499
Dated: Feb. 26/91
From Victoria Trust, $300 for reduction of bank
loan.

❑ Cash Receipt #4
Dated: Feb. 28/91
From cash register tapes (no.3981 - no.4900),
$3 400 including GST collected for food
services. Amount deposited in bank.

❑ Bank Debit Memo #VT-1564
Dated: Feb. 28/91
From Victoria Trust;

Payroll: Staff Wages	$1 800.00
Payroll: Manager's Salary	2 000.00
Payroll Services including GST	53.50
Total	$3 853.50

❑ Memo #2
Dated: Feb. 28/91
From manager to accountant: Charge $2 800
to the Cost of Goods Sold account, and
reduce the Food Inventory account.

Keystrokes

Opening Data Files

Using the instructions for accessing data files on page 9, load the data files for Carousel Café. You are prompted to enter the first using date, February 7, 1991, for this application.

Type: 02-07-91

Click on OK to enter the first using date for this application. The familiar main Ledger/Journal company window appears.

Accounting for Purchases

Click on the Purchases icon in the lower journal portion of the window to highlight it as follows:

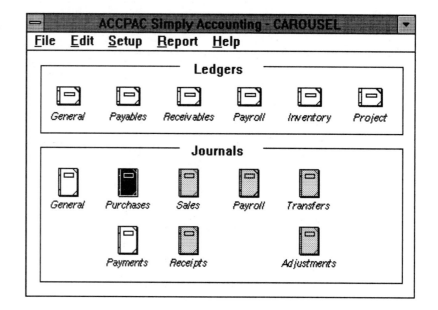

Choose **Open Journal** from the pull-down menu under **File** to open the Purchases Journal. The Purchases Journal input form appears on the screen as follows:

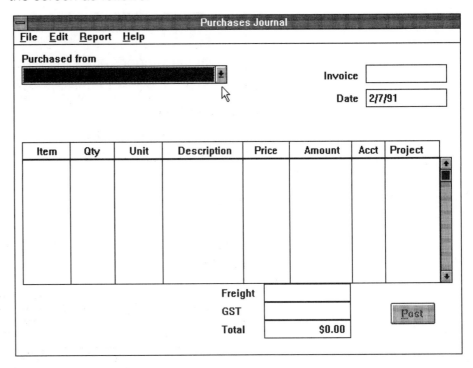

The Vendor (Purchased from) field is darkened, ready to receive information.

Click on the arrow beside the Vendor field to obtain the list of vendors as shown:

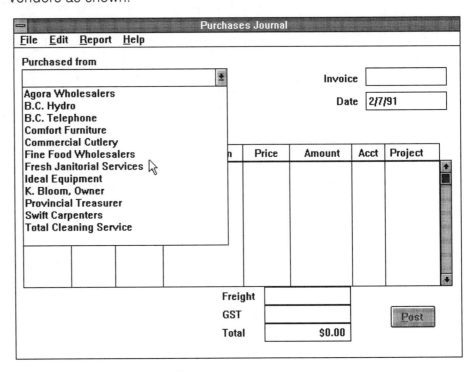

Whenever you see this arrow beside a field, a selection list is available to choose from. You may either use this list or type in the full information.

Click on Fine Food Wholesalers, the vendor for this purchase, to select and enter it.

Notice that the vendor's name and address have been added to your input form, making it easy to check whether you have selected the correct vendor. If you have made an error in your selection, click on the enter list arrow and start again. If you have selected correctly,

Press `Tab`

The cursor moves to the Invoice field, where you should type in the alphanumeric invoice number.

Type: `FF-131`

Press `Tab`

The cursor moves to the Date field. Enter the date on which the transaction took place, February 2, 1991. The using date appears automatically by default. It is highlighted, ready to be accepted or changed. You need to change the date.

Type: `02-02-91`

Press `Tab`

The cursor advances to the Item field. Because we are not using the Inventory Ledger for this application, you can ignore this field as well as the next two.

Click on the first line of the Description field to move the cursor. This field is used to enter a description or comment for the purchase.

Type: `Food & Beverages`

Press `Tab`

Even though the full description in no longer visible on the screen, all the information is stored. The cursor is now positioned in the Price field. This field relates to inventory items that have unit prices, so skip over it.

Press `Tab`

The cursor advances to the Amount field, where you will enter the total amount for this purchase. Because the business is using the **quick method** for administering the GST, purchases of non-capital expenditures, such as supplies and services, will be recorded with the GST included. Since food inventory is zero-rated, it will not include any GST. Review the Accounting Procedures section on page 51 for more information if necessary.

Type: 800

Press Tab

The cursor moves to the Account field. When you work in a subsidiary ledger, your Accounts Payable control account in the General Ledger will automatically be credited for the purchase. The Account field for this purchase only refers to the debit part of the journal entry, normally the acquistion of an asset or the incurring of an expense. It could also refer to a decrease in a liability account (e.g., for GST paid to reduce the liability owing to Revenue Canada). It also could be used to decrease an equity account, if the purchase were made for the owner's personal use. In this example, the business has acquired an asset, so you need to enter the asset account to which the purchase should be debited.

Type: 1

Press Enter

The familiar list of accounts appears with the first asset account highlighted.

Click on 1100 Food Inventory to highlight it.

Click on Select to enter the account to your Purchases Journal form. Your screen should now resemble the following:

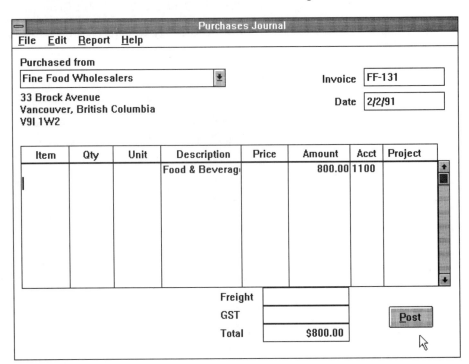

The cursor is flashing in the Item field on the second line so that you can enter additional purchases from this vendor. Since the entries for this transaction are complete, you are ready to review your transaction.

Reviewing the Purchases Journal Entry

Choose Display Purchases Journal Entry from the pull-down menu under **Report** to display the transaction you have entered on the screen:

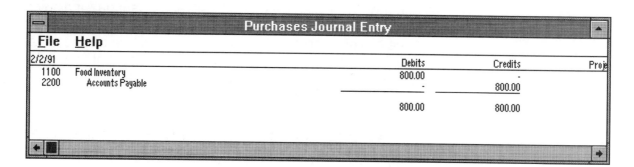

		Debits	Credits	Proj
2/2/91				
1100	Food Inventory	800.00	-	
2200	Accounts Payable	-	800.00	
		800.00	800.00	

By reviewing the journal entry, you can check for mistakes. Note that the ACCPAC Simply Accounting program automatically updates the Accounts Payable control account because the Payables and General Ledgers are fully integrated.

Close the display to return to the Purchases Journal input screen.

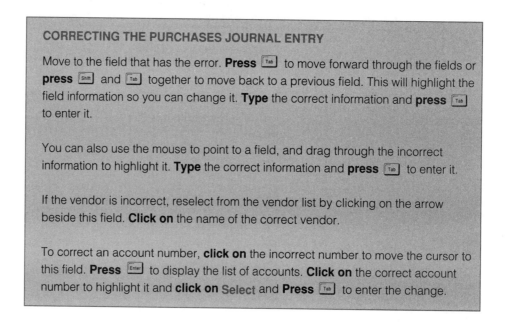

CORRECTING THE PURCHASES JOURNAL ENTRY

Move to the field that has the error. **Press** [Tab] to move forward through the fields or **press** [Shift] and [Tab] together to move back to a previous field. This will highlight the field information so you can change it. **Type** the correct information and **press** [Tab] to enter it.

You can also use the mouse to point to a field, and drag through the incorrect information to highlight it. **Type** the correct information and **press** [Tab] to enter it.

If the vendor is incorrect, reselect from the vendor list by clicking on the arrow beside this field. **Click on** the name of the correct vendor.

To correct an account number, **click on** the incorrect number to move the cursor to this field. **Press** [Enter] to display the list of accounts. **Click on** the correct account number to highlight it and **click on** Select and **Press** [Tab] to enter the change.

Posting

When you are certain that you have entered all the information correctly, you must post the transaction to save it. Notice that the Post button is no longer dimmed.

Click on Post to save your transaction.

A new blank Purchases Journal form appears on the screen. Our next transaction is a payment, however, not a purchase.

Close the Purchases Journal window to return to the main Ledger/Journal company window.

Accounting for Payments

Click on the Payments Journal icon from the Ledger/Journal company window to highlight it as shown:

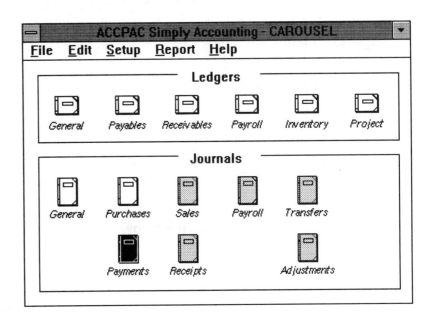

Choose **Open Journal** from the pull-down menu under **File** to open the journal. The following blank Payments Journal input screen appears:

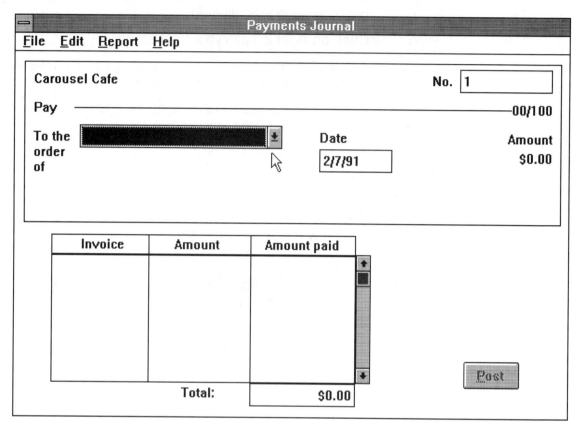

The Vendor (To the order of) field is darkened, ready to receive information.

Click on the arrow beside this field to see the familiar list of vendors displayed in alphabetical order.

Click on Comfort Furniture to choose and enter the vendor to whom the payment is made. As shown, the vendor's name, address and outstanding invoice(s) have been added automatically to your input form, making it easy to see whether you have selected correctly:

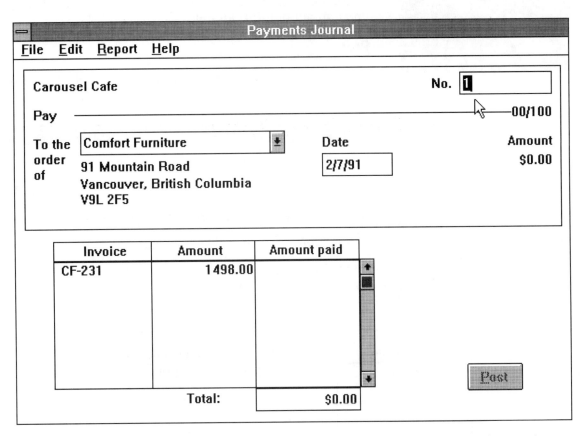

If you need to change the vendor, click on this arrow again to select from the vendor list. When you have the correct vendor,

Press `Tab`

The cursor advances to the No. field, where you should enter the cheque number.

Type: 150

Press `Tab`

The cursor moves to the Date field, where the using date appears by default. Because it is highlighted, you can change it as required for this transaction.

Type: 02-02-91

Press `Tab`

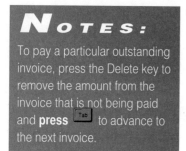
The cursor moves to the Amount field. By default, the amount owing on the first invoice is shown and highlighted. All outstanding invoices for a vendor are listed on the screen. You can accept a highlighted amount, or type in an exact amount for a partial payment. In this case, there is only one invoice and the full amount is being paid, so you can accept the default.

Press [Tab]

Your completed Payments Journal form should now appear as follows:

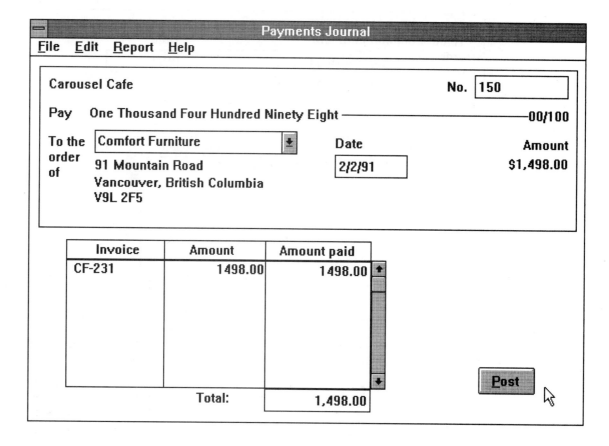

Notice that the upper cheque portion of the form is also complete.

As you work in a subsidiary ledger, your Accounts Payable control account in the General Ledger will automatically be debited for the payment and the Cash in Bank account will be credited.

The entries for this transaction are complete, so you are ready to review and post your transaction.

Reviewing the Payments Journal Entry

Choose Display Payments Journal Entry from the pull-down menu under **Report** to display the transaction you have entered:

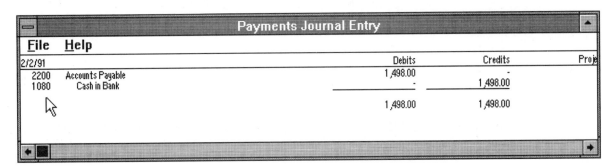

You can see that the ACCPAC Simply Accounting program has automatically updated the Accounts Payable and Cash in Bank accounts, because the Payables and General Ledgers are fully integrated.

Close the display to return to the Payments Journal input screen.

CORRECTING THE PAYMENTS JOURNAL ENTRY

Move to the field that has the error. **Press** [Tab] to move forward through the fields or **press** [Shift] and [Tab] together to move back to a previous field. This will highlight the field information so you can change it. **Type** the correct information and **press** [Tab] to enter it.

You can also use the mouse to point to a field and drag through the incorrect information to highlight it. **Type** the correct information and **press** [Tab] to enter it.

If the vendor is incorrect, reselect from the vendor list by **clicking on** the arrow beside this field. **Click on** the name of the correct vendor. You will be asked to confirm that you want to discard the current transaction. **Click on** Yes to discard the incorrect vendor entry and display the outstanding invoices for the correct vendor. Reenter the payment information for this vendor.

Posting

When you are certain that you have entered all the information correctly, you must post the transaction to save it. Notice that the Post button is no longer dimmed.

Click on Post to save your transaction.

Enter the remaining transactions for the February 7 using date. To complete transactions involving the General Journal, you must exit to the main Ledger/Journal company window and follow the keystroke instructions for the General Journal from the Pilot Plumbing application.

Adding a New Vendor

The first transaction for the February 14 using date involves a purchase from a company that is not listed as a vendor. You must add Pirri's Esso to the vendor list in order to record the transaction.

Click on the Payables Ledger icon from the upper ledger portion of the Ledger/Journal company window to highlight it as shown:

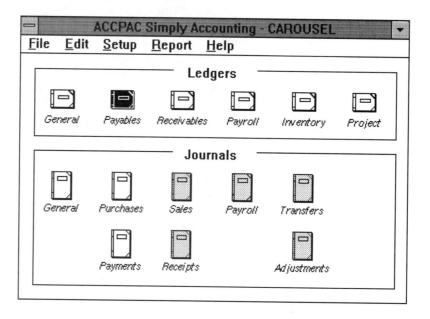

Choose Open Ledger from the pull-down menu under **File** to open the Payables Ledger.

The vendor screen for Agora Wholesalers, the first vendor, appears.

Choose **Create** from the pull-down menu under **Edit** to display the following new vendor input screen:

Payables Ledger

Edit   Report   Help

Vendor: `New Vendor`   Phone: `_____`

Contact: ⌖ `_____`   Fax: `_____`

Street: `_____`

City: `Vancouver`   Last year purchases: 0.00

Province: `British Columbia`   YTD purchases: 0.00

Postal code: `_____`   Balance owing: 0.00

☐ **Clear invoices when paid**

☒ **Include in GST report**   [Create]

You are ready to enter the new vendor. The Vendor field is highlighted, ready to receive new information.

Type: `Pirri's Esso`

Press [Tab]

The cursor advances to the Contact field, where you enter the name of Carousel Café's contact person at Pirri's. This field may be left blank by tabbing over it.

Type: `Joseph Pirri`

Press [Tab]

The cursor moves to the Street field.

Type: `33 Burnaby Drive`

Press [Tab]

The cursor moves to the City field. By default, the program has entered the name of the city and province in which Carousel Café is located. You can accept these defaults because they are correct for Pirri's Esso as well.

Press `Tab`

Press `Tab`

The cursor moves to the Postal code field. You do not need to use capital letters, and you do not need to leave a space within the postal code. The program will make these adjustments for you.

Type: v3c4p4

Press `Tab`

Notice that the format of the postal code has been corrected automatically. The cursor moves to the Phone field. You do not need to insert a dash when you enter a telephone number.

Type: 2918907

Press `Tab`

Notice that the format for the telephone number has been corrected automatically. The cursor advances to the Fax field. Pirri's Esso does not have a fax number, so ignore this field.

Two other fields appear on this form as check boxes: *Clear invoices when paid* and *Include in GST report*. The *Clear invoices* option is used to remove invoices that are fully paid. Choose not to clear the invoices so that you can keep a record of all purchases and payments. Leave the box unchecked.

Any vendor supplying goods or services that qualify as input tax credits should be included in GST reports and have this box checked. Since Carousel Café uses the quick method, only vendors supplying capital goods would fall into this category. Pirri's Esso does not supply capital goods, so you should turn the option off.

Click on the box beside **Include in GST report** to remove the "x".

Your completed new vendor input screen now appears as follows:

```
┌────────────────────────────────────────────────────────────────────┐
│ ▬                          Payables Ledger                          │
├────────────────────────────────────────────────────────────────────┤
│  Edit   Report   Help                                               │
│                                                                     │
│   Vendor:     │Pirri's Esso          │   Phone:  │291-8907        │ │
│                                                                     │
│   Contact:    │Joseph Pirri          │   Fax:    │                │ │
│                                                                     │
│   Street:     │33 Burnaby Drive      │                             │
│                                                                     │
│   City:       │Vancouver             │   Last year purchases:  0.00 │
│                                                                     │
│   Province:   │British Columbia      │   YTD purchases:        0.00 │
│                                                                     │
│   Postal code:│V3C 4P4               │   Balance owing:        0.00 │
│                                                                     │
│   ☐ Clear invoices when paid                                        │
│                                         ┌──────────┐                │
│   ☐ Include in GST report               │  Create  │                │
│                                         └──────────┘                │
│ ◄ │                                                        │ ■ │ ► │
└────────────────────────────────────────────────────────────────────┘
```

> **CORRECTING A NEW VENDOR ACCOUNT**
>
> Move to the field that contains the error by **pressing** `Tab` to move forward or `Shift` and `Tab` to go back to the previous field. **Type** the correct information.
>
> You can also highlight the incorrect information by dragging the cursor through it. You can now **type** the correct information.
>
> After a field has been corrected, **press** `Tab` to enter the correction.

NOTES:

Vendor information can be updated at any time. Find the vendor in the Payables Ledger and edit the information as necessary.

Saving a New Vendor Account

When you are certain that all of the information is correct, you must save the newly created vendor and add it to the current list.

Click on Create to save the new vendor information.

Close the Payables Ledger to return to the Ledger/Journal company window and enter the purchase transaction for the new vendor by following the procedures outlined earlier. You will see the new vendor added to the vendor list when you display it.

Displaying Vendor Reports

Displaying Vendor Lists

With the Payables Ledger open or its icon highlighted in the Ledger/Journal company window,

Choose Display Vendor List from the pull-down menu under **Report** to display the list. Scroll as necessary to see customers not visible on the screen.

Close the display when you have finished viewing it.

Displaying Vendor Aged Reports

You can display Vendor Aged reports at any time except when you are entering a transaction.

Choose Vendor Aged from the menu under **Report** The following window appears with several options for your display.

The **Summary** option provides the total balance owing to each vendor. It displays an alphabetic list of vendors with outstanding total balances organized into aged columns. By default, the program selects this option.

Select the **Detail** option if you wish to see individual outstanding invoices and payments made to vendors. This more descriptive report is also aged. Management can use it to make payment decisions. Click on the circle beside Detail to choose this option.

Click on the name in the vendor list to select the vendor for whom you want to see the report. If you want the report to include all vendors, click on **Select All**.

After you have indicated all of the options,

Click on OK to see the report.

Close the displayed report when you have finished.

Displaying the Purchases Journal

Click on the Purchases Journal icon in the Ledger/Journal company window to highlight it.

Choose Display Purchases Journal from the pull-down menu under **Report** to display the following screen:

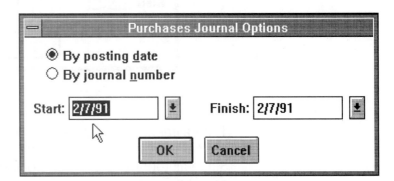

The Purchases Journal can be displayed by posting date or by journal entry number. By default, the posting date option is selected. Since all reports in this workbook use this option, leave the selection unchanged.

Type the beginning date for the journal transactions you want to display.

Press ⌈Tab⌉

Type the ending date for the transaction period you want to see.

Click on OK to see the report.

Close the display when you have finished.

Displaying the Payments Journal

Click on the Payments Journal icon in the Ledger/Journal company window to highlight it.

Choose Display Payments Journal from the pull-down menu under **Report** to see the following screen:

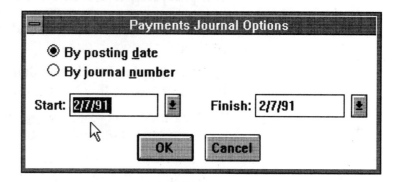

The Payments Journal can also be displayed by posting date or by journal entry number. By default, the posting date option is selected. Since all reports in this workbook request this option, leave the selection unchanged.

Type the beginning date for the journal transactions you want to display.

Press | Tab |

Type the ending date for the transaction period you want to display.

Click on OK to see the report.

Close the display when you are finished.

Printing Vendor Reports

To print vendor reports, display the report you want to print.

Choose Print from the pull-down menu under **File**. Make sure that the print options have been set correctly before you print.

Case Problems

Case One

In March 1991, Commercial Cutlery Ltd. billed Carousel Café for $482.00, including GST, for the purchase of new soup and salad bowls. At the end of the month, Commercial Cutlery informed Mr. Bloom that the correct amount for this purchase was $428.00, not $482.00.

1. What entry would Mr. Bloom have to make to correct his accounts? Describe the procedures he should follow.

2. If Mr. Bloom has already paid the original amount of $482.00, what steps should he follow to make the necessary corrections?

3. Could Mr. Bloom have detected the error himself before being notified by the vendor? How? What controls should he put in place to prevent future errors of this type?

Case Two

At the end of April 1991, Carousel Café has the following balances:

Revenue from Services	CR	$48 800
GST Paid on Capital Goods	DR	$ 664

Manually show the journal entries to reflect the GST liability incurred from café services for the quarterly period and the remittance of the balance owing to the Receiver General.

Wallstreet Wizard

Company Information

Company Profile

Wallstreet Wizard Inc. is a financial consulting business owned and operated by Lucas Vinod in the city of Winnipeg, Manitoba. Mr. Vinod had five years experience with an investment firm when he decided to use his experience and expertise to embark on his own by starting up Wallstreet Wizard Inc.

The business provides financial consulting services, counsels clients in making investment decisions and prepares investment reports for clients. Mr. Vinod also earns income from an investment portfolio.

Although many clients pay cash for the services offered by Wallstreet Wizard, Mr. Vinod has several clients who have opened accounts with him. He allows credit clients to pay their bills within 30 days.

Mr. Vinod started his business on January 1, 1991. After six months of doing his accounting manually, he decided to computerize his accounting records on June 30, 1991. In June, he purchased for cash a NEC 80486 25MHz slimline MS-DOS computer system with an NEC silentwriter2 model 90 laser printer and software (word processing, spreadsheet, database, accounting, windows, utilities and an antivirus package) for $7 600, plus GST of $532. His business is relatively small, with no employees. Occasionally, when his workload requires, he hires a secretary from a temporary services agency.

Mr. Vinod chose the ACCPAC Simply Accounting software package to keep his accounting records because it could handle all his present accounting requirements as well as the accounting for his planned business expansion. His long-term objectives for the business are the expansion of the operations into other areas of the financial business services sector and the hiring of new personnel.

Wallstreet Wizard does not owe money to any of its vendors, but Mr. Vinod has set up a list of vendors that he deals with on a regular basis. The following information summarizes the conversion from the manual to the computerized accounting system:

1. Chart of Accounts;
2. Trial Balance;
3. Vendor Information;
4. Customer Information;
5. Accounting Procedures.

WALLSTREET WIZARD INC.
CHART OF ACCOUNTS

Assets
1080 Cash in Bank
1200 Accounts Receivable
1220 Investment Portfolio
1240 Office Supplies
1260 Software Library
1500 Automobile
1520 Computers & Peripherals
1540 Office Condominium
1560 Office Equipment

Liabilities
2100 Bank Loan
2200 Accounts Payable
2600 GST Charged on Services
2610 GST Paid on Purchases
2620 GST Owing (Refund)
2920 Mortgage Payable

Equity
3560 L. Vinod, Capital

Revenue
4020 Consulting & Counselling
4040 Investment Income
4060 Reports

Expense
5020 Advertising
5040 Bank Charges
5060 General Expense
5080 Hydro Expense
5100 Secretarial Services
5120 Telephone Expense

WALLSTREET WIZARD, INC.
VENDOR INFORMATION

Vendor Name	Address & Telephone	Invoice Date	Invoice Number	Outstanding Balance
Financial Post	4 Revenue Rd. Winnipeg, Manitoba R9T 1W3 Tel: 785-1098			
Manitoba Telephone	89 Sounder Ave. Winnipeg, Manitoba R7U 2A3 Tel: 767-0123			
Midwest Hardware	5 Hammer Rd. Winnipeg, Manitoba R4E 1Y6 Tel: 786-1290			
Pro-Temp Serv Inc	10 Service Rd. Winnipeg, Manitoba R5T 9U7 Tel: 781-9876			

Vendor Name	Address & Telephone	Invoice Date	Invoice Number	Outstanding Balance
Softlink Computers	310 Prochip Ave. Winnipeg, Manitoba R9I 1K8 Tel: 781-0987			
Winnipeg Stationery	2 Brock Ave. Winnipeg, Manitoba R5U 1E3 Tel: 821-0984			

WALLSTREET WIZARD, INC.
CUSTOMER INFORMATION

Customer Name	Address & Telephone	Invoice Date	Invoice Number	Outstanding Balance
Cash Sales	56 Ozland Ave. Winnipeg, Manitoba R8I 2W3 Tel: 479-2211			
Fynetrust Finance	36 Bliss Ave. Winnipeg, Manitoba R6Y 1Q3 Tel: 761-9876	June 28/91	WW-42	$2 675.00
Josh Robyn	761 Fenwick Rd. Winnipeg, Manitoba R8U 2C3 Tel: 387-1234	June 4/91	WW-38	$ 642.00
Prima Realty	121 Prairie Rd. Winnipeg, Manitoba R9I 1A7 Tel: 392-1098	June 15/91	WW-40	$1 712.00
Teachers' Group	98 Lawrence Ave. Winnipeg, Manitoba R8J 2G4 Tel: 761-0987	June 11/91 June 26/91	WW-39 WW-41 Total	$ 856.00 $1 498.00 —— $2 354.00
			Grand Total	$7 383.00

Accounting Procedures

1. **Open-Invoice Accounting for Receivables**

   The open-invoice method of accounting for invoices issued by a business allows the business to keep track of each individual invoice and of any partial payments made against it. In contrast, other methods only keep track of the outstanding balance by combining all invoice balances owed by a customer. ACCPAC Simply Accounting uses the open-invoice method. When an invoice is fully paid, you can either retain the invoice or remove (clear) it.

2. **NSF Cheques**

   If a cheque is deposited from an account that does not have enough money to cover it, the bank may return it to the depositor as NSF (Non-Sufficient Funds). The treatment of an NSF cheque from a customer requires an entry in the Sales Journal to re-enter the original invoice (still unpaid, since the bank refused to cash the cheque) for the amount of the NSF cheque. Re-enter the original invoice number if the invoice was cleared. Otherwise, you may enter the bank debit memo number as a reference for the source of the charge. The account credited will be Cash in Bank. In most companies, the accounting department notifies the customer who wrote the NSF cheque to explain that the debt remains unpaid.

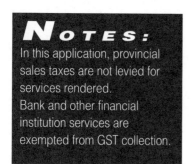

NOTES:

In this application, provincial sales taxes are not levied for services rendered.
Bank and other financial institution services are exempted from GST collection.

3. **The Goods and Services Tax (GST): Remittances**

   Wallstreet Wizard is a financial services business using the **regular method** of calculating the Goods and Services Tax. Prices quoted to customers include GST. GST charged and collected from customers will be recorded as a liability in the GST Charged on Services account. GST paid to vendors will be recorded in the GST Paid on Purchases account as a decrease in liability to Revenue Canada. The balance to be remitted or the request for a refund will be sent to the Receiver General of Canada by the last day of the month for the previous quarterly period.

4. **Cash Sales of Services**

   Cash transactions for services rendered are a normal occurrence in most service businesses. The ACCPAC Simply Accounting program does not have a point-of-sale module for over-the-counter sales. However, it can handle cash transactions. You must set up Cash Sales as a customer in the Receivables Ledger. Use the address and telephone information for the business, Wallstreet Wizard, to insert the customer called **Cash Sales**. This account is already set up for you in this application. Enter the cash transaction for services in the same way you would enter any credit sale transaction for services to customers, with these additional steps:

- When the cursor moves down to the next line on the invoice, type "Payment" in the Description field.
- Enter **code 1** in the GST field to show that the payment is non-taxable.
- Enter a **negative** amount in the Amount field for the cash, cheque or money order received from the customer.
- Enter the *Cash in Bank* account number in the Account field.
- The program will debit the Cash in Bank account instead of the Accounts Receivable control account. All the other accounts for this transaction will be appropriately debited or credited.

Instructions

1. Using the Chart of Accounts, Vendor Information, Customer Information and Accounting Procedures for Wallstreet Wizard, record entries for the source documents in ACCPAC Simply Accounting. The procedures for entering each new type of transaction in this application are outlined step by step in the keystroke section following the source documents.

2. After you have finished making your entries, print the reports indicated on the printing form below.

PRINTING

Primary Reports

☑ Balance Sheet
  date: July 28

☐ Income Statement
  Period covered:
  from: to:

☑ Trial Balance
  date: July 28

☑ General Ledger
  accounts: 1200   4020
                4040

☐ Vendor Aged
  ◯ Summary
  ◯ Detail

  Period covered:
  from: July 1 to: July 28

☑ Customer Aged
  ◯ Summary
  ⊘ Detail

Secondary Reports

GENERAL

☑ General Journal

⊘ by posting date: July 1-28

ACCOUNTS PAYABLE

☐ Vendor Address List

☐ Purchases Journal

○ by posting date:

☐ Payments Journal

○ by posting date:

ACCOUNTS RECEIVABLE

☐ Customer Address List

☑ Sales Journal

⊘ by posting date: July 1-28

☑ Receipts Journal

⊘ by posting date: July 1-28

Source Documents

USING DATE

July 8   ☑   Sales Invoice #WW-43
Dated: July 2/91
To Prima Realty, $642.00 for investment consultation and counselling including GST. Terms: net 30 days.

☑   Cash Receipt #1
Dated: July 3/91
From Josh Robyn, cheque #34, $642 in full payment of account. Reference invoice #WW-38.

☐   Purchase Invoice #FP-123
Dated: July 5/91
From Financial Post magazine, $250 for advertisement to promote business, plus GST paid $17.50. Purchase Invoice total $267.50. Terms: cash on receipt.

☐ Cheque Copy #65
Dated: July 5/91
To Financial Post magazine, $267.50 in full payment of account. Reference invoice #FP-123.

☐ Purchase Invoice #WS-65
Dated: July 5/91
From Winnipeg Stationery, $100 for the purchase of office supplies, plus GST paid $7. Purchase Invoice total $107. Terms: cash on receipt.

☐ Cheque Copy #66
Dated: July 5/91
To Winnipeg Stationery, $107 in full payment of account. Reference invoice #WS-65.

☐ Cash Sales Slip #22
Dated: July 6/91
To L. Bowen, a cash client, a cheque received for $187.25. This amount includes standard consultation and counselling fees and GST.

☐ Sales Invoice #WW-44
Dated: July 7/91
To the Teachers' Group, $321.00 for consultation and $963.00 for investment report including GST. Sales Invoice total $1 284. Terms: net 30 days.

July 14 ☐ Cash Receipt #2
Dated: July 9/91
From the Teachers' Group, cheque #65, $2 354 in payment of account. Reference invoices #WW-39 and #WW-41.

☐ Sales Invoice #WW-45
Dated: July 10/91
To the Phoenix Café (new customer), $321 for consulting and counselling services including GST. Terms: net 30 days.

☐ Bank Debit Memo #PT-981
Dated: July 11/91
From Prairie Trust, $642 for NSF cheque from Josh Robyn. Reference invoice #WW-38 and Cash Receipt #1. Josh Robyn has been notified of his unpaid account and NSF cheque by the owner.

NOTES:
☑ Phoenix Café is located at
31 Calderone Rd.
Winnipeg, Manitoba
R4T 1X3
Tel: 386-9874

HINTS:
To complete this transaction, read Accounting Procedures - NSF Cheques on page 80.

☐ Cash Sales Slip #23
Dated: July 12/91
To K. Huang, a cash client, a money order received for $187.25. This amount includes standard consultation and counselling fees and GST.

☐ Bank Debit Memo #PT-1023
Dated: July 13/91
From Prairie Trust, $500 for reduction of bank loan.

☐ Sales Invoice #WW-46
Dated: July 14/91
To the Teachers' Group, $214 for counselling services including GST. Terms: net 30 days.

☐ Bank Credit Memo #PT-456
Dated: July 14/91
From Prairie Trust, $1 400 for quarterly investment income.

July 21 ☐ Sales Invoice #WW-47
Dated: July 16/91
To Fynetrust Finance, $428 for consulting and counselling services including GST. Terms: net 30 days.

☐ Cash Receipt #3
Dated: July 16/91
From Prima Realty, cheque #231, $1 712 in payment of account. Reference invoice #WW-40.

☐ Utility Statement #MT-1123
Dated: July 17/91
From Manitoba Telephone, $120 for telephone services plus GST paid $8.40. Utility Statement total $128.40. Terms: cash on receipt.

☐ Cheque Copy #67
Dated: July 17/91
To Manitoba Telephone, $128.40 in full payment of account. Reference invoice #MT-1123.

☐ Purchase Invoice #MH-90
Dated: July 19/91
From Midwest Hardware Store, $70.00 for paint and tools to repaint office condominium, plus GST paid $4.90. Purchase Invoice total $74.90. Terms: cash on receipt.

☐ Cheque Copy #68
Dated: July 19/91
To Midwest Hardware Store, $74.90 in full payment of account. Reference invoice #MH-90.

☐ Cash Sales Slip #24
Dated: July 20/91
To G. Carver, a cash client, cash received for $187.25. This amount includes standard consultation and counselling fees and GST.

☐ Cash Recipt #4
Dated: July 21/91
From Josh Robyn, certified cheque #56, $642 in full payment of account. Reference invoice #WW-38, Cash Receipt #1 and Bank Debit Memo #PT-981.

July 28 ☐ Cash Receipt #5
Dated: July 23/91
From Fynetrust Finance, cheque #58, $2 000 in payment of account. Reference invoice #WW-42.

☐ Sales Invoice #WW-48
Dated: July 24/91
To Prima Realty, $214 for consulting and counselling services including GST. Terms: net 30 days.

☐ Bank Debit Memo #PT-1110
Dated: July 25/91
From Prairie Trust, $25 for bank service charges.

☐ Office Services Contract #PTS-109
Dated: July 26/91
From Pro-Temp Services Inc., a secreterial service company, $300 for temporary secretarial help plus GST paid $21. Service Contract total $321. Terms: cash on receipt.

☐ Cheque Copy #69
Dated: July 26/91
To Pro-Temp Services Inc., $321 in full
payment of account. Reference invoice
#PTS-109.

☐ Cash Sales Slip #25
Dated: July 28/91
To K. Wilkes, a cash client, a money order
received for $187.25. This amount includes
standard consultation and counselling fees
and GST.

☐ Purchase Invoice #SC-34
Dated: July 28/91
From Softlink Computers Inc., $100 for the
purchase of statistical software plus GST paid
$7. Purchase Invoice total $107. Terms: cash
on receipt.

☐ Cheque Copy #70
Dated: July 28/91
To Softlink Computers Inc., $107 in full
payment of account. Reference invoice
#SC-34.

☐ Cash Receipt #6
Dated: July 28/91
From Fynetrust Finance, cheque #67, $675 in
payment of account. Balance of reference
invoice #WW-42.

Keystrokes

Opening Data Files

Using the instructions for accessing data files on page 9, load the
data files for Wallstreet Wizard. Enter the first using date, July 8,
1991, for this application.

Type: 07-08-91

Click on OK

You are shown the following warning statement:

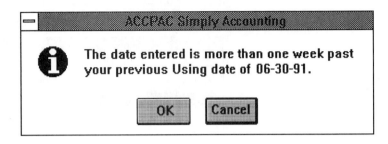

Normally a business would update its accounting records more frequently. If you have entered the correct date,

Click on OK to accept the date entered and display the familiar main Ledger/Journal company window.

Accounting for Sales

Click on the Sales icon in the lower journal portion of the window to highlight it as follows:

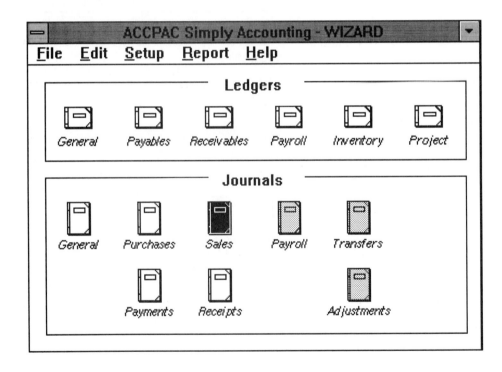

Choose **Open Journal** from the pull-down menu under **File** to open the Sales Journal. The Sales Journal input form appears on the screen as follows:

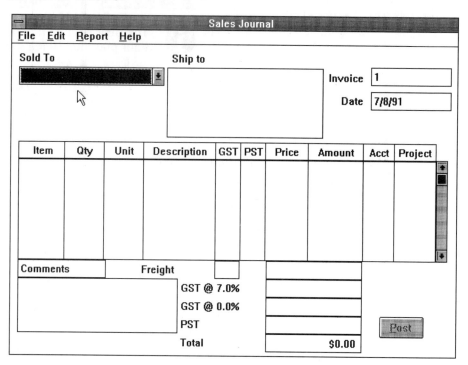

The Customer (Sold To) field is darkened, ready to receive information.

Click on the arrow beside the darkened field to obtain the list of customers as shown below:

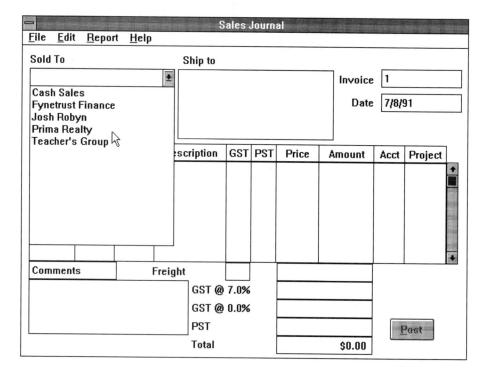

Click on Prima Realty, the customer in the first source document, to select and enter it.

Notice that the customer's name and address have been added to your input form. If you have made an error in your selection, click on the customer list arrow and start again. By default, the Sold to and the Ship to fields are the same, although they could be different if a customer has more than one business location. If you have selected correctly, you can skip over the shipping information for this customer.

Press [Tab] repeatedly until the Invoice field is highlighted.

Type: `WW-43`

Press [Tab]

The cursor moves to the Date field. The using date appears automatically by default. It is highlighted, ready to be accepted or changed. You need to change the date. Enter the date on which the transaction took place, July 2, 1991.

Type: `07-02-91`

Press [Tab]

The cursor advances to the Item field. Because we are not using the Inventory Ledger for this application, ignore this field and the next two.

Click on the first line of the **Description field** . The Description field is used to enter a description or comment concerning the sale.

Type: `Consultation & Counselling`

Press [Tab]

The cursor is now positioned in the GST field.

NOTES:

Alternatively, you could press ⎚ repeatedly until you were in the Description field.

Press `Enter` to display the following GST codes on your screen:

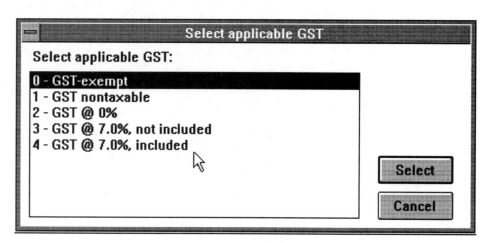

You may select from this list the appropriate GST code for the company. Since the invoice amount already includes the GST, you should choose code *4 - GST @ 7%, included*.

Click on 4 - GST @ 7.0%, included to highlight it.

Click on Select to enter the code.

The cursor is now in the Price field. Since the service provided is exempt from provincial sales tax (PST), the cursor skips over this field. When PST is applicable and is set up in the defaults for the company, the program will not skip over the PST field. The Price field also refers to inventory items with unit prices; it is not applicable to Wallstreet Wizard.

Press `Tab`

The cursor should now be positioned in the Amount field, where you will enter the total amount for this invoice, with the GST included.

Type: 642

Press `Tab`

In the Account field, you can see the list of accounts. To see revenue accounts,

Type: 4

Press `Enter`

Click on 4020 Consulting & Counselling to highlight it.

Click on Select to add it to your input form.

Press ⎡Tab⎤

The cursor is now placed in the Item field of line 2, ready for additional sale items if necessary. You can use the Comments box to type an appropriate comment such as "GST included in fees." (Click on the Comments field to move the cursor.)

The transaction is now complete, and your invoice should resemble the following:

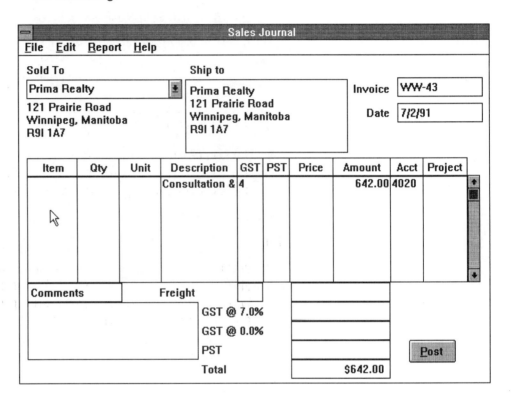

Reviewing the Sales Journal Entry

Choose Display Sales Journal Entry from the pull-down menu under **Report** to display the transaction you have entered as shown:

Review the journal entry to check for mistakes. You can see that the Accounts Receivable control account has been updated automatically by the ACCPAC Simply Accounting program because the Receivables and General Ledgers are fully integrated. The GST Charged on Services account has also been updated correctly because of the GST code you entered.

Close the display to return to the Sales Journal input screen.

CORRECTING THE SALES JOURNAL ENTRY

Move to the field that has the error. **Press** `Tab` to move forward through the fields or **press** `Shift` and `Tab` together to move back to a previous field. This will highlight the field information so you can change it. **Type** the correct information and **press** `Tab` to enter it.

You can also use the mouse to point to a field and drag through the incorrect information to highlight it. **Type** the correct information and **press** `Tab` to enter it.

If the customer is incorrect, reselect from the customer list by **clicking on** the arrow beside this field. **Click on** the name of the correct customer.

To correct an account number, **click on** the incorrect number to move the cursor to this field. **Press** `Enter` to display the list of accounts. **Click on** the correct account number to highlight it and **click on Select** and **press** `Tab` to enter the change.

Posting

When you are certain that you have entered all the information correctly, you must post the transaction to save it. Notice that the Post button is no longer dimmed.

Click on Post to save your transaction.

A new blank Sales Journal form appears on the screen. The next transaction is a receipt, however, so we must exit from the Sales Journal.

Close the Sales Journal input form to return to the main Ledger/Journal company window.

Accounting for Receipts

Click on the Receipts Journal icon from the Ledger/Journal company window to highlight it as shown:

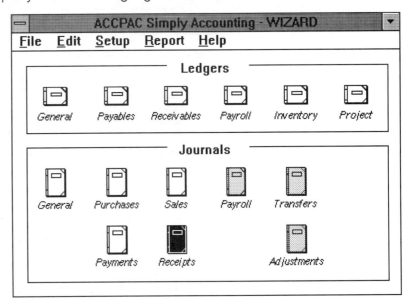

Choose Open Journal from the pull-down menu under **File** to open the Receipts Journal. The following blank Receipts Journal input screen appears:

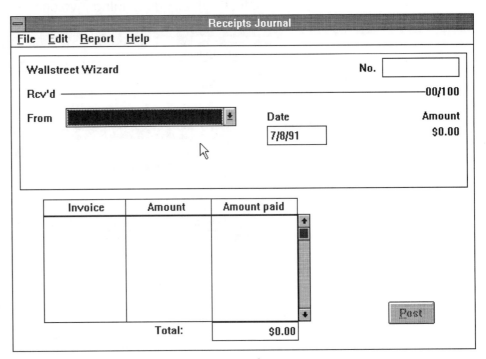

The Customer (Rcv'd From) field is darkened, ready to receive information.

Click on the arrow beside this field to display the familiar customer list as shown:

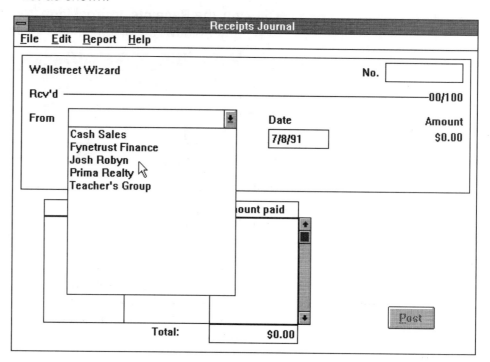

Click on Josh Robyn to choose this customer. As shown, the customer's name and address have been added to your input form, together with all outstanding invoices for Josh Robyn:

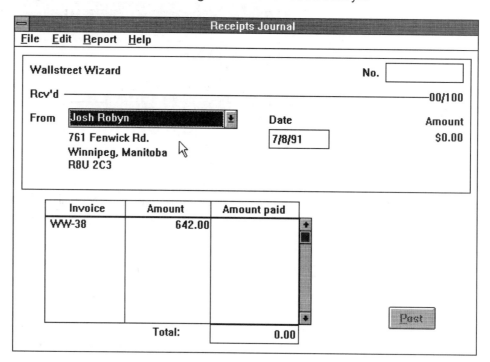

If you have chosen the wrong customer, display the list again and reselect. If you have selected correctly,

Press

The cursor advances to the No. field, where you should enter the cheque number.

Type: 34

Press Tab

The cursor moves to the Date field. Replace the using date with the date for this transaction.

Type: 07-03-91

Press Tab

The cursor moves to the Amount field. By default, the amount owing on the first invoice is shown and highlighted. All outstanding invoices are listed on the screen. You can accept a highlighted amount, or type in an exact amount for a partial payment. In this case, there is only one invoice and the full amount is being paid so you can accept the default.

Press Tab

The completed Receipts form should now appear as follows:

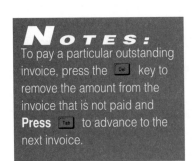

NOTES:

To pay a particular outstanding invoice, press the [Del] key to remove the amount from the invoice that is not paid and **Press** [Tab] to advance to the next invoice.

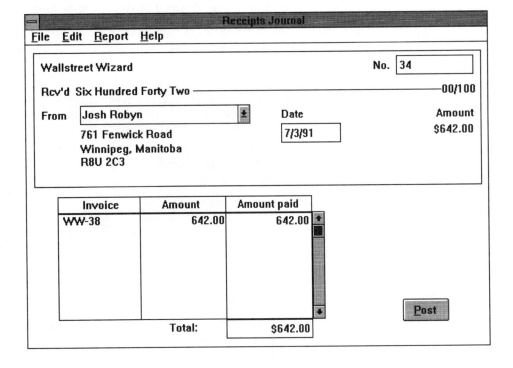

Notice that the upper cheque portion of the form has also been completed.

You have made all the entries for this transaction, so you are ready to review and post your transaction.

Reviewing the Receipts Journal Entry

Choose Display Receipts Journal Entry from the pull-down menu under **Report** to display the transaction you have entered as follows:

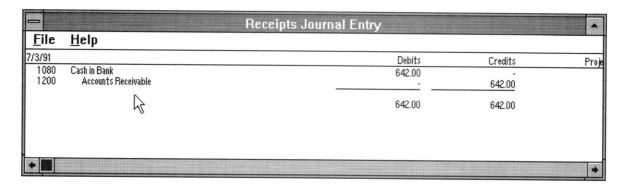

When you work in a subsidiary ledger, the ACCPAC Simply Accounting program will automatically debit the Accounts Receivable control account in the General Ledger and credit the Cash in Bank account. The Accounts Receivable and Cash in Bank accounts are updated automatically because the ledgers are fully integrated.

Close the display to return to the Receipts Journal input screen.

CORRECTING THE RECEIPTS JOURNAL ENTRY

Move to the field that has the error. **Press** [Tab] to move forward through the fields or **press** [Shift] and [Tab] together to move back to a previous field. This will highlight the field information so you can change it. **Type** the correct information and **press** [Tab] to enter it.

You can also use the mouse to point to a field and drag through the incorrect information to highlight it. **Type** the correct information and **press** [Tab] to enter it.

If the customer is incorrect, reselect from the customer list by **clicking on** the arrow beside this field. **Click on** the name of the correct customer. You will be asked to confirm that you want to discard the current transaction. **Click on** Yes to discard the incorrect entry and display the outstanding invoices for the correct customer. **Type** the receipt information for this customer.

Posting

When you are certain that you have entered all the information correctly, you must post the transaction to save it. Notice that the Post button is no longer dimmed.

Click on Post to save your transaction.

Adding a New Customer

On July 10, a new customer is listed in the source documents and must be added to your list.

Click on the Receivables Ledger icon from the upper ledger portion of the Ledger/Journal company window to highlight it as shown:

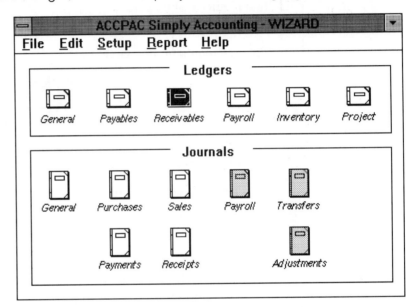

Choose Open Ledger from the pull-down menu under **File** to open the Receivables Ledger. The Cash Sales screen appears.

Choose **Create** from the pull-down menu under **Edit** to display the following new customer input screen:

```
┌─────────────────────────────────────────────────────────────────────┐
│ ▬                        Receivables Ledger                          │
├─────────────────────────────────────────────────────────────────────┤
│ E̲dit    R̲eport   Help                                                │
│                                                                       │
│  Customer:   ┌───────────────────────┐   Phone:        ┌───────────┐ │
│              │ New Customer          │                 │           │ │
│              └───────────────────────┘                 └───────────┘ │
│  Contact:  ꝂꝂ┌───────────────────────┐   Fax:          ┌───────────┐ │
│              │                       │                 │           │ │
│              └───────────────────────┘                 └───────────┘ │
│  Street:     ┌───────────────────────┐   Credit limit:  ┌──────────┐ │
│              │                       │                  │          │ │
│              └───────────────────────┘                  └──────────┘ │
│  City:       ┌───────────────────────┐   Last year sales:    0.00    │
│              │ Winnipeg              │                               │
│              └───────────────────────┘                               │
│  Province:   ┌───────────────────────┐   YTD sales:          0.00    │
│              │ Manitoba              │                               │
│              └───────────────────────┘                               │
│  Postal code:┌───────────────────────┐   Balance owing:      0.00    │
│              │                       │                               │
│              └───────────────────────┘                               │
│  ☐ Clear invoices when paid                                          │
│  ☒ Include in GST report                                             │
│  ☒ Print statements for this customer                                │
│                          ┌──────────┐                                │
│                          │  Create  │                                │
│                          └──────────┘                                │
├─────────────────────────────────────────────────────────────────────┤
│ ◄                                                             ■ ►    │
└─────────────────────────────────────────────────────────────────────┘
```

You are ready to enter your new customer. The Customer field is highlighted, ready to receive new information.

Type: `Phoenix Cafe`

Press [Tab]

The cursor moves to the contact field. If Wallstreet Wizard normally deals with a particular individual at Phoenix Café (e.g., the owner or the accountant), enter that person's name here. Leave this field blank for now.

Press [Tab]

The cursor moves to the Street field.

Type: `31 Calderone Rd.`

Press [Tab]

The cursor moves to the City field. Notice that the city and province in which Wallstreet Wizard is located have been entered by default. Because they are correct for our customer, leave them unchanged.

Press `Tab`

Press `Tab`

The cursor moves to the Postal code field. You do not need to use capital letters or to leave a space within the postal code. The program will make these adjustments for you.

Type: `r4t1x3`

Press `Tab`

Notice that the format of the postal code is corrected automatically. The cursor moves to the Phone field. You do not need to insert a dash when you enter a telephone number.

Type: `3869874`

Press `Tab`

Notice that the format for the telephone number is corrected automatically. The cursor advances to the Fax field. Phoenix Café does not have a fax number. In the next field, the Credit Limit field, you can enter the upper credit limit for a particular customer to help keep bad debts to a minimum. Customers who have previously defaulted on making their payments could be placed on a cash-only basis by setting their credit limits at zero. Wallstreet Wizard is not presently using this field, but it is analyzing customer payment trends to consider adding this feature in the future.

Three other options are available for customer records. The default settings for these options are correct so do not change them. (You can change these settings at any time.)

The *Clear invoices when paid* option removes invoices that are fully paid. Choose not to remove paid invoices by leaving this box empty. This way you can keep a record of all purchases and payments made by this customer.

You may also choose the *Print statements for this customer* option. You should use the correct statement forms, but you could also print statements on ordinary printer paper.

The *Include in GST report* option should also be left checked so that sales to this customer become part of the permanent GST record.

Your completed customer information form now appears as follows:

```
┌─────────────────────────────────────────────────────────────┐
│ ─                    Receivables Ledger                      │
├─────────────────────────────────────────────────────────────┤
│ Edit   Report   Help                                         │
│                                                              │
│ Customer:  ┌─────────────────────┐   Phone:  ┌────────────┐  │
│            │ Phoenix Cafe        │           │ 336-9874   │  │
│            └─────────────────────┘           └────────────┘  │
│ Contact:   ┌─────────────────────┐   Fax:    ┌────────────┐  │
│            │                     │           │            │  │
│            └─────────────────────┘           └────────────┘  │
│ Street:    ┌─────────────────────┐   Credit limit: ┌──────┐  │
│            │ 31 Calderone Rd.    │                 │      │  │
│            └─────────────────────┘                 └──────┘  │
│ City:      ┌─────────────────────┐   Last year sales:  0.00  │
│            │ Winnipeg            │                           │
│            └─────────────────────┘                           │
│ Province:  ┌─────────────────────┐   YTD sales:        0.00  │
│            │ Manitoba            │                           │
│            └─────────────────────┘                           │
│ Postal code: ┌───────────────────┐  Balance owing:     0.00  │
│              │ R4T 1X3           │                           │
│              └───────────────────┘                           │
│ ☐ Clear invoices when paid                                   │
│ ☒ Include in GST report                                      │
│ ☒ Print statements for this customer                         │
│                            ┌──────────┐                      │
│                            │ Create   │                      │
│                            └──────────┘                      │
└─────────────────────────────────────────────────────────────┘
```

CORRECTING A NEW CUSTOMER ACCOUNT

Move to the field that contains the error by **pressing** [Tab] to move forward or [Shift] and [Tab] to go back to the previous field. **Type** the correct information.

You can also highlight the incorrect information by dragging the cursor through it. You can now **type** the correct information.

After you have corrected a field, **press** [Tab] to enter the correction.

Saving a New Customer Account

When you are certain that all of the information is correct, you must save the newly created customer account and add it to the current list.

Click on Create to save the new customer information.

You can now return to the Sales Journal and enter the sale transaction for the new customer by following the procedures outlined earlier. When you display the customer list, note that the new customer has been added to it.

Displaying Customer Lists

With the Receivables Ledger open or its icon highlighted in the Ledger/Journal company window,

Choose Display Customer List from the pull-down menu under **Report** to display the list. Scroll to see customers not visible on the screen.

Close the display when you have finished viewing it.

Displaying Customer Aged Reports

Choose Customer Aged from the pull-down menu under **Report** at any time except when you are entering a transaction. The following window will appear, showing several options for your display:

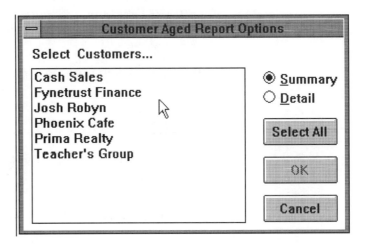

Click on the appropriate name in the customer list. If you want the report to include all customers, click on the circle beside Select All.

The **Summary** option will display an alphabetic list of the selected customers with outstanding total balances owing, organized into aged columns. By default, the program selects this option.

Select the **Detail** option if you wish to see individual outstanding invoices and payments made by customers. This more descriptive report is also aged. Management can use it to make credit decisions. Click on the circle beside Detail to choose this option.

After you have indicated all of the options you want,

Click on OK to see the report.

Close the displayed report when you have finished.

Displaying the Sales Journal

With the Sales Journal icon highlighted in the Ledger/Journal company window,

Choose Display Sales Journal from the pull-down menu under **Report** to display the following screen:

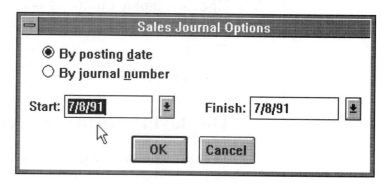

You can display the Sales Journal by posting date or by journal entry number. The default setting, the *By posting date* option, is the one used for all reports in this workbook, so leave the selection unchanged.

Type the beginning date for the journal transactions you want to display.

Press [Tab]

Type the ending date for the transaction period you want to see.

Click on OK to see the report.

Close the display when you are finished.

Displaying the Receipts Journal

With the Receipts Journal icon highlighted in the Ledger/Journal company window,

Choose Display Receipts Journal from the pull-down menu under **Report** to display the following screen:

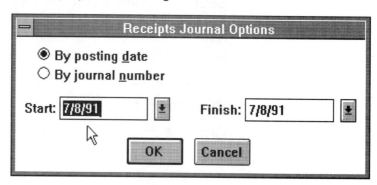

The Receipts Journal can also be displayed by posting date or by journal entry number. The default setting, the *By posting date* option, is the one requested for all reports in this workbook, so leave the selection unchanged.

Type the beginning date for the journal transactions you want to display.

Press [Tab]

Type the ending date for the transaction period you want to see.

Click on OK to see the report.

Close the display when you are finished.   .

Displaying the GST Report

Choose GST from the pull-down menu under **Report**. You may display this report at any time unless you are entering a transaction. The following dialogue window appears:

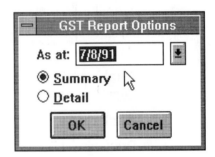

Type the date for which you want the report.

Leave the default setting at **Summary** if you want to include only the totals of the GST Paid on Purchases, GST Charged on Services and the difference between these two amounts.

Click on the button beside **Detail** if you want a detailed breakdown of all customer and vendor transactions that included GST.

Once you have set the options as you wish,

Click on OK to see the report.

Close the display window when you are finished.

NOTES:

Only the GST transactions that were entered through the Sales Journal or the Purchases Journal will be included in this report. Furthermore, only customers and vendors for whom the *Include in GST report* box was checked will be included. GST-related transactions completed in the General Journal will not be included. Therefore, the amounts shown in the GST report may differ from the balances in the General Ledger GST accounts that include all GST transactions. You should use the General Ledger accounts to determine the balance owing (or refund) and then make adjustments in the report as necessary.

Printing Customer Reports

To print customer reports, display the report you want to print.

Choose Print from the pull-down menu under **File**. Since printing will begin immediately, make sure that you have set the print options correctly.

Printing Customer Statements

Choose Customer Statements from the pull-down menu under **Report** to see the following options:

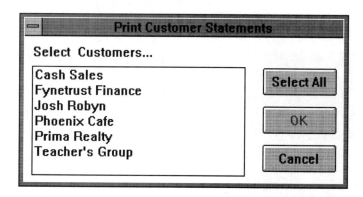

Click on the customer for whom you want to print the statement, or click on **Select All** to include all customers.

Click on OK

Printing will begin immediately, so be sure your printer is set up with the correct forms before you begin.

Case Problem

In March, a new customer, Standard Trust, contracted with Wallstreet Wizard Inc. to write a report on restructuring its financial portfolios. The work was to be completed in three months, for a total cost of $10 000. The terms of the contract required Standard Trust to prepay 25 percent of the total amount negotiated, followed by equal monthly payments for the remainder. The final payment was scheduled to coincide with the completion of the project.

1. How should Wallstreet Wizard record the prepayment using ACCPAC Simply Accounting? Hint: You may wish to refer to your ACCPAC Simply Accounting users' guide.

2. What entries need to be made when the remaining payments are received each month and when the work is completed?

3. At the end of the three months, the report was 90 percent completed and all payments from Standard Trust had been received. How should this information be recorded using Generally Accepted Accounting Principles?

CHAPTER SIX

Celine's Cleaners

OBJECTIVES

Upon completion of this chapter, you will be able to:

1. *open* the Payroll Journal;
2. *enter* employee-related payroll transactions;
3. *understand* automatic payroll deductions;
4. *post* payroll transactions;
5. *observe* and *understand* integration accounts;
6. *edit* and *review* payroll transactions;
7. *display* and *print* payroll reports.

Company Information

Company Profile

Celine's Cleaners is a dry cleaning business owned and managed by Celine Porter in the downtown Vancouver area. The business earns its money by providing dry cleaning and delivery services and by mending and repairing clothing. The business is open six days per week.

The business employs four full-time staff members and two part-time workers. The full-time employees include an assistant manager/cashier, who handles the front-end operations of the business, works at the counter and is responsible for the accounting work. Three full-time employees clean and press the clothing, handle all the equipment and share general maintenance responsibilities. The part-time employees include a person who comes in for half a day each working day to repair clothing and a person who delivers clothing to regular customers in the mornings. The owner is responsible for ordering supplies, handling customer complaints, delegating duties and making business decisions.

Celine Porter attended a business conference in Vancouver and was quite impressed by the ACCPAC Simply Accounting software package. She decided to use it for her business in the new fiscal year starting January 1, 1991 because it was able to handle all her accounting and payroll requirements. Prior to starting the new fiscal year, the business remitted all payroll liabilities to the government and other agencies. The information that summarizes Celine's Cleaners' accounting data after its conversion from a manual to a computerized accounting system is contained in the following reports:

1. Chart of Accounts;
2. Trial Balance;
3. Vendor Information;
4. Employee Information;
5. Employee Profiles and TD1 Information;
6. Accounting Procedures.

Celine will collect the Goods and Services Tax (GST) using the **regular method**. Her cash registers are programmed to accomodate the GST calculations.

CELINE'S CLEANERS
CHART OF ACCOUNTS

Assets
1080 Cash in Bank
1240 Advances Receivable
1250 Clothes Hangers
1300 Dry Cleaning Supplies
1350 Office Supplies
1500 Cash Registers
1550 Delivery Truck
1600 Dry Cleaning Equipment
1650 Pressing Machines
1700 Railings
1750 Shop

Liabilities
2100 Bank Loan
2200 Accounts Payable
2300 Vacation Payable
2310 UI Payable
2320 CPP Payable
2330 Income Tax Payable
2440 Medical Payable
2460 WCB Payable
2600 GST Charged on Services
2610 GST Paid on Purchases
2620 GST Owing (Refund)

Equity
3560 C. Porter, Capital

Revenue
4050 Dry Cleaning Services
4100 Repairs & Alterations

Expense
5020 Advertising & Promotion
5040 Bank Charges
5080 General Expense
5100 Hydro Expense
5140 Repairs & Maintenance
5160 Telephone Expense
5180 Truck Expense
5300 Wages
5310 UI Expense
5320 CPP Expense
5330 WCB Expense

```
CELINE'S CLEANERS
POST-CLOSING TRIAL BALANCE

December 31, 1990

  1080 Cash in Bank              $ 17 800.00
  1250 Clothes Hangers             1 000.00
  1300 Dry Cleaning Supplies       3 200.00
  1500 Cash Registers              2 000.00
  1550 Delivery Truck             10 000.00
  1600 Dry Cleaning Equipment     65 000.00
  1650 Pressing Machines          25 000.00
  1700 Railings                    4 000.00
  1750 Shop                      100 000.00
  2100 Bank Loan                               $  10 000.00
  2200 Accounts Payable                            1 450.00
  3560 C. Porter, Capital                        216 550.00
                                 _____    _____
                                 $228 000.00    $228 000.00
                                 ===========    ===========
```

CELINE'S CLEANERS
VENDOR INFORMATION

Vendor Name	Address & Telephone	Invoice Date	Invoice Number	Outstanding Balance
B.C. Hydro	87 Energy Ave. Vancouver, British Columbia V9P 3E4 Tel: 345-9821			
B.C. Telephone	976 Signal Rd. Vancouver, British Columbia V9I 2C3 Tel: 784-0981			
Dymond Service Centre	41 Brinks Ave. Vancouver, British Columbia V7L 2F4 Tel: 981-2367			
EuroCan Equipment Co.	981 Brunswick Rd. Vancouver, British Columbia V5T 1A3 Tel: 316-2346			
Oceanview Printers	73 Brandon Rd. Vancouver, British Columbia V3R 1D3 Tel: 672-1967			

Vendor Name	Address & Telephone	Invoice Date	Invoice Number	Outstanding Balance
Pacific Stationery	10 Surf Avenue Vancouver, British Columbia V6Y 2D5 Tel: 211-0923			
Performance Machinery	91 Grinding Rd. Vancouver, British Columbia V9L 1P8 Tel: 746-2347			
Westcoast Suppliers	5 Tafel Rd. Vancouver, British Columbia V8I 2D6 Tel: 364-2947	Dec. 15/90	WS-111	$1 450.00

CELINE'S CLEANERS
EMPLOYEE INFORMATION SHEET

Employee Number:	1	2	3
Position:	Assistant Manager	Cleaner/Presser	Cleaner/Presser
Social Insurance No.:	629 456 122	428 645 987	653 189 192
Employee Name:	Kenneth Ho	Bok Leung	Sara Marino
Address & Telephone:	45 Brooks Ave. Vancouver British Columbia V9R 1J6 604-612-9321	33 Linen Rd. Vancouver British Columbia V1S 2W3 604-212-9876	56 Silken Street Vancouver British Columbia V6Y 1J9 604-301-7654
Date of Birth (dd-mm-yy):	06-11-56	19-08-60	01-04-59
Tax Exemptions: (TD1-1991) Basic Personal Spouse (or equivalent) Children Disability Education & Tuition Other	$6 280.00 5 757.00 406.00	$6 280.00	$6 280.00
Total Exemptions Less: Family Allowances	12 443.00 392.88	6 280.00	6 280.00
Net Claim	12 050.12	6 280.00	6 280.00
Employee Earnings: Regular Wage Rate Overtime Wage Rate Regular Salary Vacation Pay	$1 350.00/period 4% (retained)	$14.50/hour $21.75/hour 4% (retained)	$14.50/hour $21.75/hour 4% (retained)

Employee Deductions:

Medical	$50.00/period	$25.00/period	$25.00/period
CPP	*	*	*
UI	*	*	*
Income Tax	*	*	*

* Calculations built into ACCPAC Simply Accounting program

CELINE'S CLEANERS
EMPLOYEE INFORMATION (continued)

Employee Number:	4	5	6
Position:	Cleaner/Presser	Delivery	Sewing
Social Insurance No.:	319 354 712	419 449 977	713 688 392
Employee Name:	Rita Polski	Farad Russey	Nirmala Vas
Address & Telephone:	12 Falstaff Ave. Vancouver British Columbia V7F 1K3	23 Hume Rd. Vancouver British Columbia V6G 9F3	68 Millet Rd. Vancouver British Columbia V6P 1K9
	604-651-9531	604-782-9356	604-841-7610
Date of Birth (dd-mm-yy):	19-08-58	15-03-69	07-11-56

Tax Exemptions:
(TD1-1991)

Basic Personal	$ 6 280.00	$ 6 280.00	$ 6 280.00
Spouse (or equivalent)	5 757.00		
Children			
Disability			
Education & Tuition		1 280.00	
Other			
Total Exemptions	12 037.00	7 560.00	6 280.00
Less: Family Allowances			
Net Claim	12 037.00	7 560.00	6 280.00

Employee Earnings:

Regular Wage Rate	$14.50/hour	$10.50/hour	$12.00/hour
Overtime Wage Rate	$21.75/hour	$15.75/hour	$18.00/hour
Regular Salary			
Vacation Pay	4% (retained)	4% (retained)	4% (retained)

Employee Deductions:

Medical	$25.00/period	$25.00/period	$25.00/period
CPP	*	*	*
UI	*	*	*
Income Tax	*	*	*

* Calculations built into ACCPAC Simply Accounting program

Employee Profiles and TD1 Information

1. Kenneth Ho is the assistant manager of the store. His duties are to look after incoming dry cleaning orders and handle the banking and accounting. He also assumes full responsibility for the store when the owner is absent by ordering supplies, delegating work to the other employees and dealing with customer complaints and concerns. Kenneth fully supports his wife. He has one child, aged 12, who has no income. Kenneth's salary is $1 350.00 per pay period ($35 100.00 per year). He does not receive any company benefits.

2. Bok Leung works as a cleaner and presser. He is single and self-supporting. He receives $14.50 per hour for regular work and $21.75 for overtime work. He does not receive any company benefits.

3. Sara Marino works as a cleaner and presser. She is single and self-supporting. She earns $14.50 per hour for regular work and $21.75 for overtime work. She does not receive any company benefits.

4. Rita Polski works as a cleaner and presser. Rita is single and supports an infirm brother, aged 19. She receives $14.50 per hour for regular work and $21.75 for overtime work. She does not receive any company benefits.

5. Farad Russey works part-time, making deliveries in the mornings. Farad is single and self-supporting. He is also a student at a local community college. Farad earns $10.50 per hour for regular work and $15.75 for overtime work. He does not receive any company benefits.

6. Nirmala Vas works in the mornings only, repairing clothing for Celine's Cleaners. She also works for another business on a part-time basis. Nirmala is single and self-supporting. She earns $12.00 per hour for regular work and $18.00 per hour for overtime work. She does not receive any company benefits.

Additional Payroll Information

1. There are 26 pay periods for all employees.

2. UI, CPP and income taxes withheld are remitted to the Receiver General of Canada monthly.

3. Medical payments are remitted to the Provincial Treasurer monthly.

4. The employer's contributions include

   - CPP contributions equal to employee contributions;
   - UI factor of 1.4;
   - WCB rate of 3.92.

Accounting Procedures

NOTES:
- Bank and other financial institution services are exempt from GST charges in this application.
- Provincial sales taxes are not levied in this application.

The Goods and Services Tax: Remittances

Celine has decided to use the **regular method** for remittance of the Goods and Services Tax. She will record the GST collected from customers as a liability in the GST Charged on Services account. GST paid by her to vendors will be recorded in the GST Paid on Purchases account as a decrease in her liability to Revenue Canada. Her GST quarterly refund or remittance will be calculated automatically in the GST Owing (Refund) clearing account. You will see this balance when you display or print the Balance Sheet. She will file for a refund or remit the balance owing to the Receiver General of Canada by the last day of the month for the previous quarterly period.

Instructions

NOTES:
- The Receivables Ledger is not integrated in this application, since Celine's Cleaners deals only in cash. Do not attempt to use the Sales or Receipts journals.
- Please print Payroll Summaries after you have completed payroll transactions for a given using date. You may also wish to print out the Payroll Journal Entry (before posting) for each employee as you complete the payroll transaction. This will assist you in making reversals and corrections if you have made any errors. (Refer to the keystrokes for Displaying and Printing Payroll Reports on page 124.)

1. Using the Chart of Accounts, Vendor Information and Employee Information, enter the transactions using the ACCPAC Simply Accounting program. The procedures for entering the first payroll transaction for this application are outlined step by step in the keystroke section following the source documents.

2. After you have finished making your entries, print the reports indicated on the printing form below.

PRINTING

Primary Reports

☐ Balance Sheet
   date:

☐ Income Statement
   Period covered:
   from: to:

☑ Trial Balance
   date: Jan. 28

☑ General Ledger
   accounts: 2310   2320
              2330   5300

☐ Vendor Aged
   ○ Summary
   ○ Detail

   Period covered:
   from: Jan. 1   to: Jan. 28

☑ Employee Summary
☐ Employee Register 1
☐ Employee Register 2
☐ T4 Slips

Secondary Reports

GENERAL

☑ General Journal

    ⊘ by posting date: Jan. 1-28

ACCOUNTS PAYABLE

☐ Vendor Address List

☐ Purchases Journal

    ○ by posting date:

☐ Payments Journal

    ○ by posting date:

PAYROLL

☐ Employee List

☑ Payroll Journal

    ⊘ by posting date: Jan. 1-28

Source Documents

USING DATE

Jan. 7   ☐   Purchase Invoice #WS-123
Dated: Jan. 2/91
From Westcoast Suppliers, $400 for dry cleaning supplies plus GST paid $28. Purchase Invoice total $428. Terms: net 30 days.

       ☐   Purchase Invoice #DSC-78
Dated: Jan. 3/91
From Dymond Service Centre, $120 for annual tune-up of delivery truck plus GST paid $8.40. Purchase Invoice total $128.40. Terms: cash on receipt.

       ☐   Cheque Copy #1
Dated: Jan. 3/91
To Dymond Service Centre, $128.40 in full payment of account. Reference invoice #DSC-78.

☐ Cheque Copy #2
Dated: Jan. 4/91
To Westcoast Suppliers, $1 450 in payment of account. Reference invoice #WS-111.

☐ Purchase Invoice #PS-901
Dated: Jan. 5/91
From Pacific Stationery, $100 for invoice forms and other stationery supplies plus GST paid $7. Purchase Invoice total $107. Terms: cash on receipt.

☐ Cheque Copy #3
Dated: Jan. 5/91
To Pacific Stationery, $107 in full payment of account. Reference invoice #PS-901.

☐ Cash Receipt #1
Dated: Jan. 7/91
From cash register #1 (tapes no.1-400), $4 000 for dry cleaning service orders completed plus GST charged $280. Cash Register total $4 280. Amount deposited in bank.

☐ Cash Receipt #2
Dated: Jan. 7/91
From cash register #2 (tapes no.1-45), $600 for repair and alteration orders completed plus GST charged $42. Cash Register total $642. Amount deposited in bank.

Jan. 14 ☐ Purchase Invoice #PM-176
Dated: Jan. 10/91
From Performance Machinery, $350 for repairs and maintenance to dry cleaning equipment plus GST paid $24.50. Purchase Invoice total $374.50. Terms: cash on receipt.

☐ Cheque Copy #4
Dated: Jan. 10/91
To Performance Machinery, $374.50 in full payment of account. Reference invoice #PM-176.

☐ Credit Invoice #1
Dated: Jan. 12/91
To Myra Grodsky, a customer, $15 allowance for dry cleaning damages (See Hint on page 115.)

❑ Cheque Copy #5
Dated: Jan. 12/91
To Myra Grodsky, $15 in full payment of credit invoice. Reference Credit Invoice #1.

❑ Cash Receipt #3
Dated: Jan. 14/91
From cash register #1 (tapes no.401-855), $4 800 for dry cleaning service orders completed plus GST charged $336. Cash Register total $5 136. Amount deposited in bank.

❑ Cash Receipt #4
Dated: Jan. 14/91
From cash register #2 (tapes no.46-104), $760 for repair and alteration orders completed plus GST charged $53.20. Cash Register total $813.20. Amount deposited in bank.

TIME SUMMARY SHEET #1
(pay period ending January 14)

Name of Employee	Week 1 Hours	Week 2 Hours	Reg. Hours	O/T Hours
☑ Bok Leung*	40	42	80	2
❑ Sara Marino	40	40	80	-
❑ Rita Polski	42	40	80	2
❑ Farad Russey	20	20	40	-
❑ Nirmala Vas	22	20	40	2

*1. Bok Leung will receive an advance of $100 for a medical emergency in addition to his normal pay. This amount will be repaid in amounts of $25 over the next four pay periods. (See keystrokes for payroll in this application)

2. Using Time Summary Sheet #1 and the Employee Information Sheet, complete the payroll for hourly employees.

❑ 3. Using the Employee Information Sheet, complete payroll for the salaried employee, Kenneth Ho.

4. Issue cheques #6 - #11.

Jan. 21 ❑ Bank Credit Memo #SB-1251
Dated: Jan. 17/91
From Scotia Bank, $8 000 loan granted to purchase new pressing machines.

☐ Purchase Invoice #EE-118
Dated: Jan. 18/91
From EuroCan Equipment Co., $8 000 for the purchase of new pressing machine plus GST paid $560. Purchase Invoice total $8 560. Terms: cash on delivery.

☐ Cheque Copy #12
Dated: Jan. 18/91
To EuroCan Equipment Co., $8 560 in full payment of account. Reference invoice #EE-118.

☐ Cash Receipt #5
Dated: Jan. 20/91
From Broadview Cleaners, $2 140 certified cheque, for the sale of old pressing machines for $2 000 plus GST charged $140. Book value of old pressing machines was $2 500. Open and charge to a new expense account called Loss on Sale of Equipment (5120).

☐ Purchase Invoice #OP-1121
Dated: Jan. 20/91
From Oceanview Printers, $50 for advertising flyers to promote end-of-the-month specials and coupons plus GST paid $3.50. Purchase Invoice total $53.50. Terms: cash on delivery.

☐ Cheque Copy #13
Dated: Jan. 20/91
To Oceanview Printers, $53.50 in full payment of account. Reference invoice #OP-1121.

☐ Cash Receipt #6
Dated: Jan. 21/91
From cash register #1 (tapes no. 866-1255), $4 710 for dry cleaning service orders completed plus GST charged $329.70. Cash Register total $5 039.70. Amount deposited in bank.

☐ Cash Receipt #7
Dated: Jan. 21/91
From cash register #2 (tapes no. 105-154), $700 for repair and alteration orders completed plus GST charged $49. Cash Register total $749. Amount deposited in bank.

Jan. 28 ☐ Utility Statement #BCT-8711
Dated: Jan. 23/91
From B.C. Telephone, $120 for telephone
services plus GST paid $8.40. Utility
Statement total $128.40. Terms: cash on
receipt.

☐ Cheque Copy #14
Dated: Jan. 23/91
To B.C. Telephone, $128.40 in full payment of
account. Reference invoice #BCT-8711.

☐ Utility Statement #BCH-811
Dated: Jan. 24/91
From B.C. Hydro, $480 for hydro services plus
GST paid $33.60. Utility Statement total
$513.60. Terms: cash on receipt.

☐ Cheque Copy #15
Dated: Jan. 24/91
To B.C. Hydro, $513.60 in full payment of
account. Reference invoice #BCH-811.

☐ Bank Debit Memo #SB-651
Dated: Jan. 25/91
From Scotia Bank, $22 for bank service
charges for previous month.

☐ Cash Receipt #8
Dated: Jan. 28/91
From cash register #1 (tapes no. 1256-1625),
$4 250 for dry cleaning service orders
completed plus GST charged $297.50. Cash
Register total $4 547.50. Amount deposited in
bank.

☐ Cash Receipt #9
Dated: Jan. 28/91
From cash register #2 (tapes no. 155-201),
$670 for repair and alteration orders
completed plus GST charged $46.90. Cash
Register total $716.90. Amount deposited in
bank.

TIME SUMMARY SHEET #2
(pay period ending January 28)

Name of Employee	Week 3 Hours	Week 4 Hours	Reg. Hours	O/T Hours
☐ Bok Leung	40	40	80	-
☐ Sara Marino	40	40	80	-
☐ Rita Polski	40	40	80	-
☐ Farad Russey	20	20	40	-
☐ Nirmala Vas	20	20	40	-

1. Using Time Summary Sheet #2 and the Employee Information Sheet, complete the payroll for hourly employees. Recover $25 advanced to Bok Leung.
☐ 2. Using the Employee Information Sheet, complete the payroll for the salaried employee, Kenneth Ho.
3. Issue cheques #16 - #21.

Keystrokes

Entering Payroll Transactions

Using the instructions for accessing data files on page 9, load the application for Celine's Cleaners. Complete the transactions for the January 7 using date. Advance the using date to January 14, and complete the transactions up to the payroll entries using the keystroke instructions covered earlier in this workbook.

Click on the Payroll Journal icon to highlight it as follows:

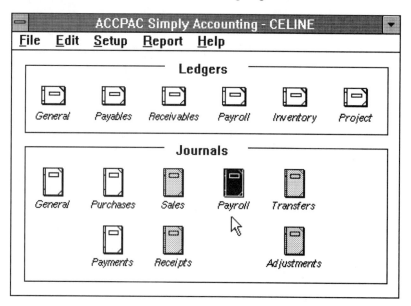

Open the Payroll Journal to display the following Payroll Journal input form:

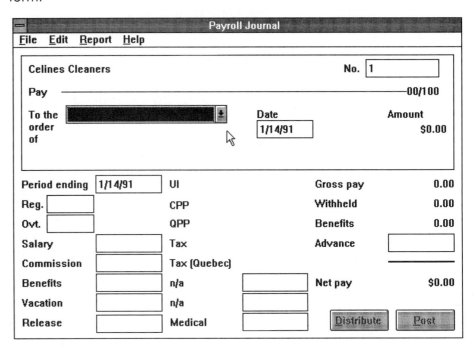

The cursor is flashing in the Employee (Pay to the order of) field.

Click on the arrow beside this field to see the list of employees as follows:

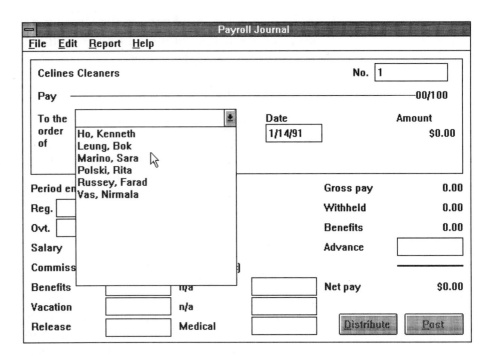

Click on Bok Leung to select this employee and add his name to the input form. If you have not chosen correctly, return to the employee list. Otherwise,

Press [Tab]

The cursor is now in the Cheque (No.) field. The employee's address has been added to the form.

Type: 6

Press [Tab]

The cursor moves to the Date field, where you should enter the date of payment. In this case, it is the same as the using date, which has been entered by default. Accept this date.

Press [Tab]

The cursor advances to the Period ending field. Since the using date is also the same as the pay period ending date, you can accept the default date again.

Press [Tab]

The cursor advances to the Regular hours (Reg.) field. This field contains the number of regular hours an employee has worked during the two-week pay period.

Type: 80

Press [Tab]

Notice that many of the remaining fields have been calculated automatically. The cursor advances to the Overtime (Ovt.) field. This field contains the number of overtime hours an employee has worked during the two-week pay period.

Type: 2

Press [Tab]

Notice that the remaining fields have been recalculated to include the additional pay. The cursor advances to the Salary field. This and the next several fields do not apply to this employee. The Salary field is used only for salaried employees. Since Bok Leung is not a salaried employee, ignore this field.

The Commission field is used for employees who earn a commission to be paid in this pay period. For applications in which employees are commissioned, you will have to calculate manually the amount of the commission and enter it in this field. Since employees at Celine's Cleaners are not commissioned, ignore this field.

The Benefits field is used to enter the total amount of benefits a business offers to its employees, such as health insurance, or dental plans. Celine's Cleaners does not offer any employee benefits, so ignore this field.

The ACCPAC Simply Accounting program automatically calculates an amount in the Vacation pay field and displays it as a default. This default amount is calculated at the vacation pay rate of four percent entered for this employee and will be retained by the business until the employee takes a vacation or leaves the employ of the business. (See the Employee Information Sheet.) You should accept the default.

The Release field is used to release any vacation pay retained for an employee. The amount to be released appears as a default. For this application, none of the employees are taking vacations or leaving the business, so ignore this field.

Advance the cursor to the Medical field so you can record the medical deduction.

Type: 25
Press ⌜Tab⌟

The cursor advances to the Advance field. This field is used to enter an amount advanced to an employee in addition to his or her normal pay from wages or salary. Advances are given for emergencies and other personal reasons upon approval by management. An advance offered to an employee is shown as a positive amount. An advance recovered on a regular basis is indicated as a negative amount in this same field. An advance of $100 for Bok Leung has been approved.

Type: 100
Press ⌜Tab⌟

Notice that the upper cheque portion of your input form window has been updated continuously as you added information about

NOTES:

If the employee were taking a vacation or leaving the business, you would release the accumulated vacation pay by selecting the default amount. The retain option should be changed to "no" in the Payroll Ledger for an employee when that employee leaves. You would click on the check box beside Retain Vacation to turn it off.

deductions or pay. Your complete payroll form should look like the one shown below:

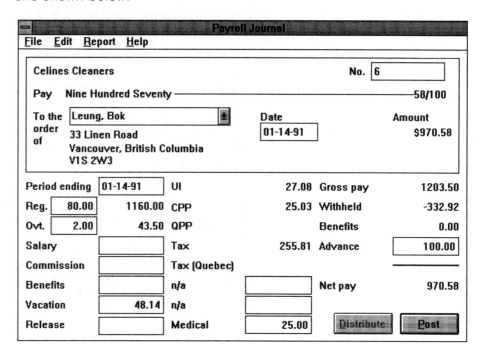

Reviewing the Payroll Journal Transaction

When you have completed entering all the information, you should review the completed transaction before posting.

Choose Display Payroll Journal Entry from the pull-down menu under **Report.** The transaction you have just completed appears as follows:

01-14-91		Debits	Credits	Proje
1240	Advances Receivable	100.00	-	
5300	Wages	1,251.64	-	
5310	UI Expense	37.91	-	
5320	CPP Expense	25.03	-	
5330	WCB Expense	47.18	-	
1080	Cash in Bank	-	970.58	
2300	Vacation Payable	-	48.14	
2310	UI Payable	-	64.99	
2320	CPP Payable	-	50.06	
2330	Income Tax Payable	-	255.81	
2440	Medical Payable	-	25.00	
2460	WCB Payable	-	47.18	
		1,461.76	1,461.76	

Notice that all the relevant wage expense accounts have been debited. In addition, all the wage-related liability accounts and the cash account have been updated automatically because the Payroll Ledger is integrated with the General Ledger.

Close the display to return to the Payroll Journal input screen.

CORRECTING THE PAYROLL JOURNAL ENTRY

Move the cursor to the field that contains the error. **Press** [Tab] to move forward through the fields or **press** [Shift] and [Tab] together to move back to a previous field. This will highlight the field information so that you can change it. **Type** the correct information and **press** [Tab] to enter the change.

You can also use the mouse to point to a field and drag through the incorrect information to highlight it. **Type** the correct information. **Press** [Tab] to save the corrections.

If you have selected the wrong employee, return to the employee list by **clicking on** the arrow beside this field. **Click on** the name of the correct employee and **press** [Tab] . When prompted, confirm that you wish to discard the incorrect entry. **Click on** **Yes**, and start again from the beginning.

Posting

When all the information in your journal entry is correct, you must post the transaction to save your work.

Click on Post

A new blank Payroll Journal input screen appears for you to enter the next payroll transaction.

To complete transactions involving other ledgers, you must close the Payroll Journal input form window to return to the Ledger/Journal company window.

Displaying Employee Reports

Choose Employee from the pull-down menu under **Report** to see the following Employee Report Options window:

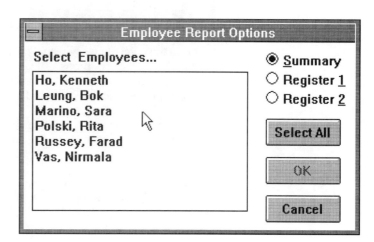

Click on the employee for whom you want the report, or click on **Select All** to include all employees in the report.

The **Summary** option allows you to see an employee's payroll report in summary form. The summary report will give you the accumulated totals only for all deductions and payments, which are updated each pay period. You will not be able to see earlier summary reports unless you have a backup copy for that specific time period (i.e., using date) or if you have a hard copy of the summary output.

The **Register 1** option will show you the deductions made to date for taxes, UI and CPP for each employee for each pay period. The **Register 2** option will provide the number of hours worked and the remaining employee deductions, including medical deductions for each pay period.

Once you have selected your employees and report options,

Click on OK

Displaying the Payroll Journal

With the Payroll Journal icon highlighted,

Choose Display Payroll Journal from the pull-down menu under **Report** to display the following Payroll Journal Options window:

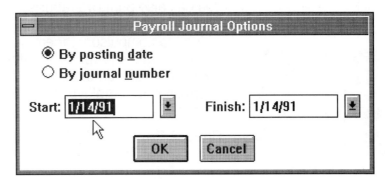

By default, the *By posting date* option is selected. This option is used for all reports in this application. The last using date appears by default in both the Start and Finish date fields. The start date is highlighted, ready for editing.

Type the beginning date for the report you want to see.

Press ⌐Tab⌐

Type the ending date for the report you want to see.

Click on OK

Close the display when you are finished.

Displaying Employee Lists

With the Payroll Ledger icon highlighted on the Ledger/Journal company window,

Choose Employee List from the pull-down menu under **Report** to display a list of all current employees, together with their addresses and telephone numbers.

Close the display when you are finished.

Printing Payroll Reports

Choose **Print** from the pull-down menu under **File** while you are displaying any of the reports listed in the section Displaying Payroll Reports.

You can also print two reports that are not available for display: **T4 Slips** and **Releve 1 Slips**. The **T4** option will allow you print T4 slips, which are compulsory for employees for income tax return filing. You should have the proper tax statement forms from Revenue Canada to take full advantage of this option. You should retain payroll information for employees who leave during the year so that you can prepare T4 slips to mail to them.

Choose **Print T4 Slips** (or **Print Releve 1 Slips**) from the pull-down menu under **Report** to display the following options:

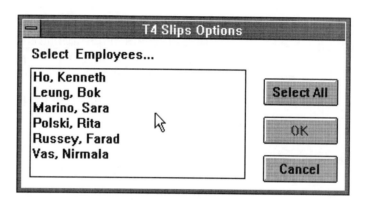

Click on **Select All** or on the name of the employee for whom you want the report printed.

Click on **OK**

Printing will begin immediately, so be sure that you have set up your printer correctly before you begin.

Case Problem

Celine Porter has obtained advice from a consultant to improve the image of her dry cleaning business and to gain the confidence of her workers by implementing an employee benefit package. As a result of this advice, she is planning a major renovation and expansion of her store in the next few months. The consultant is not a employee of the business.

1. Is the payment to the non-employee consultant free of GST, as it is for regular employees of this business? Explain.

2. Are the proposed employee benefits, namely a pension, health and dental care package, subject to GST? Explain.

CHAPTER SEVEN
Classic Clothes

OBJECTIVES

Upon completion of this chapter, you will be able to:

1. *enter* inventory-related purchase transactions;
2. *enter* inventory-related credit sale transactions of goods and services;
3. *enter* inventory-related cash sale transactions of goods and services;
4. *make* inventory adjustments;
5. *post* transactions;
6. *understand* the integration of the Inventory Ledger with the Payables and Receivables ledgers;
7. *enter* new inventory items;
8. *display* and *print* inventory reports.

Company Information

Company Profile

Classic Clothes is a business owned and operated by Enda Salt. Enda studied fashion and design and had a career as a model in Montreal. When she started Classic Clothes in Montreal, her intention was to provide women with the highest quality fashionable clothes and accessories. Enda also works as a corporate image consultant, counselling women on the types of clothing, hairstyle and makeup that are suitable for their job situations. Her clients include successful women moving up in the corporate world and various business organizations that hire her to speak to employees on image building.

The business earns revenue from two sources:

1. the sale of clothing and accessories;
2. consultation services provided to individuals and corporate clients.

Enda opened her store in November 1989 and ran it with her mother's assistance. Her mother looks after the store while Enda is away consulting. Enda has opened accounts for some of her regular customers. Her mother handles all the clerical and accounting functions. During busy periods she hires temporary help, but generally Enda and her mother handle the duties of the business.

Enda was interested in converting her manual accounting records to a computerized system. A software consulting company recommended ACCPAC Simply Accounting software because it could handle all of her business records efficiently and easily. The program could handle all inventory purchases, sales and adjustments. In addition to these features, it could deal with the consulting services as inventory items, so that Enda could keep track of the number of full- and half-day contracts she has carried out. The ACCPAC Simply Accounting program could also record cash transactions for goods and services and could generate invoices if needed. Enda and her mother prefer to use the cash register and generate manual invoices for the present time, but they were considering adapting to a computer-generated invoice system within the next few months.

Enda purchased an MS-DOS computer system and printer and, with a little bit of training from an accounting teacher and friend, Larry Sardinha, she and her mother set up the accounts at the end of June 1991.

The information in the following reports summarizes the state of the accounting records of Classic Clothes at the time of conversion:

1. Chart of Accounts;
2. Trial Balance;
3. Vendor Information;
4. Customer Information;
5. Inventory Information;
6. Accounting Procedures.

CLASSIC CLOTHES
CHART OF ACCOUNTS

Assets
1080 Cash in Bank
1200 Accounts Receivable
1220 Prepaid Insurance
1240 Software Library
1260 Store Supplies
1520 Accessories
1540 Blouses
1560 Jackets
1580 Skirts
1720 Cash Register
1760 Computers & Peripherals
1800 Display Fixtures
1840 Shop

Liabilities
2100 Bank Loan
2200 Accounts Payable
2600 GST Charged on Sales
2610 GST Paid on Purchases
2640 PST Payable
2840 Mortgage Payable

Equity
3560 E. Salt, Capital
3580 E. Salt, Drawings

Revenue
4020 Revenue from Sales
4040 Revenue from Consulting

Expense
5020 Advertising & Promotion
5040 Bank Charges
5060 Cost of Goods Sold
5080 Damaged Inventory
5100 Freight Expense
5120 Hydro Expense
5140 Sales Discount
5160 Telephone Expense
5180 Temporary Services

CLASSIC CLOTHES
POST-CLOSING TRIAL BALANCE

June 30, 1991

Account	Debit	Credit
1080 Cash in Bank	$ 7 109.75	
1200 Accounts Receivable	6 821.25	
1220 Prepaid Insurance	250.00	
1240 Software Library	500.00	
1260 Store Supplies	600.00	
1520 Accessories	5 900.00	
1540 Blouses	7 500.00	
1560 Jackets	12 000.00	
1580 Skirts	6 225.00	
1720 Cash Register	1 200.00	
1760 Computers & Peripherals	5 000.00	
1800 Display Fixtures	1 450.00	
1840 Shop	85 000.00	
2100 Bank Loan		$ 8 000.00
2200 Accounts Payable		6 206.00
2600 GST Charged on Sales		1 148.00
2610 GST Paid on Purchases	795.00	
2640 PST Payable		1 403.84
2840 Mortgage Payable		75 000.00
3560 E. Salt, Capital		48 593.16
	$140 351.00	$140 351.00

CLASSIC CLOTHES
VENDOR INFORMATION

Vendor Name	Address & Telephone	Invoice Date	Invoice Number	Outstanding Balance
Euroclothes Mfg.	21 McGill Ave. Montreal, Quebec H3R 1A6 Tel: 921-5432	June 14/91	EM-43	$3 317.00
Quality Clothes	54, rue Leonard Montreal, Quebec H8U 2C3 Tel: 781-9064	June 17/91	QC-671	$2 889.00
Quebec Hydro	234, chemin Chambly Montreal, Quebec H4Y 2S3 Tel: 659-1234			
Vendome Printers	23, rue Galibois Montreal, Quebec H2P 1T4 Tel: 285-1234			
		GRAND TOTAL		$6 206.00

CLASSIC CLOTHES
CUSTOMER INFORMATION

Customer Name	Address & Telephone	Invoice Date	Invoice Number	Outstanding Balance
Aries Public Relations	35, rue Champlain Montreal, Quebec H9W 3F4 Tel: 871-0943	June 4/91	142	$1 792.25
Cash Sales	89, rue Couture Montreal, Quebec H2W 0O1 Tel: 912-4521			
JTV Studios	65, rue Laurier Montreal, Quebec H8U 2C4 Tel: 912-9087	June 12/91	144	$3 424.00
Piroux & Prince Inc.	43, rue St-Jacques Montreal, Quebec H9T 2B6 Tel: 919-0091	June 8/91	143	$1 605.00
		GRAND TOTAL		$6 821.25

CLASSIC CLOTHES
INVENTORY INFORMATION

Item Number & Name	Unit Description	Selling Price	Quantity on Hand	Amount (cost)	Minimum Stock Level
101 Accessories:belts	item(s)	$ 25.00	30	$300.00	5
102 Accessories:brooches	item(s)	$ 40.00	50	$1 000.00	15
103 Accessories:collar-pins	item(s)	$ 40.00	50	$1 000.00	15
104 Accessories:hats	item(s)	$ 75.00	50	$1 500.00	15
105 Accessories:scarves-silk	item(s)	$ 50.00	60	$1 200.00	20
106 Accessories:scarves-wool	item(s)	$ 40.00	60	$900.00	20
				$5 900.00	
107 Blouses:Dolman slve-silk	item(s)	$125.00	20	$1 100.00	5
108 Blouses:crew cut-silk	item(s)	$110.00	20	$1 000.00	5
109 Blouses:padded-cotton	item(s)	$ 60.00	20	$500.00	5
201 Blouses:padded-polyester	item(s)	$ 75.00	20	$700.00	5
202 Blouses:padded-silk	item(s)	$110.00	20	$1 000.00	5
203 Blouses:shirt style-cotton	item(s)	$ 60.00	20	$500.00	5
204 Blouses:shirt style-silk	item(s)	$100.00	20	$900.00	5
205 Blouses:v neck-polyester	item(s)	$ 80.00	20	$800.00	5
206 Blouses:v neck-silk	item(s)	$110.00	20	$1 000.00	5
				$7 500.00	
301 Jackets:dble breasted-wool	item(s)	$400.00	25	$4 500.00	8
302 Jackets:regular-wool	item(s)	$350.00	25	$4 000.00	8
303 Jackets:short-wool	item(s)	$325.00	25	$3 500.00	8
				$12 000.00	
401 Skirts:3/4-wool	item(s)	$175.00	15	$1 200.00	3
402 Skirts:A line-wool	item(s)	$175.00	15	$1 200.00	3
403 Skirts:pleated-silk	item(s)	$225.00	15	$1 350.00	3
404 Skirts:pleated-wool	item(s)	$200.00	15	$1 275.00	3
405 Skirts:straight-wool	item(s)	$175.00	15	$1 200.00	3
				$6 225.00	
901 Srvc:1 day consultation	unit(s)	$500.00	60	$0.00	0
902 Srvc:1/2 day consultation	unit(s)	$300.00	80	$0.00	0

NOTES:

Classic Clothes offers two types of services: half-day consultation for a fee of $300, and full-day consultation for a fee of $500. These service charges are included in the inventory list (numbers 901 and 902). They will be treated like any other inventory item on the list. Classic Clothes can keep track of the number of half-day and full-day consulting service contracts it carries out. This ability to use the inventory database for both goods and services is a convenient feature of the ACCPAC Simply Accounting software. Although not done in this workbook, generating computerized invoices for goods and services is another convenient feature of the software.

Accounting Procedures

1. **The Goods and Services Tax: Remittances**

   Enda Salt uses the **regular method** for remittance of the Goods and Services Tax. GST collected from customers is recorded as a liability in the GST Charged on Sales account. GST paid to vendors is recorded in the GST Paid on Purchases account as a decrease in liability to Revenue Canada. Enda files her return to the Receiver General of Canada by the last day of the month for the previous quarterly period, either requesting a refund or remitting the balance owing.

2. **Provincial Sales Tax (PST)**

   Provincial sales tax of eight percent is applied to all cash and credit sales of goods in the province of Quebec. This amount must be remitted monthly to the Provincial Treasurer. Provincial sales taxes are not applied to services in this application. At the time this workbook was written, the province of Quebec ruled that the provincial sales tax would apply to the amount of the invoice with GST included. This is often referred to as a "tax on a tax" or a "piggy-backed" tax. The defaults for this application are set so that the program will automatically calculate the PST rate on the amount with GST included.

   The province of Ontario applies the provincial sales tax on the base amount of the invoice, which excludes the GST. Accounting examples for the provinces of Quebec and Ontario follow:

Quebec

Sold goods on account to customer for $500. GST charged is 7% PST charged is 8%.

GST = (0.07 * 500) = $35.00
PST = (0.08 * 535) = $42.80
Total amount of invoice = $500.00 + $35 + $42.80 = $577.80

Date	Particulars	Ref	Debit	Credit
xx/xx	Accounts Receivable		577.80	
	GST Charged on Sales			35.00
	PST Payable			42.80
	Revenue from Sales			500.00

Ontario

Sold goods on account to customer for $500. GST charged is 7%. PST charged is 8 %.

GST = (0.07 * 500) = $35.00
PST = (0.08 * 500) = $40.00
Total amount of invoice = $500.00 + $35 + $40 = $575.00

Date	Particulars	Ref	Debit	Credit
xx/xx	Accounts Receivable		575.00	
	GST Charged on Sales			35.00
	PST Payable			40.00
	Revenue from Sales			500.00

3. **Sales Invoices**

Sales invoices are prepared manually in this application; they are not generated by the ACCAPC Simply Accounting program. The user, of course, has the option of generating invoices through the software.

If you want to print the sales invoice through the program, complete the Sales Journal transaction as you would otherwise. *Before* posting the transaction, choose **Print** from the pull-down menu under **File**. Printing will begin immediately, so be sure you have the correct forms for your printer before you begin.

4. **Cash Sales of Inventory Items and Services**

Cash transactions for goods and services occur normally in most types of businesses. The ACCPAC Simply Accounting program does not have a point-of-sale module for over-the-counter sales. However, it can handle cash transactions through the Sales Journal. The process is fairly simple although it will appear to be unorthodox to the uninitiated. You must set up **Cash Sales** as a customer in the Receivables Ledger, using the business address and telephone information. This account is already set up for you in this application. You then enter the cash transaction the same way as you would enter any credit sale transaction to customers, with these additional steps:

- After recording all of the items sold, when the cursor moves down to the next line on the invoice, type "Payment" in the Description field.
- Enter **code 1** in the GST field to show that the payment is non-taxable .
- Enter a **negative** amount in the Amount field for the cash or cheque received from the customer.
- Enter the *Cash in Bank* account number in the Account field. Leave the PST field blank.

The program will then debit the Cash in Bank account instead of the Accounts Receivable control account. All the other relevant accounts for this transaction will be debited and credited as in other transactions.

The source document for cash transactions for this application is a cash register summary. This summary lists individual cash sales transactions obtained from cash register tapes and invoices issued to various customers. You use it in the same way that you would use an individual customer's source document for a cash sale. Including a summary form eliminates the need to prepare a large number of source documents for this application.

5. **Freight Expense**
When a business purchases inventory items, the cost of any freight that cannot be directly allocated to a specific item must be charged to the Freight Expense account. This amount will be regarded as an expense rather than being charged to an inventory asset account.

6. **Sales Discounts**
Discounts may be offered to encourage customers to settle their accounts early. When earned by the customers, these discounts should be considered as negative invoices. They are handled in a similar way to cash sales transactions:

- Type "discount" or some other appropriate comment in the Description field.
- Enter GST **code 1** in the GST field to indicate that the discount is non-taxable.
- Enter a **negative** (-) amount in the Amount field for the discount.
- Enter the *Sales Discount* account number in the Account field.
- Leave the PST field blank to show that the discount is non-taxable.
- Leave the remaining fields blank because they pertain to the sale of inventory items.

Instructions

1. Using the Chart of Accounts, Trial Balance, Vendor Information, Customer Information and Inventory Information provided, record entries for the source documents for July 1991 using ACCPAC Simply Accounting. The procedures for entering each new type of transaction are outlined step by step in the keystroke section that follows the source documents.

2. After you have finished making your entries, print the reports indicated on the printing form below.

PRINTING

Primary Reports

☑ Balance Sheet
    date: July 14

☑ Trial Balance
    date: July 14

☐ Vendor Aged

    ◯ Summary

    ◯ Detail

☐ Customer Aged

    ◯ Summary

    ◯ Detail

☑ Inventory

    ⊘ Synopsis

☐ Income Statement
    Period covered:
    from: to:

☑ General Ledger
    accounts: 1200   4020
                2600   2640

    Period covered:
    from: July 1   to: July 14

Secondary Reports

GENERAL

☑ General Journal

    ⊘ by posting date: July 1-14

ACCOUNTS RECEIVABLE

☐ Customer Address List

☐ Sales Journal

    ◯ by posting date:

☐ Receipts Jouranl

    ◯ by posting date:

INVENTORY

☑ Inventory List

☑ Inventory Adjustment

    ⊘ by posting date: July   1-14

ACCOUNTS PAYABLE

☐ Vendor Address List

☐ Purchases Journal

    ◯ by posting date:

☐ Payments Journal

    ◯ by posting date:

PAYROLL

☐ Employee List

☐ Payroll Journal

    ◯ by posting date:

Source Documents

USING DATE

July 7 ☑ Sales Invoice no. 150
Dated: July 2/91
To JTV Studios;

two Jackets:dble breasted-wool	$400.00 each
two Skirts:A line-wool	$175.00 each
four Blouses:Dolman slve-silk	$125.00 each
one Blouse:Crew cut-silk	$110.00
five Accessories:brooches	$40.00 each
Goods & Services Tax	7%
Provincial Sales Tax	8%

Terms of Sale:1/10, n/30 days.

☑ Purchase Invoice #EM-58
Dated: July 3/91
From Euroclothes Mfg.;

five Jackets:dble breasted-wool	$ 900.00
five Jackets:regular-wool	$ 800.00
Goods & Services Tax (7%) Paid	$ 119.00
Total	$1 819.00

Terms: net 30 days.

☑ Memo #1
Dated: July 3/91
From Owner: Adjust inventory records for one Blouse:padded-silk, valued at $50 and accidently torn on clothes railing. Charge to Damaged Inventory account.

☐ Cash Receipt #1
Dated: July 3/91
From Aries Public Relations, cheque #67, $1 792.25 in full payment of account. Reference invoice no.142.

☐ Purchase Invoice #VP-451
Dated: July 5/91
From Vendome printers, $125 for brochures to promote business plus GST paid $8.75. Purchase Invoice total $133.75. Terms: C.O.D.

☐ Cheque Copy #31
Dated: July 5/91
To Vendome Printers, $133.75 in full payment of account. Reference invoice #VP-451.

NOTES:
Remember that there is no PST charged on services

☐ Sales Invoice no. 151
Dated: July 6/91
To Aries Public Relations;
  one Srvc:1 day consultation $500.00
  Goods & Services Tax   7%
Terms: 1/10, net 30 days

☐ Bank Debit Memo #BM-511
Dated: July 7/91
From Bank of Montreal, $27 for bank service charges.

☑ Cash Receipt #2a
Dated: July 7/91
From Cash Register Summary Sheet (1) - Sales.
Amount deposited in bank.

Item	Qty	Price	Amount
Accessories:belts	4	$ 25.00	$ 100.00
Accessories:hats	3	$ 75.00	225.00
Blouses:v neck-silk	4	$ 110.00	440.00
Blouses:v neck-polyester	3	$ 80.00	240.00
Jackets:regular-wool	3	$ 350.00	1 050.00
Jackets:short-wool	3	$ 325.00	975.00
Skirts:pleated-silk	2	$ 225.00	450.00
Skirts:pleated-wool	4	$ 200.00	800.00
		Gross Sales	$4 280.00
		GST (7%)	299.60
		PST (8%)	366.37
Cash Received July 1-7:			$4 945.97

☐ Cash Receipt #2b
Dated: July 7/91
From Cash Register Summary Sheet (1) - Services.
Amount deposited in bank.

Item	Qty	Price	Amount
Srvc:1/2 day consultation	1	$ 300.00	$ 300.00
Srvc:1 day consultation	1	$ 500.00	500.00
		Gross Sales	$ 800.00
		GST (7%)	56.00
Cash Received July 1-7:			$ 856.00

☐ Cash Receipt #3
Dated: July 7/91
From Piroux & Prince Inc., cheque #112, $1 605 in
full payment of account. Reference invoice no. 143.

July 14 ☐ Purchase Invoice #QC-755
Dated: July 10/91
From Quality Clothes (new inventory);

five Suits:classic-wool	$1 250.00
five Suits:classic-silk	1 500.00
Freight Expense	25.00
GST Paid (7%)	194.25
Total	$2 969.25

Terms: net 30 days.

☐ Insert new inventory asset account in the General
Ledger - Suits (1600).

☑ Insert new inventory records listed below in the
Inventory Ledger:

Item Number & Name	Selling Price	Min. Stock Level
501 Suits:classic-wool	$450.00	2
502 Suits:classic-silk	$550.00	2

☐ Purchase Invoice #QH-9812
Dated: July 11/91
From Quebec Hydro, $90 for hydro services plus
GST paid $6.30. Purchase Invoice total $96.30.
Terms: cash on receipt.

☐ Cheque Copy #32
Dated: July 11/91
To Quebec Hydro, $96.30 in full payment of
account. Reference invoice #QH-9812.

☐ Cash Receipt #4
Dated: July 11/91
From JTV Studios, cheque #214, $3 424 in payment
of account. Reference invoice no. 144.

☐ Cheque Copy #33
Dated: July 12/91
To Euroclothes Mfg., $3 317 in payment of account.
Reference invoice #EM-43.

❑ Sales Invoice no. 152
Dated: July 13/91
To Piroux & Prince Inc.;

two Blouses:padded-silk	$110.00 each
two Blouses:shirt style-silk	$100.00 each
two Jackets:regular-wool	$350.00 each
one Suit:classic-silk	$550.00
two Accessories:collar pins	$40.00 each
Goods & Services Tax	7%
Provincial Sales Tax	8%

Terms:1/10, n/30 days.

❑ Cash Receipt #5a
Dated: July 14/91
From Cash Register Summary Sheet (2) - Sales.
Amount deposited in bank.

Item	Qty	Price	Amount
Accessories:scarves-silk	3	$ 50.00	$ 150.00
Accessories:hats	1	$ 75.00	75.00
Blouses:shirt style-cotton	4	$ 60.00	240.00
Blouses:v neck-silk	2	$ 110.00	220.00
Jackets:regular-wool	2	$ 350.00	700.00
Jackets:short-wool	4	$ 325.00	1 300.00
Skirts:straight-wool	2	$ 175.00	350.00
Skirts:3/4-wool	3	$ 175.00	525.00
		Gross Sales	$3 560.00
		GST (7%)	249.20
		PST (8%)	304.74
Cash Received from July 8-14:			$4 113.94

❑ Cash Receipt #5b
Dated: July 14/91
From Cash Register Summary Sheet (2) - Services.
Amount deposited in bank.

Item	Qty	Price	Amount
Srvc:1/2 day consultation	2	$ 300.00	$ 600.00
Srvc:1 day consultation	1	$ 500.00	500.00
		Gross Sales	$1 100.00
		GST (7%)	77.00
Cash Received from July 8-14:			$1 177.00

HINT:
Read about Sales Discounts in the Accounting Procedures section on page 135.

☐ Cash Receipt #6
Dated: July 14/91
From Aries Public Relations, cheque #83, $529.65 in full payment of account. Reference invoice no. 151.

☐ Negative Invoice no. 1
Dated: July 14/91
To Aries Public Relations, $5.35, discount for early payment of account. Reference invoice no. 151 and Cash Receipt #6. Charge to Sales Discount expense account.

Keystrokes

Accounting for the Sale of Inventory Items on Credit

Using the instructions for accessing data files on page 9, open the files for Classic Clothes.

Type: 07-07-91

This will enter the using date July 7, 1991. The familiar main Ledger/Journal company window appears.

Click on the Sales Journal icon to highlight it as shown:

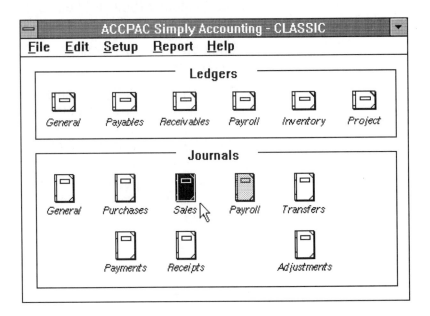

Open the Sales Journal to display the familiar Sales Journal input screen:

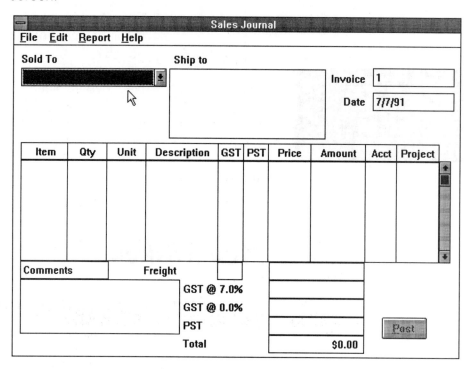

The first transaction involves the sale of inventory items. Many of the steps are identical to those you have been using for sales in previous applications. You will be using the inventory database and all of the input form fields to complete this transaction.

The Customer (Sold To) field is darkened, ready for you to enter the information.

Click on the arrow beside the Customer field to display the list of customers.

Click on JTV Studios to enter the customer's name and address on the form. If you have selected an incorrect customer, return to the customer list and select again. If you have selected correctly, you should enter the invoice number.

Press [Tab] repeatedly to skip over the Ship to field information (because the default information is correct) and advance to the Invoice field.

Type: 150

Press [Tab]

The cursor advances to the Date field. Here you must enter the source document date because the default using date is incorrect.

Type: 07-02-91

Press [Tab]

The cursor advances to the first line of the Item field. One line is used for each different inventory item or service sold by the business. A separate line would also be used to enter cash received, discounts offered, or returns and allowances made.

Press [Enter]

The following inventory list appears:

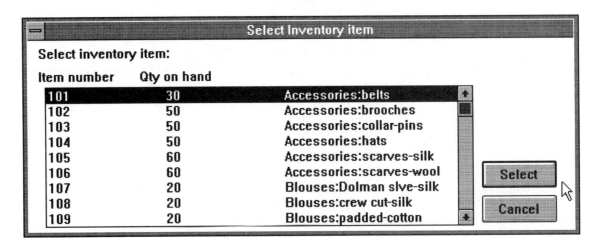

All inventory items the business offers are listed in numerical order. Quantities available are also included in this display to prevent the company from overselling an item.

Click on 301 Jackets:dble breasted-wool from the list.

Click on Select to add the inventory item to your form.

The cursor moves to the Quantity field. If you try to enter a quantity greater than the available stock, the program will not permit you to continue without changing the quantity. If you have made an incorrect selection, return to the Item field and reselect from the inventory list. Then enter the number of units of this item sold.

Type: 2

Press [Tab] repeatedly to advance to the GST field. Notice that the program adds information in each of the fields automatically, based on the inventory record information. Since it is correct, you do not need to change it.

Press ⏎[Enter] to see the list of available GST codes. Some goods and services are tax-exempt or zero-rated and will not have GST applied. You would select **codes 0** or **2** respectively for these items. **Code 1** applies to non-taxable items. You would use this code for cash received from cash sales transactions. Some imported goods would also fall into this category. **Code 3** is used if the GST is not already included in the sale price. This option is used for most applications in this workbook. **Code 4** would be selected if the GST were already included in the sale price, as it was in the Wallstreet Wizard application.

Click on 3 - GST @ 7.0%, not included because GST has not yet been included in the selling price.

Click on Select

Press [Tab] to advance through the remaining fields until you reach the next line because the default information based on the records is correct. If you needed to change the selling price for a particular item or customer, you could edit this field. The program automatically calculates an amount based on the selling price per unit. This figure appears in the Amount field.

The default revenue account appears and can be accepted or changed. You can obtain a list of accounts by pressing [Enter] while in this field. You would change the default account for cash transactions, discounts, returns and allowances, or unusual entries. Accept the default revenue account for this sale.

You may now enter the second and remaining sale items using the same steps that you used to enter the first item. Notice that the GST code is now added by default to match the entry on line one. As you complete each line and advance to the next, the totals and tax amounts at the bottom of the form are updated to include the last item entered.

If there are no further items on your input form to enter, your screen should look like the one shown here:

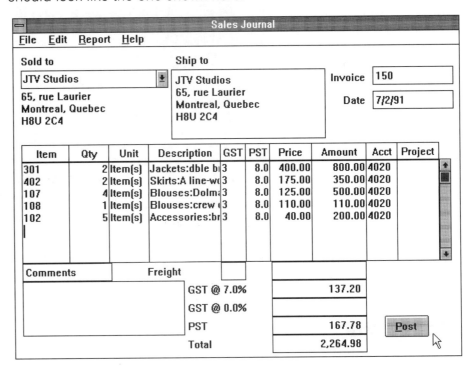

Item	Qty	Unit	Description	GST	PST	Price	Amount	Acct	Project
301	2	Item(s)	Jackets:dble b	3	8.0	400.00	800.00	4020	
402	2	Item(s)	Skirts:A line-w	3	8.0	175.00	350.00	4020	
107	4	Item(s)	Blouses:Dolm	3	8.0	125.00	500.00	4020	
108	1	Item(s)	Blouses:crew	3	8.0	110.00	110.00	4020	
102	5	Item(s)	Accessories:br	3	8.0	40.00	200.00	4020	

Reviewing the Inventory Sales Journal Transaction

Choose Display Sales Journal Entry from the pull-down menu under **Report** to display the transaction you have entered:

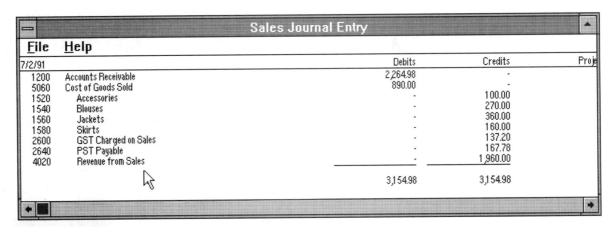

7/2/91		Debits	Credits	Proj
1200	Accounts Receivable	2,264.98	-	
5060	Cost of Goods Sold	890.00	-	
1520	Accessories	-	100.00	
1540	Blouses	-	270.00	
1560	Jackets	-	360.00	
1580	Skirts	-	160.00	
2600	GST Charged on Sales	-	137.20	
2640	PST Payable	-	167.78	
4020	Revenue from Sales	-	1,960.00	
		3,154.98	3,154.98	

Notice that all the relevant accounts have been updated automatically because the different ledgers are integrated in ACCPAC Simply Accounting. The appropriate asset, liability, revenue and expense accounts have all been debited and credited as required. The inventory database is also updated.

Close the display to return to the journal input screen.

WARNING!

Please be careful when reviewing your transaction to make sure you have entered the correct information. Otherwise, you will have to make a reversing entry to correct it.

Posting

When all the information in your journal entry is correct, you must post the transaction to save your work.

Click on Post to save the transaction.

The next transaction is an inventory purchase, not a sale. Close the Sales Journal window to exit to the Ledger/Journal company window.

Accounting for Purchases of Inventory on Credit

Click on the Purchases Journal icon in the Ledger/Journal company window to highlight it as shown:

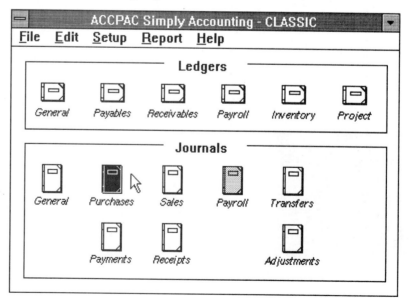

Open the Purchases Journal to display the familiar Purchases Journal input form window:

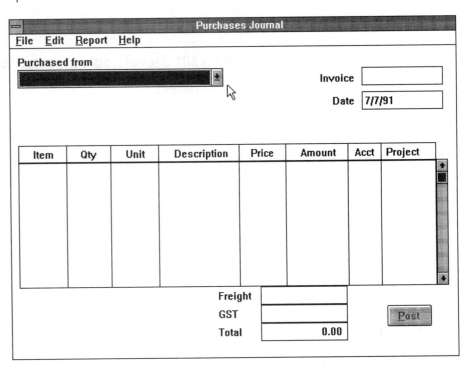

The second transaction involves the purchase of inventory items. Many of the steps in completing this entry are the same as those you have been using for other credit purchase transactions. Now you will be completing all the parts of this form, using the inventory database for the additional information.

You are now ready to enter the second transaction on the input screen. The Vendor (Purchased from) field is darkened, ready for you to enter the information.

Click on the arrow beside the Vendor (Purchased from) field to display the list of vendors.

Click on Euroclothes Mfg. from the list to add it to your input form. You now have the opportunity to check your selection. If you have selected an incorrect vendor, select again from the vendor list. If you have selected correctly, proceed by entering the invoice number.

Press ⌈Tab⌉

Type: EM-58

Press ⌈Tab⌉

The cursor advances to the Date field. Here you should enter the source document date, unless it is the same as the default using date.

Type: 07-03-91

The cursor advances to the Item field.

Press ⌈Enter⌉ to see the list of inventory items.

Click on 301 Jackets:dble breasted-wool from the list to highlight it.

Click on Select

The cursor advances to the Quantity field. The Description field should now show the name, **Jackets:dble breasted-wool.** If you have made an incorrect selection, return to the Item field and select again. The default price contained in the inventory records is entered automatically. Now enter the quantity for this item.

Type: 5

Press ⌈Tab⌉

The cursor advances to the Price field, which is used to record the unit price paid for the purchase of the inventory items. This amount should not include any GST paid that can be used as an input tax credit. The default information is correct so do not change it.

Press ⌈Tab⌉ repeatedly to advance to the next line, with the cursor blinking in the Item field again. Enter the second item on the input form or source document, using the same steps that you used to record the first item.

When there are no further items to record,

Click on the GST field to move the cursor to this field. Here you should enter the GST paid for the purchase to the vendor. Some goods and services are zero-rated or tax-exempt and will not have GST applied. Your source document will indicate the amount of GST paid.

Type: 119

Press ⌈Tab⌉

The Freight field is used to enter any freight charges that cannot be allocated to a specific item purchased. There are no freight charges for this entry. Your completed input form should appear as follows:

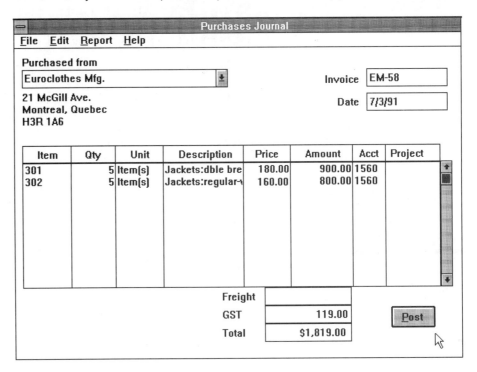

Reviewing the Inventory Purchases Journal Transaction

Choose Display Purchases Journal Entry from the pull-down menu under **Report** to display the transaction you have entered as shown:

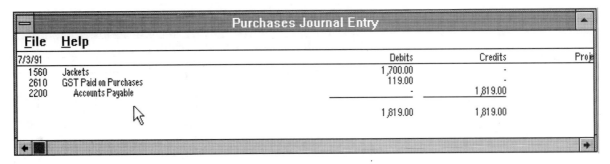

You can see that the ACCPAC Simply Accounting program has automatically updated all accounts relevant to this transaction. The appropriate inventory asset account (Jackets), Accounts Payable, and GST Paid on Purchases accounts have been updated as required because the ledgers are integrated. The inventory database is also updated.

Close the display to return to the Purchases Journal input screen.

WARNING!

Please be careful when reviewing your transaction to make sure you have entered the correct information. Otherwise, you will have to make a reversing entry to correct it.

Posting

When all the information in your journal entry is correct, you must post the transaction to save your work.

Click on Post

The next transaction is an inventory adjustment. Close the Purchases Journal to exit to the Ledger/Journal company window.

Making Inventory Adjustments

Click on the Adjustments Journal icon on the Ledger/Journal company window to highlight it as shown:

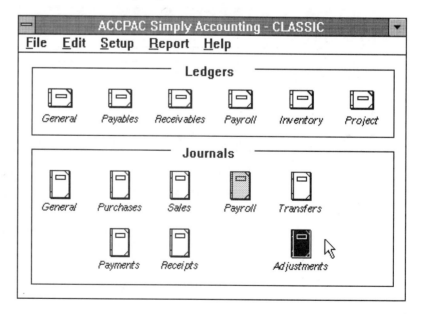

Open the Adjustments Journal to display the following blank inventory Adjustments Journal input screen:

Item	Qty	Units	Description	Unit Cost	Amount	Acct	Project

Adjustments Journal

File Edit Report Help

Source _____   Date 7/7/91

Comment _____

Total $0.00

Post

The cursor is in the Source field. The source for an adjustment will normally be a memo from a manager or owner.

Type: `Memo #1`

Press `Tab`

The cursor is now in the Date field, with the using date entered and highlighted as usual.

Type: `07-03-91`

Press `Tab`

The cursor is now in the Comment field, where you can enter a brief explanation for this transaction.

Type: `Damaged blouse - torn on railing`

Press `Tab`

The cursor is now in the Item field.

Press `Enter` to display the familiar inventory list.

Click on 202 Blouses:padded-silk from the list to highlight it.

Click on Select to enter it onto the form.

The item name, *Blouses:padded-silk*, the unit, the unit cost and the account have been added automatically. The cursor advances to the Quantity field. You need to indicate that the inventory has been reduced because of the damaged item. You do this typing a negative number in the field.

Type: –1

Press | Tab |

The cursor advances to the Amount field. A negative amount, reflecting the inventory loss, automatically appears as a default. Choose the default.

Press | Tab |

The cursor advances to the Account field. A default Cost of Goods Sold account appears automatically for this entry. However, you want the loss to be reflected in another account, *Damaged Inventory*, also an expense account.

Press | Enter | to display the list of accounts.

Click on 5080 Damaged Inventory from the account list.

Click on Select to enter the account number on the form.

The cursor advances to the Project field. This field is not used by Classic Clothes so ignore it. We will discuss it in a later application.

Press | Tab |

Your entry is complete as shown and you are ready to review it:

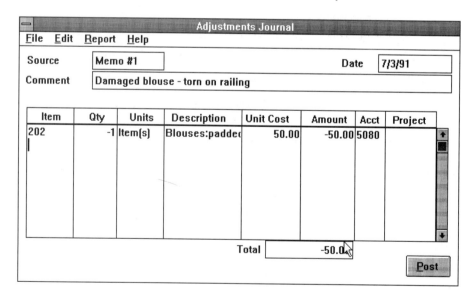

Reviewing the Adjustments Journal Entry

Choose Display Adjustments Journal Entry from the pull-down menu under **Report** to display the transaction you have entered as shown here:

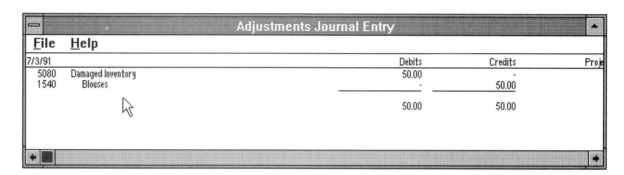

You can see that the ACCPAC Simply Accounting program has automatically updated all the relevant accounts for this transaction. The appropriate inventory asset and expense accounts and the inventory database have also been updated.

Close the display to return to the Adjustments Journal input screen.

CORRECTING THE ADJUSTMENTS JOURNAL ENTRY

Move to the field that has the error. **Press** [Tab] to move forward through the fields or **press** [Shift] and [Tab] together to move back to a previous field. This will highlight the field information so you can change it. **Type** the correct information and **press** [Tab] to enter it.

You can also use the mouse to point to a field and drag through the incorrect information to highlight it. **Type** the correct information and **press** [Tab] to enter it.

If the inventory item is incorrect, reselect from the inventory list by **pressing** [Enter] while in this field. **Click on Select** to add the item to your form. **Type** the quantity purchased and **press** [Tab]. If you have changed any information on an inventory item line, you must advance the cursor to the next line in order to update the totals.

Posting

When all the information in your journal entry is correct, you must post the transaction to save your work.

Click on Post

The next keystroke transaction is an inventory cash sales transaction.

Accounting for the Sale of Inventory for Cash

The second source document on the date July 7, 1991 is **Cash Receipt #2a**. The receipt is a total of individual cash sales transactions for the week ending July 7. It is summarized from cash register tapes and from invoices issued.

The keystrokes for cash sales transactions are similar to those for credit sales of inventory up to the recording of the cash amount received. We will review these steps very briefly. Refer to the earlier keystroke instructions if you encounter difficulties.

Open the Sales Journal.

Choose Cash Sales from the list of customers.

Press Tab to advance to the Invoice field.
Type: CR-2a

Press Tab to enter the source document number and advance to the Date field.

Press Tab to advance to the Item field, accepting the using date because it is the same as the transaction date.

Choose 101 Accessories:belts from the list of inventory items and enter it.

Type: 4 to enter the quantity.

Press Tab repeatedly to advance to the GST code field.

Choose GST code 3 - GST @ 7.0%, not included

Press Tab as needed to accept the default values entered for price and account and to move to the next line of the input form.

Repeat the above steps for each different line of information in your source document.

When you have completed entering all of the inventory items, advance the cursor to the next blank line on the input form. You are now ready to enter the total cash received from the sales. This procedure is similar to entering non-inventory sales, because inventory information is not applicable.

Press ⌈Tab⌋ repeatedly until the cursor is in the Description field, where you can add a brief explanation for this line.

Type: `Cash received`

Press ⌈Tab⌋

The cursor advances to the GST field. You must indicate that the cash received is non-taxable.

Press ⌈Enter⌋ to see the GST code list.

Click on 1 - GST nontaxable from the list.

Click on Select to enter it on your input form.

The cursor advances to the PST field. You need to indicate that PST should not be applied.

Press ⌈Tab⌋ to skip over this field.

The cursor advances to the Price field. Ignore this field. The PST field remains blank.

Press ⌈Tab⌋

The cursor advances to the Amount field. Here you will enter the total cash received from your sales transactions as shown at the bottom of the input screen. This amount is indicated with a **negative** sign, reflecting a decrease in the Accounts Receivable Ledger account, *Cash Sales*. The negative amount has the effect of cancelling the amount owing by the customer, Cash Sales.

Type: `-4945.97`

Press ⌈Tab⌋

The cursor advances to the Account field. Here you should enter the bank account, *Cash in Bank*. The decrease in the Accounts Receivable account (credit) will be reflected by an increase in the Cash in Bank account (debit).

Press ⌈Enter⌋ while you are in the Account field to display the list of accounts.

Click on 1080 Cash in Bank

Click on Select to enter it on your sales input form.

Press $\boxed{\text{Tab}}$ to advance to the next line of the form and update the totals. Notice that the Total field shows the balance owing as zero.

You have now completed all the entries for this transaction and are ready to review your transaction. Your completed form should look like the one shown here:

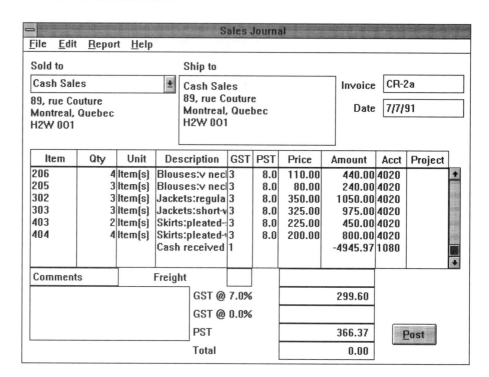

NOTES:

Scroll up to see the first two items on the list.

Reviewing the Cash Sales Journal Entry

Choose Display Sales Journal Entry from the pull-down menu under **Report** to display the transaction you have entered:

		Debits	Credits	Proj
91-07-07				
1080	Cash in Bank	4,945.97	-	
5060	Cost of Goods Sold	1,870.00	-	
1520	Accessories	-	130.00	
1540	Blouses	-	320.00	
1560	Jackets	-	900.00	
1580	Skirts	-	520.00	
2600	GST Charged on Sales	-	299.60	
2640	PST Payable	-	366.37	
4020	Revenue from Sales	-	4,280.00	
		6,815.97	6,815.97	

Take a little time to absorb what you have just accomplished. It *does* make sense. Note that the Cash in Bank account is debited instead of the Accounts Receivable control account, which is zeroed. The ACCPAC Simply Accounting program has automatically updated all other accounts relevant to this transaction as well as the inventory database.

Close the display to return to the Sales Journal input screen.

CORRECTING THE INVENTORY CASH SALES JOURNAL ENTRY

The steps for correcting entries are the same as those provided on page 146 for correcting credit sales of inventory items. Please refer to them if you encounter difficulties.

Posting

When all the information in your journal entry is correct, you must post the transaction to save it.

Click on Post

Adding a New Inventory Item

The source document on July 10 requires you to add Suits as a new inventory item to the current list. When you check the Chart of Accounts, you can see that suits do not belong in any of the existing inventory asset accounts. Therefore you must create a new asset account called **Suits** and give it a new account number, **1600**.

The keystrokes for inserting a new General Ledger account are provided in the Pilot Plumbing application.

After you have entered the new General Ledger account, you should display or print your Chart of Accounts to make sure the information for the new account is entered correctly.

To add the new inventory items,

Click on the Inventory Ledger icon on the Ledger/Journal company window to highlight it as shown below:

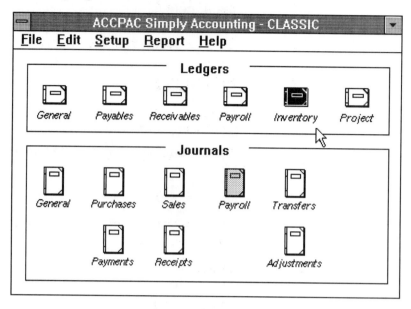

Open the Ledger to display *101 Accessories: belts,* the first inventory record.

Choose Create from the pull-down menu under **Edit** to provide the following Inventory Ledger input screen:

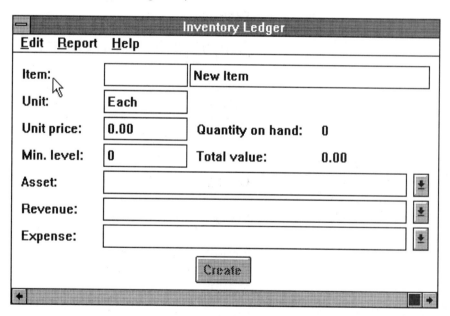

The cursor is flashing in the Item field, ready for you to enter information. From your source document information, you must enter the item number and description. The first part of the Item field contains the number of the inventory item; the second part contains the description or item name.

Type: `501`

Press ⌈Tab⌉

Type: `Suits:classic-wool`

Press ⌈Tab⌉

The cursor advances to the Unit field, which shows the way in which goods are sold (e.g., by the dozen, by the tonne or by item).

Type: `Item(s)`

Press ⌈Tab⌉

The cursor advances to the Unit price field. Here you must enter the selling price of the item.

Type: `450`

Press ⌈Tab⌉

The cursor advances to the Minimum level field. Here you must enter the stock level at which you wish to reorder the item in question. If you print out inventory reports, items that have fallen below the minimum level will be flagged.

Type: `2`

Press ⌈Tab⌉

The cursor advances to the Asset field. Here you must enter the number of the asset account affected by purchases and sales of this item. You must enter the number of the asset account you were asked to create from the account list provided when you click on the arrow to the right of the field.

Choose 1600 Suits from this list and enter it on your form.

Press ⌈Tab⌉

The cursor advances to the Revenue field. Here you must enter the revenue account that will be credited when this inventory item is sold.

Choose 4020 Revenue from Sales from the list of revenue accounts provided when you click on the arrow beside the field and enter it on your form.

Press ⌈Tab⌉

NOTES:
Only asset accounts are available in this list.

NOTES:
Only revenue accounts are available in this list.

The cursor advances to the Expense field. Here you must enter the expense account that will be debited when this inventory item is sold.

Choose 5060 Cost of Goods Sold from the list of expense accounts displayed when you click on the arrow beside the field and enter it on your form.

Press `Tab`

The completed form is shown below:

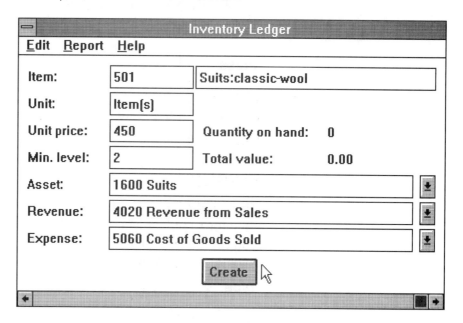

Correct the information if necessary by returning to the field that contains the error. Highlight the error and type the correct information.

Press `Tab` to enter the correction.

When all the information is correct, you must save your information.

Click on Create to save the new record and add it to your list of inventory items.

Repeat the procedures above for the second new inventory item on the source document. You should use the same asset, revenue and expense accounts that you used for the first new inventory item. Save your information and proceed to record the purchase invoice, using the keystroke instructions provided earlier in this application.

Displaying Inventory Reports

Displaying Inventory Lists

Click on the **Inventory Ledger icon** to highlight it on the Ledger/Journal company window

Choose Display Inventory List from the pull-down menu under **Report**.

Close the display when you are finished.

Displaying the Adjustments Journal

With the Adjustments Journal highlighted on the Ledger/Journal company window,

Choose Display Adjustments Journal from the pull-down menu under **Report**. The following screen appears asking for the dates for your report:

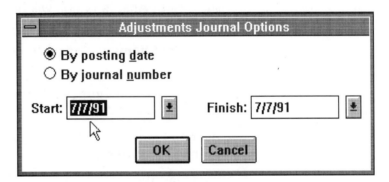

As usual, the using date and the *By posting date* option are provided by default.

Type the beginning date for the report you want.

Press Tab

Type the ending date for the report.

Click on OK

Close the display when you are finished.

Displaying Inventory Reports

Choose Inventory from the pull-down menu under **Report** to display the following report options:

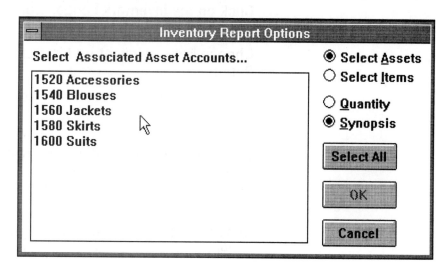

The **Select Assets** option will provide information for all inventory items in the asset group(s) chosen.

The **Select Items** option will provide information for the inventory item selected.

You can obtain information for all items through either option by choosing **Select All**.

Inventory reports can be displayed with two types of information, **quantity** or **synopsis**.

The **Quantity** option provides current information about the quantity on hand, the minimum stock levels, and whether the item has fallen below the minimum level and needs to be reordered. The information is given for the item requested or for all items in the asset group(s), according to the option you selected.

The **Synopsis** option lists selling price; quantity on hand; the cost of the inventory on hand; the total value of inventory on hand; and the profit margin for the item requested or for all items in the asset group(s) according to the option you selected. Total value of the inventory in an asset group is also given if you choose **Select Assets**

Choose the options you need for your report.

Click on OK

Close the display when you are finished.

Printing Reports

To print an inventory report, first display the report. Then,
Choose Print from the pull-down menu under **File**.

Case Problem

What must Enda Salt do to the Classic Clothes' Chart of Accounts if
she wishes to determine the cost of goods sold for each category of
stock items? What adjustments would she have to make to the
Inventory Ledger?

CHAPTER EIGHT
Careful Carpenters

Company Information

Company Profile

Careful Carpenters is located in Summerside, Prince Edward Island. This carpentry business, owned and operated by Kevin Purbhoo, began operations on January 1, 1991 and has just completed a successful year. The business earns its income by providing carpentry services to homes, businesses, offices and local farms.

At the end of the fiscal year, Careful Carpenters wishes to complete the adjustments necessary to bring its books up to date. This includes adjusting for prepaid expenses, bad debt expense, accrued liabilities, and depreciation on plant and equipment.

The following information is provided to complete the adjustments using ACCPAC Simply Accounting:

1. Chart of Accounts;
2. Trial Balance dated December 30, 1991;
3. Additional Information Memo.

CAREFUL CARPENTERS
CHART OF ACCOUNTS

Assets
1080 Cash in Bank
1200 Accounts Receivable
1220 Allowance for Bad Debts
1240 Carpentry Supplies
1260 Lumber Supplies
1280 Office Supplies
1300 Prepaid Advertising
1320 Prepaid Insurance
1340 Prepaid Rent
1520 Equipment
1540 Accum Deprec - Equipment
1560 Tools
1580 Accum Deprec - Tools
1600 Truck
1620 Accum Deprec - Truck

Liabilities
2100 Bank Loan
2200 Accounts Payable
2220 Unearned Income
2240 Interest Accrued:Bank Loan
2600 GST Payable

Equity
3560 K. Purbhoo, Capital

Revenue
4100 Revenue from Carpentry

Expense
5020 Advertising Expense
5040 Bad Debts Expense
5060 Bank Charges
5080 Carpentry Supplies Used
5100 Depreciation:Equipment
5120 Depreciation:Tools
5140 Depreciation:Truck
5160 Hydro Expense
5180 Interest: Bank Loan
5200 Insurance Expense
5220 Lumber Supplies Used
5240 Office Supplies Used
5260 Rent Expense
5280 Telephone Expense
5300 Truck Expense

```
CAREFUL CARPENTERS
TRIAL BALANCE

December 30, 1991

1080 Cash in Bank              $ 21 615.00
1200 Accounts Receivable        18 000.00
1240 Carpentry Supplies          3 000.00
1260 Lumber Supplies            10 500.00
1280 Office Supplies             1 500.00
1300 Prepaid Advertising           660.00
1320 Prepaid Insurance           1 050.00
1340 Prepaid Rent                3 600.00
1520 Equipment                  18 000.00
1560 Tools                       4 500.00
1600 Truck                      13 500.00
2100 Bank Loan                              $    7 500.00
2200 Accounts Payable                            8 200.00
2220 Unearned Income                             3 600.00
2600 GST Payable                                   408.00
3560 K. Purbhoo, Capital                        16 000.00
4100 Revenue from Carpentry                     70 100.00
5060 Bank Charges                  128.00
5160 Hydro Expense               1 350.00
5180 Interest: Bank Loan           825.00
5260 Rent Expense                6 000.00
5280 Telephone Expense             480.00
5300 Truck Expense               1 100.00
                             _____     _____
                             $105 808.00     $105 808.00
                             ===========     ===========
```

Additional Information Memo

1. Careful Carpenters purchased a regular weekly advertisement on October 1, 1991 to run in a local newspaper for six months. Three months of this prepaid expense have expired.

2. The company purchased insurance coverage for a three-year period on January 1, 1991. One year of insurance coverage has expired.

3. The company prepaid rent on November 1, 1991 for a six-month period to expire on April 30, 1992. Calculate and charge the expired portion of the prepaid rent to the Rent Expense account on December 31, 1991.

4. The amount of supplies on hand (based on a physical count on December 31, 1991) follows:

   - Carpentry Supplies $1 200.00
   - Lumber Supplies $2 300.00
   - Office Supplies $900.00

5. Careful Carpenters purchased its equipment new on January 1, 1991. The capital cost allowance rate for this class of fixed asset for tax purposes is 20 percent.

6. The company purchased its tools new on January 1, 1991. The capital cost allowance rate for this class of fixed asset for tax purposes is 20 percent.

7. The new delivery truck was purchased on March 1, 1991. The capital cost allowance rate for this class of fixed asset for tax purposes is 30 percent.

8. Careful Carpenters' accumulated unpaid interest on its bank loan is $75.00.

9. On December 1, 1991, a farmer paid $3 600 in advance for carpentry work on his barn. The work was estimated to take four months to complete. At the end of December 31, 1991, 25 percent of the work is completed.

10. Estimated uncollectible accounts is 0.5 percent of the Revenue from Carpentry account.

Instructions

1. Using the Additional Information Memo provided, record the adjusting entries using the General Journal in ACCPAC Simply Accounting. Since no source document numbers are provided, you may enter ADJ1, ADJ2, ADJ3, etc., in the Source field. The using date is December 31, 1991.

2. After you have finished making your entries, print the reports indicated on the printing form below:

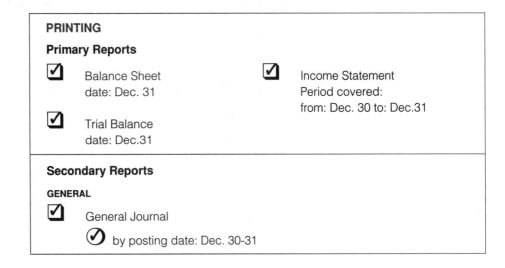

PRINTING

Primary Reports

☑ Balance Sheet
date: Dec. 31

☑ Income Statement
Period covered:
from: Dec. 30 to: Dec.31

☑ Trial Balance
date: Dec.31

Secondary Reports

GENERAL

☑ General Journal

⊘ by posting date: Dec. 30-31

CHAPTER NINE

Melody Music Centre

OBJECTIVES

Upon completion of this chapter, you will be able to:

1. *access* the ACCPAC Simply Accounting program;
2. *access* the data files for this application;
3. *enter* transactions;
4. *distribute* revenues and expenses in the Sales, Purchases and Payroll journals;
5. *edit* and *review* transactions;
6. *post* transactions;
7. *display* and *print* transactions and reports.

Company Information

Company Profile

Melody Music Centre is owned by L. Segovia. The business has three divisions or profit centres. Division One earns revenue from the sale of musical instruments. Division Two earns revenue from servicing and repairing musical instruments. Division Three earns revenue from providing musical instruction to students in the local school district. The business employs three full-time salaried employees (a manager, a service and repairperson, and a music instructor) and one part-time hourly employee (a student who does clerical and accounting tasks).

Mr. Segovia, the owner, is not involved in the daily operations of the business. The daily operations are handled by the manager, Valerie Chaikovsky. She has run the business efficiently since the owner became ill and was unable to handle the work. Mr. Segovia is considering making Ms. Chaikovsky, a working partner within the next few months, and contract negotiations to finalize the details have begun.

At the end of December 1990, a decision was made to convert the store's manual accounting system to a computerized one. Ms. Chaikovsky was impressed with the demonstration of ACCPAC Simply Accounting at a recent conference she had attended because it was able to handle all the accounting routines and to prepare the types of reports she wanted for the business. She was especially pleased that the program could very easily provide reports by divisions, departments or profit centres.

With the assistance of Jasmine Yaegar, the part-time helper, the manual accounting system was converted to ACCPAC Simply Accounting and ready for use in the new fiscal year beginning January 1, 1991. All payroll and provincial sales tax liabilities were remitted before the end of the fiscal year when the books were closed.

The following information is provided to start the new fiscal year:

1. Chart of Accounts;
2. Post-Closing Trial Balance;
3. Vendor Information;
4. Customer Information;
5. Employee Information;
6. Employee Profiles and TD-1 Information;
6. Inventory Information;
7. Division Jobcost Information;
8. Accounting Procedures.

**MELODY MUSIC CENTRE
CHART OF ACCOUNTS**

Assets
1080 Cash in Bank
1200 Accounts Receivable
1220 Musical Parts Inventory
1240 Software Library
1260 Supplies
1500 Brass
1520 Musical Sheets
1540 Percussion
1560 Strings
1580 Woodwind
1680 Computers & Peripherals
1700 Delivery Truck
1720 Equipment
1740 Furniture & Fixtures

Liabilities
2100 Bank Loan
2200 Accounts Payable
2300 Vacation Payable
2310 UI Payable
2320 CPP Payable
2330 Income Tax Payable
2390 EHT Payable
2420 CSB-Plan Payable
2460 WCB Payable
2600 GST Charged on Sales
2610 GST Paid on Purchase
2640 PST Payable

Equity
3560 L. Segovia, Capital
3570 L. Segovia, Drawings

Revenue
4020 Revenue from Sales
4030 Revenue from Services
4040 Revenue from Instruction

Expense

Cost of Goods Sold
5020 Brass
5040 Musical Sheets
5060 Percussion
5080 Strings
5100 Woodwind
5140 Freight Expense

Operating Expenses
5220 Advertising Expense
5240 Bank Charges
5260 Delivery Expense
5280 Hydro Expense
5300 Legal Expense
5320 Musical Parts Used
5340 Rent Expense
5360 Telephone Expense
5380 Truck Expense

Payroll Expenses
5500 Wages
5510 UI Expense
5520 CPP Expense
5530 WCB Expense
5560 EHT Expense

```
MELODY MUSIC CENTRE
POST-CLOSING TRIAL BALANCE

December 31, 1990

1080 Cash in Bank              $  15 000.00
1200 Accounts Receivable          11 000.00
1220 Musical Parts Inventory       2 500.00
1240 Software Library                500.00
1260 Supplies                        500.00
1500 Brass                         5 250.00
1520 Musical Sheets                1 000.00
1540 Percussion                   31 900.00
1560 Strings                      20 400.00
1580 Woodwind                      7 100.00
1680 Computers & Peripherals       4 500.00
1700 Delivery Truck               10 000.00
1720 Equipment                     7 000.00
1740 Furniture & Fixtures          2 590.00
2100 Bank Loan                                   $   9 700.00
2200 Accounts Payable                                4 800.00
3560 L. Segovia, Capital                           104 740.00
                                  _____      _____
                                  $119 240.00      $119 240.00
                                  ===========      ===========
```

MELODY MUSIC CENTRE
VENDOR INFORMATION

Vendor Name	Address & Telephone	Invoice Date	Invoice Number	Outstanding Balance
Acoustical Furniture Store	12 Bass Avenue Toronto, Ontario M4R 1Q9 Tel: 969-3234	Dec. 13/90	AF-X33	$ 600.00
Bell Telephone	155 Eglinton Ave. Toronto, Ontario M4R 1K8 Tel: 484-1298			
L. Segovia, Drawings	n/a			
Musicland Corporation	8 Recorder Road Toronto, Ontario M9A 1U2 Tel: 925-1619	Dec. 15/90 Dec. 18/90 Total	MC-634 MC-651	$1 800.00 $1 200.00 _____ $3 000.00
Schimmel Piano Inc.	23 Ivory Rd. Queenston, Ontario K2L 1Y2 Tel: 621-3462			

Vendor Name	Address & Telephone	Invoice Date	Invoice Number	Outstanding Balance
Song & Dance Inc.	455 Jive Road Scarborough, Ontario M8U 1Q3 Tel: 284-1524	Dec. 20/90	SDI-511	$ 800.00
Sound Transport Co.	2 Deliverance Blvd. Toronto, Ontario M4C 1K3 Tel: 923-1614	Dec. 20/90	ST-116	$ 400.00
Toronto Hydro	55 University Ave. Toronto, Ontario M5T 1J7 Tel: 923-1123			
Toronto Star	1 Yonge Street Toronto, Ontario M5E 1E6 Tel: 368-3611			
			GRAND TOTAL	$4 800.00

MELODY MUSIC CENTRE
CUSTOMER INFORMATION

Customer Name	Address & Telephone	Invoice Date	Invoice Number	Outstanding Balance
Access Card	58 Visa Avenue Tutorial Bank Plaza Toronto, Ontario M1Q 8E3 Tel: 978-1280	Dec. 16/90 Dec. 16/90 Dec. 19/90 Dec. 22/90 Dec. 29/90	MMC-818 MMC-824 MMC-856 MMC-860 MMC-867	$1 250.00 $1 100.00 $1 100.00 $ 800.00 $1 000.00
			Total	$5 250.00
Cash Sales	2001 Yonge St. Toronto, Ontario M5R 1J2 Tel: 486-1816			
Metro School Board	155 Collegiate Ave. Toronto, Ontario M1G 4S2 Tel: 927-4513	Dec. 4/90	MMC-782	$2 750.00
School of Performing Arts	21 Drama Drive Toronto, Ontario M6A 1M1 Tel: 933-0837	Dec. 6/90	MMC-790	$1 250.00

Tivoli Theatre	156 College St. Toronto, Ontario M6R 1W2 Tel: 922-4435	Dec. 15/90	MMC-805	$ 750.00
The Music Conservatory	12 Symphony Rd. North York, Ontario M2N 1E4 Tel: 531-6711	Nov. 30/90	MMC-765	$ 1 000.00
The Junction Band	35 Bluegrass Road East York, Ontario M5N 4H8 Tel: 691-8125		**GRAND TOTAL**	$11 000.00

MELODY MUSIC CENTRE
EMPLOYEE INFORMATION SHEET

	1	2	3	4
Employee Number:	1	2	3	4
Position:	Manager & Sales	Repairs & Service	Instructor	Accountant/Clerical
Social Insurance Number:	382-764-072	511-881-192	342-579-192	467-123-222
Employee Name:	Valerie Chaikovsky	Joachim Pinchez	Margaret Worrell	Jasmine Yaegar
Address & Telephone:	21 Clinton Blvd. Toronto, Ontario M4J 3S4 416-477-6123	3 Runnymede Road Toronto, Ontario M4K 2S1 416-485-1393	881 Chaplin Cres. Toronto, Ontario M5P 2E9 416-422-1118	82 Chudley Cres. Toronto, Ontario M1P 2W9 416-833-1318
Date of Birth (dd-mm-yy):	15-10-53	5-02-41	12-11-63	14-01-66
Tax Exemptions: **(TD1-1991)** Basic Personal Spouse Children Disability Education & Tuition Other	$6 280.00	$6 280.00 $5 757.00 $406.00	$6 280.00	$6 280.00 $1 080.00
Total Exemptions Less: Family Allowance	$6 280.00	$12 443.00 $392.88	$6 280.00	$7 360.00
Net Claim	$6 280.00	$12 050.12	$6 280.00	$7 360.00
Employee Earnings: Regular Wage Rate Overtime Wage Rate Regular Salary Commissions Vacation Pay	 $4 500/period 1% of sales 6% (retained)	 $3 200/period 2% of services 4% (retained)	 $2 850/period 5% of instruction 4% (retained)	$12.00/hour $18.00/hour 4% (retained)

Employee Number:	1	2	3	4
Employee Deductions:				
CSB-Plan *	$50.00/period	$50.00/period	$50.00/period	-
CPP	**	**	**	**
UI	**	**	**	**
Income Tax	**	**	**	**

* Canada Savings Bond Plan
** Calculations built into ACCPAC Simply Accounting program

Employee Profiles and TD1 Information

1. Valerie Chaikovsky is the salesperson and manager of the store. Her duties are to delegate work duties and to handle the daily operations of the business. Valerie is single and supports herself. Her salary is $4 500 per pay period ($54 000 per year), and she receives a commission of one percent, calculated on the monthly revenue from sales and payable each pay period. She receives no company benefits.

2. Joachim Pinchez is the service and repairperson. He works both inside and outside the store on work orders. Joachim is married and fully supports his wife and a child age 13 who have no income. Joachim will receive $392.88 in family allowances for 1991. His salary is $3 200 per pay period ($38 400 per year), and he receives a commission of two percent, calculated on the monthly revenue from services and payable each pay period. He receives no company benefits.

3. Margaret Worrell is the musical instructor. She provides instructions on the flute, guitar, piano and violin to students in the local school district. Margaret is single and self-supporting. She earns a salary of $2 850 per pay period ($34 200 per year), and she receives a commission of five percent, calculated on the monthly revenue from instruction and payable each pay period. She receives no company benefits.

4. Jasmine Yaegar works part-time performing general clerical and accounting duties. She is a full-time student at the local community college. Jasmine is single and self-supporting. Her tuition fees are $600 for 1991 and she is allowed the education deduction of $60 per month for eight months of the academic year. Her hourly rate is $12.00 for regular work and $18.00 for overtime work. She receives no company benefits.

Additional Payroll Information

1. There are 12 pay periods in the year for salaried employees.

2. There are 26 pay periods in the year for the hourly employee.

3. The employer's contributions include:

    - CPP contributions equal to employee contributions;
    - UI factor of 1.4;
    - WCB rate of 1.12;
    - EHT factor of 0.98.

MELODY MUSIC CENTRE
INVENTORY INFORMATION

Item Number & Name	Unit Description	Selling Price	Quantity on Hand	Amount (cost)	Minimum Stock Level
11 Brass: Cornet	item(s)	$300.00	6	$900.00	2
12 Brass: Horn	item(s)	$400.00	6	$1 500.00	2
13 Brass: Trombone	item(s)	$400.00	6	$1 500.00	2
14 Brass: Trumpet	item(s)	$400.00	6	$1 350.00	2
				$5 250.00	
15 Music Instruction	hour(s)	$25.00	2 000	$0.00	0
16 Musical Sheets (various)	item(s)	$2.00	1 000	$1 000.00	400
17 Percussion: Bongos	set(s)	$100.00	24	$1 200.00	6
18 Percussion: Drum	item(s)	$400.00	12	$2 400.00	4
19 Percussion: Piano 120cm	item(s)	$6 000.00	4	$12 000.00	1
20 Percussion: Piano 130cm	item(s)	$7 500.00	4	$16 000.00	1
21 Percussion: Tambourine	item(s)	$40.00	12	$300.00	3
				$31 900.00	
22 Services and Repairs	hour(s)	$50.00	2 000	$0.00	0
23 Strings: Cello	item(s)	$1 200.00	3	$2 400.00	1
24 Strings: Guitar/cl	item(s)	$500.00	12	$3 600.00	3
25 Strings: Guitar/sp	item(s)	$400.00	12	$2 400.00	3
26 Strings: Violin type-a	item(s)	$750.00	12	$4 800.00	3
27 Strings: Violin type-b	item(s)	$1 000.00	12	$7 200.00	3
				$20 400.00	
28 Woodwind: Clarinet	item(s)	$400.00	6	$1 500.00	2
29 Woodwind: Flute	item(s)	$300.00	12	$2 400.00	3
30 Woodwind: Oboe	item(s)	$300.00	8	$1 600.00	3
31 Woodwind: Saxophone	item(s)	$600.00	4	$1 600.00	1
				$7 100.00	

MELODY MUSIC CENTRE
DIVISION JOBCOST INFORMATION

(Percentage [%] allocation)

Account	Sales Division	Service Division	Instruction Division
Revenue:			
Sales	100		
Service		100	
Instruction			100
Cost of Goods Sold:			
Brass	100		
Musical Sheets	100		
Percussion	100		
Strings	100		
Woodwind	100		
Freight Expense	100		
Operating Expenses:			
Advertising	60	20	20
Bank Charges	60	30	10
Delivery Expense	90	10	
Hydro Expense	50	25	25
Legal Expense	100		
Musical Parts Used		98	2
Rent Expense	70	20	10
Telephone Expense	60	20	20
Truck Expense	10	90	
Payroll Expenses:			
Wages: Manager	90	5	5
UI: Manager	90	5	5
CPP: Manager	90	5	5
WCB: Manager	90	5	5
Wages: Serviceperson		100	
UI: Serviceperson		100	
CPP: Serviceperson		100	
WCB: Serviceperson		100	
Wages: Instructor			100
UI: Instructor			100
CPP: Instructor			100
WCB: Instructor			100
Wages: Accountant/CI	60	20	20
UI: Accountant/CI	60	20	20
CPP: Accountant/CI	60	20	20
WCB: Accountant/CI	60	20	20

AccountingProcedures

1. **The Employer Health Tax (EHT)**
The Employer Health Tax (EHT) replaced the Ontario Health Insurance Plan premium payments on January 1, 1990. The health tax is paid by all employers who have a permanent establishment in Ontario and who pay remuneration to employees who report to work. It also includes employees who are not required to report for work as long as an employer-employee relationship exists. The EHT is based on the total annual remuneration paid to employees. The EHT rate ranges from 0.98 percent to 1.95 percent. The lowest rate (0.98%) applies if the total remuneration is under $200 000. The highest rate (1.95%) applies to employers paying total remuneration exceeding $400 000.

ACCPAC Simply Accounting will calculate the employer's liability to the Provincial Treasurer automatically once the information is set up correctly in the payroll defaults and integration accounts. A later application, Artistic Interiors, will provide you with the keystrokes necessary for setting up the EHT information. The EHT can be remitted monthly or quarterly.

2. **The Goods and Services Tax: Remittances**
Melody Music Centre will use the **regular method** for remittance of the Goods and Services Tax. GST collected from customers will be recorded as a liability in the GST Charged on Sales account. GST paid to vendors will be recorded in the GST Paid on Purchases account as a decrease in liability to Revenue Canada. The report will be filed with the Receiver General of Canada by the last day of the month for the previous quarterly period, either including the balance owing or requesting a refund.

3. **Access Card Sales**
The Access Card issued by the Tutorial Bank allows customers to purchase items on credit. It is similar to a Visa, Mastercard or American Express card. The ACCPAC Simply Accounting program does not have a point-of-sale module (over-the-counter sales). Therefore, all Access Card sales are processed in the Sales Journal. In this way the business is able to keep track of all credit card sales. Melody Music Centre has set up an Accounts Receivable account called Access Card. When a credit card sale is made, the Access Card account in the Receivables Ledger is debited, the appropriate revenue, GST Charged on Sales and PST Payable accounts are credited and the inventory accounts are changed. The business accumulates credit card receipts and prepares a Sales Recap Slip every two weeks. The Sales Recap Slip is then submitted as a deposit to the Tutorial Bank. After the deposit is made, it is recorded as a receipt in the Payments Journal just like any other receipt from a customer.

NOTES:
- Most bank and other financial institution services are exempt from GST collection in this application.
- Provincial sales taxes are levied in this application.

NOTES:
- Although it is customary for businesses allowing credit card purchases to pay a service charge to the credit card company, the Melody Music Centre application omits this detail for the sake of simplicity.
- It is also customary to prepare a Sales Recap Slip on a daily basis rather than biweekly as our application shows.
- The accounting procedures for credit cards may vary among different credit card companies.

4. **Cash Sales of Inventory Items and Services**

Cash transactions for goods and services occur normally in most types of businesses. The ACCPAC Simply Accounting program does not have a point-of-sale module for over-the-counter sales. However, it can handle cash transactions through the Sales Journal. The process is fairly simple although it will appear to be unorthodox to the uninitiated. You must set up **Cash Sales** as a customer in the Receivables Ledger, using the business address and telephone information. This account is already set up for you in this application. You then enter the cash transaction the same way as you would enter any credit sale transaction to customers, with these additional steps:

- After recording all of the items sold, when the cursor moves down to the next line on the invoice, type "Payment" in the Description field.
- Enter **code 1** in the GST field to show that the payment is non-taxable .
- Enter a **negative** amount in the Amount field for the cash or cheque received from the customer.
- Enter the *Cash in Bank* account number in the Account field.
- Leave the PST field blank.

The program will then debit the Cash in Bank account instead of the Accounts Receivable control account. All the other relevant accounts for this transaction will be debited and credited as in other transactions.

The source document for cash transactions for this application is a cash register summary. This summary lists individual cash sales transactions obtained from cash register tapes and invoices issued to various customers. You use it in the same way that you would use an individual customer's source document for a cash sale. Including a summary form eliminates the need to prepare a large number of source documents for this application.

5. **Freight Expense**

When a business purchases inventory items, the cost of any freight that cannot be directly allocated to a specific item must be charged to the Freight Expense account. This amount will be regarded as an expense rather than being charged to any inventory asset account.

6. **PST**

The province of Ontario has ruled that PST is calculated on the base amount of the invoice, which does not include the GST.

In this application, provincial sales taxes of 8% are applied to cash and credit sales of musical instruments and to service and repair work orders. PST is not applied to revenue from instruction.

7. **Sales Invoices**

   Sales Invoices are prepared manually in this application. They are not generated by the program. The user of course, has the option of generating invoices through the software. Before posting a journal transaction, choose **Print** from the pull-down menu under **File**.

8. **Parts Requisition Summary Form**

   Musical parts are requisitioned for work orders by the service and repairperson. These requisition forms are summarized every two weeks in a Parts Requisition Summary Form. When this form is completed, an adjusting entry must be made in the General Journal to reduce the Musical Parts inventory asset account and increase the Musical Parts Used expense account.

Instructions

1. Using the Chart of Accounts, Trial Balance and other information, record entries for the source documents for January, 1991 using ACCPAC Simply Accounting. The procedures for entering each new type of transaction are outlined step by step in the keystroke section that follows the source documents.

2. After you have finished making your entries, print the reports indicated on the printing form below.

PRINTING

Primary Reports

☑ Balance Sheet
date: Jan. 31

☑ Income Statement
Period covered:
from: Jan. 1   to: Jan. 31

☑ Trial Balance
date: Jan. 31

☑ General Ledger
accounts: 1240 _____ 4030 _____
5100 _____ 2390 _____

☑ Vendor Aged
  ⊘ Summary
  ◯ Detail

Period covered:
from: Jan. 1 to: Jan. 31

☑ Customer Aged
  ⊘ Summary
  ◯ Detail

☑ Employee Summary
☑ Employee Register 1
☐ Employee Register 2
☐ T4 Slips

☑ Inventory
  ⊘ Synopsis

☑ Division Summary
  ⊘ Summary
  ⊘ Detail

Secondary Reports

GENERAL

☑ General Journal
  ⊘ by posting date: Jan. 1-31

ACCOUNTS PAYABLE

☑ Vendor Address List

☐ Purchases Journal
  ◯ by posting date:

☐ Payments Journal
  ◯ by posting date:

ACCOUNTS RECEIVABLE

☑ Customer Address List
☐ Sales Journal
  ◯ by posting date:
☐ Receipts Journal
  ◯ by posting date:

PAYROLL

☑ Employee List
☐ Payroll Journal
  ◯ by posting date:

INVENTORY

☑ Inventory List
☐ Inventory Adjustments Journal
  ◯ by posting date:

DIVISION

☐ Division List

Source Documents

USING DATE

Jan. 7 ☑ Purchase Invoice #TS-1231
Dated: Jan. 2/91
From Toronto Star, $400 for newspaper
advertisement, plus GST paid $28. Purchase
Invoice total $428. Terms: cash on receipt.

☐ Cheque Copy #101
Dated: Jan. 2/91
To Toronto Star, $428 in full payment of account.
Reference invoice #TS-1231.

☐ Sales Invoice #MMC-1
Dated: Jan. 2/91
To The Music Conservatory;
    10 hours - Services and Repairs $50.00/hour
    Goods & Services Tax   7%
    Provincial Sales Tax   8%
Terms: net 60 days.

☐ Sales Invoice #MMC-2
Dated: Jan. 2/91
To Phil Maturi;
    one Brass: Trumpet $400.00
    Goods & Services Tax   7%
    Provincial Sales Tax   8%
Payment: Access Card (no. 347238674)

☐ Sales Invoice #MMC-3
Dated: Jan. 3/91
To Darka Gallo;
    one Strings: Violin type-b $1 000.00
    Goods & Services Tax   7%
    Provincial Sales Tax   8%
Payment: Access Card (no. 543265241)

☐ Sales Invoice #MMC-4
Dated: Jan. 3/91
To Tivoli Theatre;
    12 hours - Services and Repairs $50.00/hour
    Goods & Services Tax   7%
    Provincial Sales Tax   8%
Terms: net 60 days.

☐ Sales Invoice #MMC-5
Dated: Jan. 4/91
To Rick Kollins;
 one Strings: Guitar/sp $400.00
  Goods & Services Tax 7%
  Provincial Sales Tax 8%
Payment: Access Card (no. 245675432)

☐ Sales Recap Slip #1
Dated: Jan. 4/91
Deposited with Tutorial Bank, $5 250 for Access
Card purchases (reference invoices #MMC-818,
824, 856, 860 and 867).

☐ Sales Invoice #MMC-6
Dated Jan. 5/91
To Maido Musta;
 one Percussion: Tambourine $40.00
  Goods & Services Tax 7%
  Provincial Sales Tax 8%
Payment: Access Card (no. 564736632)

☐ Sales Invoice #MMC-7
Dated: Jan. 5/91
To Metro School Board;
 one Percussion: Piano 120cm $6 000.00
 one Strings: Cello $1 200.00
 two Strings: Violin type-a $ 750.00 each
 two Brass: Trombones $ 400.00 each
  Goods & Services Tax 7%
  Provincial Sales Tax 8%
Terms: net 60 days.

☐ Purchase Invoice #SP-13
Dated: Jan. 5/91
From Schimmel Piano Inc.;
 two Percussion: Pianos 130cm $8 000.00
 Goods & Services Tax (7%) paid 560.00
         ———————
     Total $8 560.00
         ═══════

Freight included. Terms: net 30 days.

☐ Purchase Invoice #SP-14
Dated: Jan. 5/91
From Schimmel Piano Inc.;
   two Percussion: Pianos 120cm $6 000.00
   Goods & Services Tax (7%) paid   420.00

               Total $6 420.00

Freight included. Terms: net 30 days.

☐ Purchase Invoice #ST-143
Dated: Jan. 5/91
From Sound Transport Co., $300 for delivery of
musical instruments to Metro School Board and
other customers plus GST paid $21. Purchase
Invoice total $321. Terms: net 30 days.

☐ Purchase Invoice #SDI-564
Dated: Jan. 6/91
From Song & Dance Inc.,
   200 Musical Sheets (various) $200.00
   Goods & Services Tax (7%) paid   14.00

               Total $214.00

Freight included. Terms: net 30 days.

☐ Cheque Copy #102
Dated: Jan. 7/91
To Musicland Corporation, $3 000 for payment of
invoices #MC-634 and #MC-651 on account.

☐ Bank Debit Memo #TB-97
Dated: Jan. 7/91
From Tutorial Bank, $36.50 for bank service
charges.

☐ Cash Receipt #1
Dated: Jan. 7/91
From Cash Register Summary Sheet (1) - Sales.
Amount deposited in bank.

Item	Qty	Price	Amount
Brass: Cornet	1	$300.00	$300.00
Woodwind: Oboe	1	$300.00	300.00
		Gross Sales	$600.00
		GST (7%)	42.00
		PST (8%)	48.00
Total Cash Received Jan. 1-7:			$690.00

Cash Receipt #2
Dated: Jan. 7/91
From Cash Register Summary Sheet (2) - Services and Repairs. Amount deposited in bank.

Item	Qty	Price	Amount
Services and Repairs	14	$50.00	$700.00
		GST (7%)	49.00
		PST (8%)	56.00
Total Cash Received Jan. 1-7:			$805.00

Cash Receipt #3
Dated: Jan. 7/91
From Cash Register Summary Sheet (3) - Instruction. Amount deposited in bank.

Item	Qty	Price	Amount
Music Instruction	32	$25.00	$800.00
		GST (7%)	56.00
Total Cash Received Jan. 1-7:			$856.00

Jan. 14 Sales Invoice #MMC-8
Dated: Jan. 10/91
To The Junction Band;
   one Percussion: Piano 120cm $6 000.00
   Goods & Services Tax 7%
   Provincial Sales Tax 8%
Terms: net 60 days.

☐ Sales Invoice #MMC-9
Dated: Jan. 11/91
To Angus W. LeeSing;
　　one Woodwind: Saxophone　　　$600.00
　　Goods & Services Tax　　　　　7%
　　Provincial Sales Tax　　　　　8%
Payment: Access Card (no. 354626262)

☐ Sales Invoice #MMC-10
Dated: Jan. 11/91
To Metro School Board;
　　13 hours - Services and Repairs　$50.00/hour
　　Goods & Services Tax　　　　　7%
　　Provincial Sales Tax　　　　　8%
Terms: net 60 days.

☐ Cheque Copy #103
Dated: Jan. 12/91
To Sound Transport Co., $400 for payment of
invoice #ST-116 on account.

☐ Cash Receipt #4
Dated: Jan. 12/91
From Tivoli Theatre, cheque #13, $750 for payment
of invoice #MMC-805 on account.

☐ Cash Receipt #5
Dated: Jan. 13/91
From The Music Conservatory, cheque #152, $1 000
for payment of invoice #MMC-765 on account.

☐ Utility Statement #TH-901
Dated: Jan. 13/91
From Toronto Hydro, $160 for hydro services plus
GST paid $11.20. Utility Statement total $171.20.
Terms: cash on receipt.

☐ Cheque Copy #104
Dated: Jan. 13/91
To Toronto Hydro, $171.20 in full payment of
account. Reference invoice #TH-901.

☐ Sales Invoice #MMC-11
Dated: Jan. 13/91
To Robert Buerkle;
　　one Strings: Guitar/cl　　　$500.00
　　one Woodwind: Flute　　　　$300.00
　　Goods & Services Tax　　　　7%
　　Provincial Sales Tax　　　　8%
Payment: Access Card (no. 237195631)

☐ Purchase Invoice #ST-171
Dated: Jan. 14/91
From Sound Transport Co., $280 for delivery of
musical instruments to customers plus GST paid
$19.60. Purchase Invoice total $299.60. Terms: net
30 days.

☐ Purchase Invoice #MC-78
Dated: Jan. 14/91
From Musicland Corporation;

two Brass: Trombones	$ 500.00
one Brass: Trumpet	225.00
one Strings: Guitar/sp	200.00
one Strings: Violin type-a	400.00
one Strings: Violin type-b	600.00
Freight Expense	75.00
Goods & Services Tax (7%) paid	140.00
Total	$2 140.00

Terms: net 60 days.

☐ Sales Invoice #MMC-12
Dated: Jan. 14/91
To School of Performing Arts;

one Brass: Cornet	$300.00
one Brass: Horn	$400.00
one Brass: Trombone	$400.00
Goods & Services Tax	7%
Provincial Sales Tax	8%

Terms: net 60 days.

☐ Cash Receipt #6
Dated: Jan. 14/91
From The Junction Band, cheque #35, $2 900 for
partial payment of invoice #MMC-8 on account.

☐ Parts Requisition Summary Form #1
Dated: Jan. 14/91
From manager: Charge $225 to Musical Parts Used
account, and reduce the Musical Parts Inventory
account for the two weeks ending January 14.

☐ Cash Receipt #7
Dated: Jan. 14/91
From Cash Register Summary Sheet (4) - Sales.
Amount deposited in bank.

Item	Qty	Price	Amount
Woodwind: Saxophone	1	$600.00	$600.00
		Gross Sales	$600.00
		GST (7%)	42.00
		PST (8%)	48.00
Total Cash Received Jan. 8-14:			$690.00

Cash Receipt #8
Dated: Jan. 14/91
From Cash Register Summary Sheet (5) - Services and Repairs. Amount deposited in bank.

Item	Qty	Price	Amount
Services and Repairs	16.2	$50.00	$810.00
		GST (7%)	56.70
		PST (8%)	64.80
Total Cash Received Jan. 8-14:			$931.50

Cash Receipt #9
Dated: Jan. 14/91
From Cash Register Summary Sheet (6) - Instruction. Amount deposited in bank.

Item	Qty	Price	Amount
Music Instruction	32	$25.00	$800.00
		GST (7%)	56.00
Total Cash Received Jan. 8-14:			$856.00

Memo #1
Dated: Jan. 14/91
From owner: Complete payroll for hourly employee. Issue cheque #105.

TIME SUMMARY SHEET #1
(pay period ending January 14)

Name of Employee	Week 1 Hours	Week 2 Hours	Reg. Hours	O/T Hours
☑ Jasmine Yaegar	10	12	22	-

Jan. 21 ☐ Bank Debit Memo #TB-151
Dated: Jan. 16/91
From Tutorial Bank, $2 900 for NSF cheque #35
from The Junction Band. Reference invoice #MMC-8
and Cash Receipt #6.

☐ Bank Credit Memo #TB-L96
Dated: Jan. 16/91
From Tutorial Bank, $15 000 loan granted to pay off
Schimmel Piano Inc. account.

☐ Cheque Copy #106
Dated: Jan. 17/91
To Schimmel Piano Inc., $14 980 in full payment of
account. Reference invoices #SP-13 and #SP-14.

☐ Sales Invoice #MMC-13
Dated: Jan. 17/91
To Julius Bell;
   one Strings: Cello $1 200.00
   Goods & Services Tax   7%
   Provincial Sales Tax   8%
Payment: Access Card (no. 342334551)

☐ Cash Receipt #10
Dated: Jan. 18/91
From Metro School Board, cheque #87, $2 750 for
payment of invoice #MMC-782 on account.

☐ Cash Receipt #11
Dated: Jan. 18/91
From School of Performing Arts, cheque #145,
$1 250 for payment of invoice #MMC-790 on
account.

☐ Sales Invoice #MMC-14
Dated: Jan. 19/91
To Larry Chin;
   one Strings: Violin type-a $750.00
   Goods & Services Tax   7%
   Provincial Sales Tax   8%
Payment: Access Card (no. 451932722)

☐ Sales Invoice #MMC-15
Dated: Jan. 19/91
To Tivoli Theatre;
   one Percussion: Piano 130cm $7 500.00
   one Brass: Trumpet $ 400.00
   Goods & Services Tax   7%
   Provincial Sales Tax   8%
Terms: net 60 days.

☐ Cash Receipt #12
Dated: Jan. 19/91
From Tivoli Theatre, cheque #37, $2 085 for partial payment of invoice #MMC-15 on account.

☐ Sales Invoice #MMC-16
Dated: Jan. 20/91
To Metro School Board;
   one Brass: Horn $400.00
   one Brass: Trombone $400.00
   two Woodwind: flutes $300.00
   300 Music Sheets (various) $ 2.00 each
   Goods & Services Tax   7%
   Provincial Sales Tax   8%
Terms: net 60 days.

☐ Cheque Copy #107
Dated: Jan. 20/91
To Song & Dance Inc., $800.00 for payment of invoice #SDI-511 on account.

☐ Legal Statement #JH-35
Dated: Jan. 20/91
From Julia Henry, lawyer (new vendor), $300 for payment of legal fees to recover piano from The Junction Band plus GST paid $21. Statement total $321. Terms: cash on receipt.

NOTES:

☐ Julia Henry is located at
3 Erskine Avenue
Toronto, Ontario
M4R 1G5

Tel: 484-1234

☐ Cheque Copy #108
Dated: Jan. 20/91
To Julia Henry, $321 in full payment of account.
Reference statement #JH-35.

☐ Utility Statement #BT-8123
Dated: Jan. 20/91
From Bell Telephone, $80 for telephone services
plus GST paid $5.60. Utility Statement total $85.60.
Terms: cash on receipt.

☐ Cheque Copy #109
Dated: Jan. 20/91
To Bell Telephone, $85.60 in full payment of
account. Reference invoice #BT-8123.

☐ Bank Debit Memo #TB-221
Dated: Jan. 21/91
From Tutorial Bank, $400 for reduction of bank loan.

☐ Sales Invoice #MMC-17
Dated: Jan. 21/91
To The Music Conservatory;
   two Strings: Violin type-b $1 000.00 each
   100 Musical Sheets (various) $ 2.00 each
   Goods & Services Tax   7%
   Provincial Sales tax   8%
Terms: net 60 days.

☐ Memo #2
Dated: Jan. 21/91
From manager: Repossession of piano from The
Junction Band. Complete a reversing entry in the
Sales Journal to adjust all the required accounts.

☐ Purchase Invoice #AF-Y87
Dated: Jan. 21/91
From Acoustical Furniture Store, $300 for a new
piano stool for the instructor plus GST paid $21.
Purchase Invoice total $321. Terms: net 60 days.

☐ Purchase Invoice #ST-223
Dated: Jan. 21/91
From Sound Transport Co., $300 for delivery of
musical instruments to customers plus GST paid
$21. Purchase Invoice total $321. Terms: net 30
days.

Cash Receipt #13
Dated: Jan. 21/91
From Cash Register Summary Sheet (7) - Sales.
Amount deposited in bank.

Item	Qty	Price	Amount
Strings: Violin type-a	1	$750.00	$750.00
Musical Sheets (various)	25	$2.00	50.00
		Gross Sales	$800.00
		GST (7%)	56.00
		PST (8%)	64.00
Total Cash Received Jan. 15-21:			$920.00

Cash Receipt #14
Dated: Jan. 21/91
From Cash Register Summary Sheet (8) - Services
and Repairs. Amount deposited in bank.

Item	Qty	Price	Amount
Services and Repairs	18	$50.00	$ 900.00
		GST (7%)	63.00
		PST (8%)	72.00
Total Cash Received Jan. 15-21:			$1 035.00

Cash Receipt #15
Dated: Jan. 21/91
From Cash Register Summary Sheet (9) -
Instruction. Amount deposited in bank.

Item	Qty	Price	Amount
Music Instruction	32	$25.00	$800.00
		GST (7%)	56.00
Total Cash Received Jan. 15-21:			$856.00

Sales Recap Slip #2
Dated: Jan. 21/91
Deposited with Tutorial Bank, $3 726 for Access
Card purchases. Reference invoices #MMC-2, 3, 5,
6, 9 and 11.

Jan. 28 **Sales Invoice #MMC-18**
Dated: Jan. 23/91
To Metro School Board;
| | |
14 hours - Music Instruction $25.00/hour
Goods & Services Tax 7%
Terms: net 60 days.

Cheque Copy #110
Dated: Jan. 23/91
To Acoustical Furniture Store, $600 for payment of
invoice #AF-X33 on account.

Sales Invoice #MMC-19
Dated: Jan. 23/91
To Bill MacKay;
one Strings: Violin type-a $750.00
one Woodwind: Oboe $300.00
Goods & Services Tax 7%
Provincial Sales Tax 8%
Payment: Access Card (no. 233124428)

Memo #3
Dated: Jan. 24/91
From manager to accountant: For audit and internal
control purposes, set up a liability for withdrawal of
$1 500 from the business by the owner for personal
use.

Cheque Copy #111
Dated: Jan. 24/91
To L. Segovia, owner, $1 500 in full payment of
account. Reference Memo #3.

Bank Debit Memo #TB-154
Dated: Jan. 24/91
From the Tutorial Bank, $5 000 for reducing bank
loan outstanding as requested by account holder.

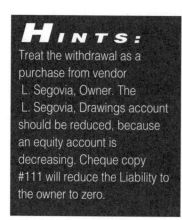

HINTS:
Treat the withdrawal as a
purchase from vendor
L. Segovia, Owner. The
L. Segovia, Drawings account
should be reduced, because
an equity account is
decreasing. Cheque copy
#111 will reduce the Liability to
the owner to zero.

❑ Sales Invoice #MMC-20
Dated: Jan. 25/91
To School of Performing Arts;
   8 hours - Services and Repairs $50.00/hour
   Goods & Services Tax   7%
   Provincial Sales Tax   8%
Terms: net 60 days.

❑ Sales Invoice #MMC-21
Dated: Jan. 25/91
To School of Performing Arts;
   one Percussion: Piano 130 cm $7 500.00
   one Woodwind: Clarinet $ 400.00
   Goods & Services Tax   7%
   Provincial Sales Tax   8%
Terms: net 60 days.

❑ Purchase Invoice #ML-141
Dated: Jan. 26/91
From Musicland Corporation;

two Brass: Trombones	$ 500.00
two Strings: Cello	1 600.00
three Strings: Violins type-a	1 200.00
two Strings: Violins type-b	1 200.00
three Woodwind: Flutes	600.00
one Woodwind: Saxophone	400.00
Freight Expense	115.00
Goods & Services Tax (7%) paid	393.05
Total	$6 008.05

Terms: net 30 days.

❑ Sales Invoice #MMC-22
Dated: Jan. 27/91
To Interplay Ballet School (new customer);
   one Percussion: Piano 130 cm $7 500.00
   Trade-in allowance:
   Used Wagner Piano   1 000.00

   Net Difference $6 500.00
   six Percussion: Tambourines   40.00 each
   Goods & Services Tax   7%
   Provincial Sales Tax   8%
Terms: net 60 days.

NOTES:

❑ Interplay Ballet School is
located at
91 Grace Road\
Toronto, Ontario
M1Q 1G3

Tel: 483-1233

☐ Memo #4
Dated: Jan. 27/91
From manager: Insert a new inventory record, **Percussion: Used Piano** (for trade-in piano, reference invoice #MMC-22), and make the necessary inventory adjustments to reflect acquisition of used piano. Selling price of used Wagner piano will be $1 750.00, and the minimum stock level will be zero.

☐ Sales Invoice #MMC-23
Dated: Jan. 28/91
To Ian Urquhart;

two Woodwind: flutes	$300.00	each
Goods & Services Tax	7%	
Provincial Sales Tax	8%	

Payment: Access Card (no. 421375935)

☐ Parts Requisition Summary Form #2
Dated: Jan. 28/91
From manager: Charge $190 to Musical Parts Used account, and reduce the Musical Parts Inventory account for the two weeks ending January 28.

☐ Memo #5
Dated: Jan. 28/91
From manager: Complete payroll for hourly employee. Issue cheque #112.

TIME SUMMARY SHEET #2
(pay period ending January 28)

Name of Employee	Week 1 Hours	Week 2 Hours	Reg. Hours	O/T Hours
☐ Jasmine Yaegar	14	14	24	4

☐ Cash Receipt #16
Dated: Jan. 28/91
From Cash Register Summary Sheet (10) - Sales. Amount deposited in bank.

Item	Qty	Price	Amount
Percussion: Bongos	2	$100.00	$ 200.00
Percussion: Drums	2	$400.00	800.00
		Gross Sales	$1 000.00
		GST (7%)	70.00
		PST (8%)	80.00
Total Cash Received Jan. 22-28:			$1 150.00

Cash Receipt #17
Dated: Jan. 28/91
From Cash Register Summary Sheet (11) - Services and Repairs. Amount deposited in bank.

Item	Qty	Price	Amount
Services and Repairs	16	$50.00	$800.00
		GST (7%)	56.00
		PST (8%)	64.00
Total Cash Received Jan. 22-28:			$910.00

Cash Receipt #18
Dated: Jan. 28/91
From Cash Register Summary Sheet (12) - Instruction. Amount deposited in bank.

Item	Qty	Price	Amount
Music Instruction	32	$25.00	$800.00
		GST (7%)	56.00
Total Cash Received Jan. 22-28:			$856.00

☐ Cash Receipt #19
Dated: Jan. 28/91
From Tivoli Theatre, cheque #65, $690 for payment
of invoice #MMC-4 on account.

☐ Rental Statement #1991-1
Dated Jan. 28/91
From Richard Fostka, new landlord (new vendor),
$2 200 for rental lease plus GST paid $154. Rental
Statement total $2 354. Terms: cash on receipt.

☐ Cheque Copy #113
Dated: Jan. 28/91
To R. Fostka, landlord, $2 354 in full payment of
account. Reference invoice #1991-1.

☐ Memo #6
Dated: Jan. 28/91
From manager to accountant: The owner, Mr.
Segovia, paid Perry's Esso from his own pocket,
$64.20, for minor repairs to delivery truck. The
repair bill was $60. GST paid for these services
amounted to $4.20.

☐ Purchase Invoice #ST-254
Dated: Jan. 28/91
From Sound Transport Co., $300 for delivery of
musical instruments to customers plus GST paid
$21. Purchase Invoice total $321. Terms: net 30
days.

Jan. 31 ☐ Memo #6
Dated: Jan. 31/91
From manager: Complete payroll for salaried
employees. Issue Cheques #114 - #116.

Keystrokes

Entering Transactions for Distributing Costs

Open the files for Melody Music Centre.

Type: 01-07-91

Click on OK

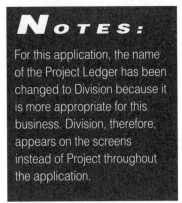

This will enter the using date, January 7, 1991. The main Ledger/Journal company window appears:

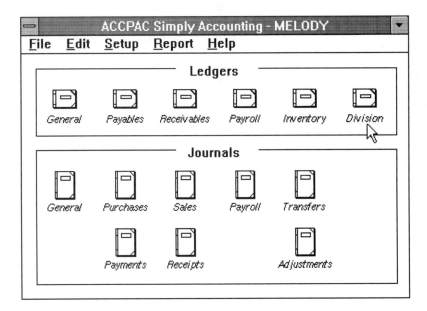

Open the Purchases Journal to see the familiar Purchases Journal input form as follows:

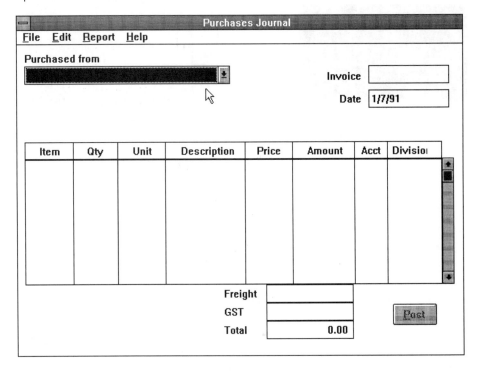

The first transaction does not involve the purchase of inventory items so you will not use the inventory database to complete this transaction.

The cursor is flashing in the Vendor field, ready to receive information. From the list of vendors,

Click on Toronto Star

Press [Tab]

The cursor moves to the Invoice field so you can enter the alphanumeric invoice number.

Type: TS-1231

Press [Tab]

The cursor moves to the Date field. Enter the date on which the transaction took place, January 2, 1991. The using date appears automatically by default, ready to be accepted. You need to change the date.

Type: 01-02-91

Press [Tab]

The cursor moves to the Item field.

Press [Tab] repeatedly to advance to the Description field.

Type: Newspaper Advertising

Press [Tab]

Press [Tab] again to move to the Amount field.

In the Amount field, you should enter the actual amount to be allocated to each division separately, not including GST, because the business is using the regular method for remitting the GST to the Receiver General. The first division is Sales, which incurs 60 percent of the total advertising expense according to the Division Jobcost Information chart. The allocation for the Sales Division is 60 percent of $400, or $240.

Type: 240

Press [Tab]

The cursor moves to the Account field. When you are working in a subsidiary ledger, your Accounts Payable control account in the General Ledger will automatically be credited for purchases you enter. You must enter the expense or debit part of this entry.

Press [Enter] to display the list of accounts.

Click on 5220 Advertising Expense

Click on Select to add the account to the input form.

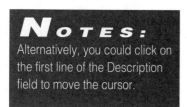

The cursor advances to the Division field because the account you selected above was an expense account.

Press [Enter] while the cursor is in this field to display a list of divisions as follows:

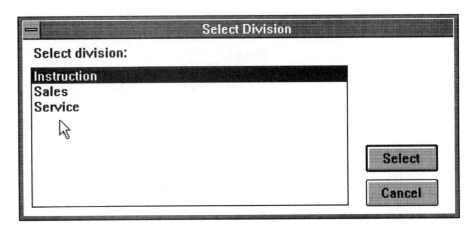

Click on Sales to highlight it.

Click on Select to enter it on your form.

The cursor advances to the next line. Now you are ready to enter the amounts for the other two divisions, 20 percent each. You need to repeat the steps outlined above in order to allocate the remainder of the expense.

NOTES:

Alternatively, you can click on the next line in the Amount field to advance the cursor.

Press [Tab] repeatedly to advance to the Amount field.

Calculate 20 percent of $400 to determine the allocation for the Service Division (20% * $400 = $80).

Type: 80

Press [Tab]

You should use the same expense account for each of the three divisions.

Type: 5220

Press [Tab]

The cursor returns to the Division field so that you can distribute the allocation to the next division.

Press [Enter] to display the list of divisions.

Click on Service

Click on Select to enter it on your form and advance to the next line.

Enter the final amount and the account number and select the Instruction Division to complete the distribution.

Click on the GST field to move the cursor.

Type: 28

Press `Tab`

Your form is now completed as shown below, and you are ready to review your work:

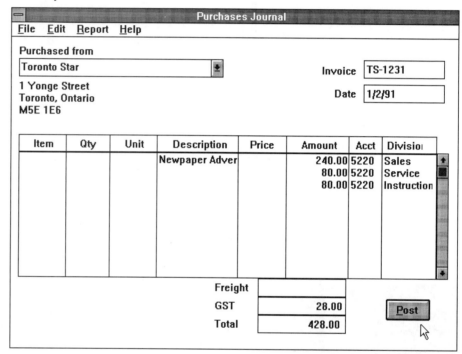

Reviewing the Purchases Journal Entry and Distribution

Choose Display Purchases Journal Entry from the pull-down menu under **Report** to display the transaction you have entered:

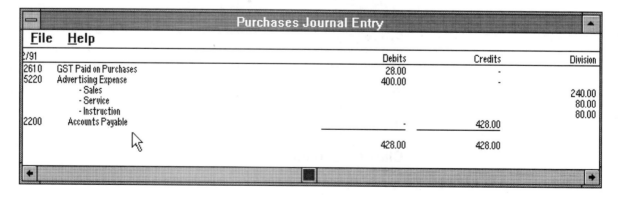

You may need to scroll to see all of the information. Notice that the ACCPAC Simply Accounting program has automatically updated the Accounts Payable control account because the Payables and General ledgers are fully integrated. Notice also that the advertising expense has been distributed among the three divisions.

Close the display to return to the Purchases Journal input screen.

CORRECTING THE PURCHASES JOURNAL ENTRY AND DISTRIBUTION

Move to the field that has the error. **Press** Tab to move forward through the fields or **press** Shift and Tab together to move back to a previous field. This will highlight the field information so you can change it. **Type** the correct information and **press** Tab to enter it. You must advance the cursor to the next invoice line to enter a change.

You can also use the mouse to point to a field and drag through the incorrect information to highlight it. **Type** the correct information and **press** Tab to enter it.

If the vendor is incorrect, reselect from the vendor list by **clicking on** the arrow beside this field. **Click on** the name of the correct vendor and **press** Tab .

To correct an account number or division, **click on** the incorrect number or division to move the cursor to this field. **Press** Enter to display the appropriate list. **Click on** the correct selection to highlight it and **click on Select** to enter the change.

Posting

When you are certain that you have entered all the information correctly, you must post the transaction to save it.

Click on Post to save the transaction.

Entering Transactions for Distributing Revenue

Use the same principles outlined above for expenses to distribute revenue in the Sales Journal to divisions, departments or profit centres.

Distributing Costs in the Payroll Journal

Distributing costs in the Payroll Journal uses a different approach than the one described above.

Record the entries for the source documents for the January 7 and 14 using dates up to the payroll entry for Jasmine Yaegar.

Open the Payroll Journal. Complete the payroll form for Ms. Yaegar by entering her name, the cheque number and the number of regular hours she worked. You should not change the using date because it is the same as the transaction date. Your Payroll Journal form should now appear as below:

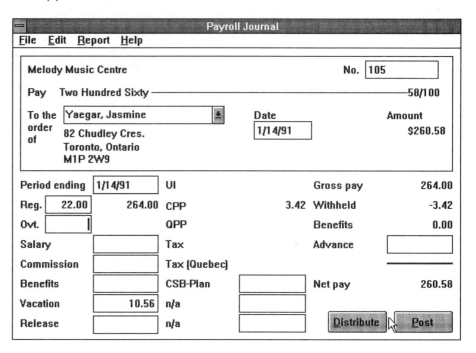

Notice that the Distribute button at the bottom of the form is darkened. You will use it to enter the distribution information.

Click on Distribute

The following Division Distribution window appears on your screen:

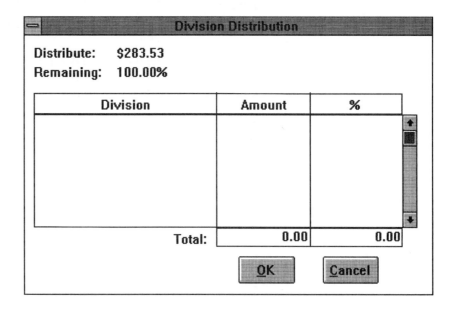

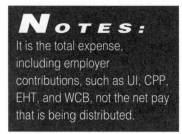
The total amount of the payroll expense to be allocated is shown at the top. The cursor is blinking in the Division field.

Press `Enter` to display the familiar list of divisions.

Click on Sales from this list and enter it on your form.

The cursor advances to the Percent (%) field. This field is used for the percentage of the total expense that is to be allocated to this division. According to the Division Jobcost Information chart, this amount is 60 percent.

Type: 60

Press `Tab`

Notice that the percentage remaining to be distributed, shown near the top of your form, has changed to 40 percent. The program calculates the dollar amount automatically. The cursor advances to the next line in the Division field.

Press `Enter` to display the list of divisions.

Click on Service

Click on Select to enter it.

The cursor moves to the Percent (%) field.

Type: 20

Press `Tab` to advance to the Division field again.

Press `Enter` to display the list of divisions.

Click on Instruction from the list of divisions. (This division is the only one remaining because you have used the other two already.)

The cursor moves to the Percent (%) field.

Click on Select to enter it.

Type: 20

Press `Tab`

When the entire expense has been allocated, your distribution should appear as follows:

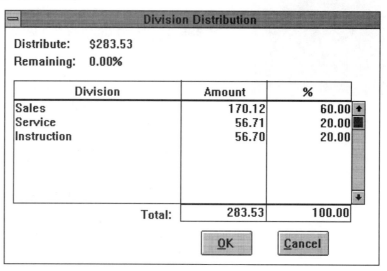

Check your information for accuracy and make any corrections necessary.

Click on OK to return to your Payroll Journal entry form. Note that this form has not changed. When you review your transaction, however, you will see that the distribution information has been saved.

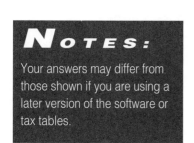

NOTES:

Your answers may differ from those shown if you are using a later version of the software or tax tables.

Reviewing the Payroll Distribution Entry

Choose Review Payroll Journal Entry from the pull-down menu under **Report** to display your transaction as follows:

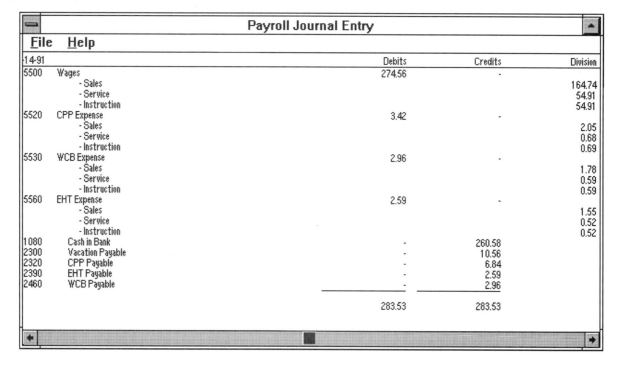

Notice that all of the payroll-related expenses have been divided among the three divisions according to the percentages you entered. They are shown under the Division column. You may have to scroll the display to see all of the information.

Close the display to return to the Payroll Journal form when you are finished.

CORRECTING THE PAYROLL DISTRIBUTION

Move the cursor to the field that contains the error. **Press** `Tab` to move forward through the fields or **press** `Shift` and `Tab` together to move back to a previous field. This will highlight the field information so that you can change it. **Type** the correct information and **press** `Tab` to enter the change.

You can also use the mouse to point to a field and drag through the incorrect information to highlight it. **Type** the correct information. **Press** `Tab` to save the corrections.

If you have selected the wrong employee, return to the employee list by **clicking on** the arrow beside this field. **Click on** the name of the correct employee and **press** `Tab` . When prompted, confirm that you wish to discard the incorrect entry. **Click on Yes**, and start again from the beginning.

If you have made an error in the distribution, **click on Distribution** to return to the distribution window. Return to the field that has the error. Highlight the incorrect information by dragging the cursor through it if necessary. **Type** the correct information. **Press** `Tab` to save the correction.

Posting

When you are certain that all of the information is correct, you can post the entry to save it.

Click on Post

Displaying Division Reports

Displaying the Division List

With the Division Ledger icon highlighted on the main Ledger/Journal company window,

Choose Display Division List from the pull-down menu under **Report**.

Close the display when you are finished viewing it.

Displaying Division Reports

Choose Division from the pull-down menu under **Report** to display the following Division Report Options window:

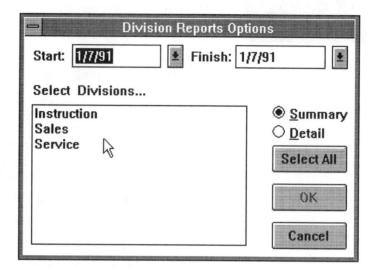

As usual, the program gives the using date as the default.

Type the beginning date for the report you want.

Press `Tab`

Type the ending date for the report.

Click on Select All to include all the divisions in the report or choose a single division by clicking on its name.

Leave the **Summary** option, as it is selected by default, if you want your report to show summary information for each account selected for each division. The **Detail** option provides complete journal information for each account for each division selected, including the names of all customers, vendors and employees, as well as the reference document number, journal entry number and date. Both options provide a calculation for revenue minus expense.

After you have indicated which options you want,

Click on OK

The program then asks you to select the particular revenue or expense account that you want the report for.

Click on Select All or on a particular account.

Click on OK to display the report.

Close the display when you are finished.

Printing Division Reports

Display the report you want on the screen by following the instructions above.

Choose **Print** from the pull-down menu under **File**.

Case Problem

Melody Music Centre has decided to refurbish and renovate its premises. It will install new shelving and floors throughout the entire centre, add new lighting fixtures and paint the entire centre.

1. How would you distribute the cost of the renovation to the various divisions? Explain what criteria you would use to divide the costs.

2. Why is it important to distribute the cost of the renovation correctly among the different divisions?

CHAPTER TEN

Artistic Interiors

OBJECTIVES

Upon completion of this chapter, you will be able to:

1. *plan and design* an accounting system for a small business;
2. *prepare* procedures for converting from a manual system;
3. *understand* the objectives of a computerized system;
4. *create* company files;
5. *set up* company accounts using set-up input forms;
6. *make* the accounting system ready for operation;
7. *enter* journal transactions using ACCPAC Simply Accounting;
8. *insert* new vendors, customers and employees as required;
9. *add* new accounts as required;
10. *display* and *print* reports;
11. *export* reports;
12. *use* spreadsheets for analysing, planning and decision making;
13. *enter* end-of-accounting-period adjustments;
14. *perform* end-of-accounting-period closing routines;
15. *analyse and interpret* case studies;
16. *develop* further group interpersonal skills;
17. *develop* further oral and written skills.

Introduction

This application provides a complete accounting cycle for a merchandising business. It is a comprehensive application covering a three-month fiscal period. You will use ACCPAC Simply Accounting to convert a manual accounting system to a computerized accounting system and then enter transactions for each month. The routines in this application are part of the demands of many small businesses, so you should find them useful. The information in this application reflects the business realities of Ontario in January 1992.

You may substitute information relevant to other provinces or the latest payroll and tax regulations wherever it is appropriate to do so. Rules for the application of the federal Goods and Services Tax (GST), provincial sales taxes and payroll may vary from one province to another.

Because of the length of the application, instructions for working with the source documents are presented with those documents, on page 295.

Company Information

NOTES:

Artistic Interiors is located at
22 Harridge Road
Toronto, Ontario
M4R 1J2

Company Profile

Artistic Interiors is a business owned by Joyce Klassen. It earns its income from the sale of office furniture, carpets, lamps and accessories. Customers include doctors, lawyers, businesses, banks and other institutions. The business began operations on July 1, 1991. It has completed a successful first quarter ending September 30, 1991. Now the owner, at the suggestion of the manager of the store and after advice from a business consultant, has decided to shift from a manual accounting system to a computerized one. This decision was in keeping with the goals of the company concerning growth and expansion. The long-range objectives of the business include:

- expansion to other lines, such as interior decorating services (many customers have enquired about such services);
- expansion of the store for further market penetration in the office furniture business;
- a wider range of inventory items to satisfy a more diverse group of customers and to keep up with new trends in office furniture design.

The consultant's report summarized below recommends that the popular ACCPAC Simply Accounting software be used for the conversion. ACCPAC Simply Accounting offers many advantages over the the company's current manual system.

CONSULTANT'S REPORT

1. Using ACCPAC Simply Accounting would allow the business to process all source documents in a timely fashion. It would automatically prepare the usual accounting reports for planning, making decisions and controlling operations within the business.

2. The software would eliminate some of the time-consuming clerical functions that are performed manually. For example, it can automatically prepare invoices, cheques and statements, and can perform all the necessary arithmetic calculations. Being freed from these chores, the accountant could extend his or her role to assume a much higher level of responsibility. For example, the accountant would have more time to spend analysing reports with the owner and could work more directly with the owner in making business decisions.

3. ACCPAC Simply Accounting can easily export reports to spreadsheets so that comparisons can be made between different fiscal periods. These comparisons would permit the owner to analyse past trends and to make better predictions about the future behaviour of the business.

4. As the business grows, the manager could divide work more meaningfully among new accounting personnel. Since ACCPAC Simply Accounting provides subsidiary ledgers, which are integrated to control accounts in the General Ledger, it could automatically co-ordinate accounting work performed by different individuals.

5. It would allow the owner to exercise controls in the operation of the business in a number of areas:

   In General

   - Access to confidential accounting records and editing capability can be restricted to authorized personnel by using passwords.
   - Mechanical errors can be virtually eliminated, since journal transactions with unequal debits and credits cannot be posted. Customer, vendor, employee, inventory and jobcost names appear in full on the journal entry input forms, making it less likely for errors to occur. Furthermore, ACCPAC Simply Accounting does not permit duplication of source document numbers.

   General Ledger

   - The software provides a directory of accounts used by the business, including all the integration accounts for the other ledgers in ACCPAC Simply Accounting. The information in these accounts can be used to prepare and analyse financial reports such as the Balance Sheet and Income Statement.
   - ACCPAC Simply Accounting provides an audit trail for all types of journal transactions.

   Receivables Ledger

   - ACCPAC Simply Accoounting provides a directory of customers.
   - Credit limit entries for each customer should reduce the losses from non-payment of accounts. Customers with poor payment histories can have their credit limits reduced or their credit purchase privileges removed.
   - Accounts receivable can be aged, and each customer's payment behaviour can be analysed. This allows for the accurate calculation of provisions for bad debts.

Payables Ledger
- ACCPAC Simply Accounting provides a directory of vendors.
- The information from the review of transactions with vendors and from the accounts payable aged analysis can be combined to make payment decisions. ACCPAC Simply Accounting helps to predict short-term cash needs in order to establish priorities for making payments and to schedule payments to vendors.
- ACCPAC Simply Accounting provides an audit trail for the Accounts Payable and Accounts Receivable journals.
- The GST remittance or refund is calculated automatically because of the integration of the GST accounts in the Payables and Receivables ledgers.

Payroll Ledger
- ACCPAC Simply Accounting maintains employee records with both personal and payment information for personnel files.
- Once the information has been set up, the program automatically withholds several employee deductions including income tax, CPP (Canada Pension Plan) and UI (Unemployment Insurance) and is therefore less prone to error. These payroll deductions are updated regularly by Computer Associates in later versions of the software.
- Summaries of employer contributions, such as EHT (Employer Health Tax), WCB (Workers' Compensation Board), UI and CPP, permit easy analysis of payroll expenses for compulsory and optional fringe benefits.
- ACCPAC Simply Accounting automatically integrates payroll with control accounts in the General Ledger to keep a cumulative record of amounts owing to various agencies for monthly or quarterly remittance.

Inventory Ledger
- ACCPAC Simply Accounting provides an inventory summary or database of all inventory items.
- Inventory reports flag items that need to be reordered and can be used to make purchase decisions.
- ACCPAC Simply Accounting automatically updates inventory records when inventory is purchased, sold, transferred, lost, recovered or returned. It does not permit the overselling of inventory.

6. In summation, ACCPAC Simply Accounting provides an integrated management accounting information system.

After the owner decided to use ACCPAC Simply Accounting, the manager, Vivian Young, began to organize the manual accounting records in preparation for the conversion to the computerized accounting system on September 30, 1991. These accounting records include the following, which you will use to set up the company accounts:

1. Chart of Accounts;
2. Income Statement;
3. Balance Sheet;
4. Post-Closing Trial Balance;
5. Vendor Information;
6. Customer Information;
7. Employee and Payroll Information;
8. Inventory Information;
9. Accounting Procedures.

ARTISTIC INTERIORS
CHART OF ACCOUNTS

ASSETS

Current Assets
1080 Cash in Bank
1200 Accounts Receivable
1220 Allowance for Bad Debts
1240 Advances Receivable
1260 Interest Receivable
1300 Prepaid Insurance
1320 Supplies: Computer
1360 Supplies: Office

Inventory Assets
1500 Accessories
1520 Carpets
1540 Chairs
1560 Lamps
1580 Sofas
1600 Tables
1620 Wall Units

Plant and Equipment
1700 Buildings
1720 Accum Deprec: Buildings
1760 Computers
1780 Accum Deprec: Computers
1820 Land
1840 Van
1860 Accum Deprec: Van

LIABILITIES

Current Liabilities
2100 Bank Loan
2120 Interest Payable:Mortgage
2200 Accounts Payable
2300 Vacation Payable
2310 UI Payable
2320 CPP Payable
2330 Income Tax Payable
2390 EHT Payable
2400 RRS-Plan Payable
2420 CSB-Plan Payable
2460 WCB Payable
2640 PST Payable
2650 GST Charged on Sales
2670 GST Paid on Purchases
2710 GST Adjustments
2730 ITC Adjustments

Long Term Debt
2850 Mortgage Payable

EQUITY

Owners' Equity
3560 J. Klassen, Capital

REVENUE

General Revenue
4020 Revenue from Sales
4040 Sales Returns & Allowances
4100 Interest Earned
4120 Purchases Discount
4160 Sales Tax Commission

EXPENSE

Operating Expenses
5020 Advertising
5030 Bad Debts Expense
5040 Bank Charges
5060 Cost of Goods Sold
5070 Adjustment Write-off
5080 Depreciation: Buildings
5100 Depreciation: Computers
5120 Depreciation: Van
5140 Delivery Expense
5150 Freight Expense
5160 Hydro Expense
5170 Insurance Expense
5190 Interest: Mortgage
5220 Maintenance & Repairs
5230 Property Taxes
5260 Supplies Used:Computers
5280 Supplies Used:Office
5290 Telephone Expense
5300 Wages
5310 UI Expense
5320 CPP Expense
5330 WCB Expense
5360 EHT Expense

The Chart of Accounts includes numbers for *postable* accounts only. It does not include account names or numbers for headings, sub-headings, totals or subtotals. These are included in the financial statements that follow.

You will need these additional postable accounts and their numbers to complete transactions for the three months ending December 31, 1991:

1290 Prepaid Advertising
1340 Supplies: Decorating
2140 Accrued Payroll
4080 Revenue from Decorating
5200 Lost Inventory
5240 Sales Discount
5180 Interest: Bank Loan
5270 Supplies Used: Decorating

You will be instructed to add these new accounts when they are required to complete transactions. Instead, you may include them when you are setting up the Chart of Accounts for Artistic Interiors.

GST Accounts

The Chart of Accounts includes four postable liability accounts for the federal Goods and Services Tax:

- 2650 GST Charged on Sales
- 2670 GST Paid on Purchases
- 2710 GST Adjustments
- 2730 ITC Adjustments

The first two, GST Charged on Sales and GST Paid on Purchases, are the integration accounts used in previous applications.

The accounts 2710 GST Adjustments and 2730 ITC Adjustments are used to adjust for changes in bad debts. When a bad debt is written off, the GST liability should be reduced because GST Charged on Sales was part of the original invoice. Remove the GST portion of the invoice from GST Owing by debiting this amount to the ITC (Input Tax Credits) Adjustments account. If the debt is later recovered, the GST liability should be restored as well. Record the recovery of GST as a credit to the GST Adjustments account.

The non-postable (subtotal) account 2750 GST Owing (Refund) is used as the GST clearing account.

NOTES:

A fifth postable GST account, Payroll Adjustments, is provided by the program to record the GST portion of taxable employee benefits that the employer withholds. It is not currently used by Artistic Interiors.

ARTISTIC INTERIORS
INCOME STATEMENT

For the Three Months Ending September 30, 1991

REVENUE

4000	GENERAL REVENUE		
4020	Revenue from Sales	$ 126 000.00	
4040	Sales Returns & Allowances	1 000.00-	
4060	Net Sales		$ 125 000.00
4100	Interest Earned		312.00
4120	Purchases Discount		847.20
4160	Sales Tax Commission		256.00
4390	TOTAL GENERAL REVENUE		126 415.20
	TOTAL REVENUE		$ 126 415.20

EXPENSE

5000	OPERATING EXPENSES	
5020	Advertising	$ 240.00
5030	Bad Debts Expense	1 260.00
5040	Bank Charges	75.00
5060	Cost of Goods Sold	63 240.00
5080	Depreciation: Buildings	1 500.00
5100	Depreciation: Computers	225.00
5120	Depreciation: Van	1 125.00
5140	Delivery Expense	820.00
5150	Freight Expense	400.00
5160	Hydro Expense	410.00
5170	Insurance Expense	150.00
5190	Interest: Mortgage	6 800.00
5220	Maintenance & Repairs	250.00
5230	Property Taxes	425.00
5260	Supplies Used: Computers	140.00
5280	Supplies Used: Office	150.00
5290	Telephone Expense	135.00
5300	Wages	29 090.88
5310	UI Expense	743.75
5320	CPP Expense	568.00
5330	WCB Expense	255.28
5360	EHT Expense	274.12
5390	TOTAL OPERATING EXPENSES	108 277.03
	TOTAL EXPENSE	$ 108 277.03
	INCOME	$ 18 138.17

ARTISTIC INTERIORS
BALANCE SHEET

September 30, 1991

ASSETS

1000	CURRENT ASSETS		
1080	Cash in Bank		$ 23 964.68
1200	Accounts Receivable	$ 10 200.00	
1220	Allowance for Bad Debts	1 260.00-	
1260	Interest Receivable	312.00	
1280	Net Receivables		9 252.00
1300	Prepaid Insurance		1 050.00
1320	Supplies: Computer		360.00
1360	Supplies: Office		450.00
1390	TOTAL CURRENT ASSETS		35 076.68
1450	INVENTORY ASSETS		
1500	Accessories		11 300.00
1520	Carpets		68 900.00
1540	Chairs		13 700.00
1560	Lamps		2 900.00
1580	Sofas		19 200.00
1600	Tables		38 400.00
1620	Wall Units		19 000.00
1640	TOTAL INVENTORY ASSETS		173 400.00
1650	PLANT AND EQUIPMENT		
1700	Buildings	120 000.00	
1720	Accum Deprec: Buildings	1 500.00-	
1740	Net Buildings		118 500.00
1760	Computers	6 000.00	
1780	Accum Deprec: Computers	225.00-	
1800	Net Computers		5 775.00
1820	Land		180 000.00
1840	Van	15 000.00	
1860	Accum Deprec: Van	1 125.00-	
1880	Net Van		13 875.00
1900	TOTAL PLANT AND EQUIPMENT		318 150.00
	TOTAL ASSETS		$526 626.68

LIABILITIES

2000	CURRENT LIABILITIES			
2100	Bank Loan			$ 75 000.00
2120	Interest Payable:Mortgage			565.00
2200	Accounts Payable			6 850.00
2300	Vacation Payable			1 118.88
2310	UI Payable		460.86	
2320	CPP Payable		404.72	
2330	Income Tax Payable		2 259.65	
2340	Receiver General Payable			3 125.23
2390	EHT Payable			274.12
2400	RRS-Plan Payable *			175.00
2420	CSB-Plan Payable *			175.00
2460	WCB Payable			255.28
2640	PST Payable			3 600.00
2650	GST Charged on Sales		3150.00	
2670	GST Paid on Purchases		2100.00-	
2750	GST Owing (Refund)			1050.00
2800	TOTAL CURRENT LIABILITIES			92 188.51
2820	LONG TERM DEBT			
2850	Mortgage Payable			249 300.00
2900	TOTAL LONG TERM DEBT			249 300.00
	TOTAL LIABILITIES			$341 488.51

EQUITY

3000	OWNER'S EQUITY		
3560	J. Klassen, Capital		167 000.00
3600	Net Income		18 138.17
3690	UPDATED CAPITAL		185 138.17
	TOTAL EQUITY		$185 138.17
	LIABILITIES & EQUITY		$526 626.68

* RRS-Plan [DeductionA]
  CSB-Plan [DeductionB]

ARTISTIC INTERIORS
POST-CLOSING TRIAL BALANCE

September 30, 1991

1080	Cash in Bank	$ 23 964.68	
1200	Accounts Receivable	10 200.00	
1220	Allowance for Bad Debts		$ 1 260.00
1260	Interest Receivable	312.00	
1300	Prepaid Insurance	1 050.00	
1320	Supplies: Computer	360.00	
1360	Supplies: Office	450.00	
1500	Accessories	11 300.00	
1520	Carpets	68 900.00	
1540	Chairs	13 700.00	
1560	Lamps	2 900.00	
1580	Sofas	19 200.00	
1600	Tables	38 400.00	
1620	Wall Units	19 000.00	
1700	Buildings	120 000.00	
1720	Accum Deprec: Buildings		1 500.00
1760	Computers	6 000.00	
1780	Accum Deprec: Computers		225.00
1820	Land	180 000.00	
1840	Van	15 000.00	
1860	Accum Deprec: Van		1 125.00
2100	Bank Loan		75 000.00
2120	Interest Payable:Mortgage		565.00
2200	Accounts Payable		6 850.00
2300	Vacation Payable		1 118.88
2310	UI Payable		460.86
2320	CPP Payable		404.72
2330	Income Tax Payable		2 259.65
2390	EHT Payable		274.12
2400	RRS-Plan Payable		175.00
2420	CSB-Plan Payable		175.00
2460	WCB Payable		255.28
2640	PST Payable		3 600.00
2650	GST Charged on Sales		3 150.00
2670	GST Paid on Purchases	2 100.00	
2850	Mortgage Payable		249 300.00
3560	J. Klassen, Capital		185 138.17
		$ 532 836.68	$ 532 836.68

ARTISTIC INTERIORS
VENDOR INFORMATION

Vendor Name (Contact)	Address, Telephone & Fax	Invoice Date	Invoice Number	Outstanding Balance
Artworks Inc. (Joan Miro)	33 Granite Rd. Toronto, Ontario M5T 1A2	Sep. 16/91 Sep. 18/91	AW-121 AW-130	$ 500.00 $ 500.00
			Total	$1 000.00
	Tel: 476-2234 Fax: 476-2290			
Ayre Office Supplies	59 Hilda Ave. Toronto, Ontario M8I 1A3			
	Tel: 881-0976			
Bell Canada	483 Bay St. Toronto, Ontario M5T 1S3			
	Tel: 923-0987			
City Treasurer	Box 2500 Terminal A Toronto, Ontario M5W 1H2			
	Tel: 392-7115			
Custom Craft Woodworks (Ashleigh Oakes)	18 Pineview Hts. Toronto, Ontario M9U 1S3			
	Tel: 468-1290			
Direct Connections (Van Ford)	2 Speedster Way East York, Ontario M9L 1Z3	Sep. 15/91	DC-271	$ 250.00
	Tel: 393-0321 Fax: 393-0333			
Equity Investment Corporation (Group Plan Dept.)	300 Bloor Ave. E. Toronto, Ontario M3K 1W3			
	Tel: 477-2134 Fax: 477-2000			
Excel Computer Store (Serge Power)	87 Pascal Rd. Toronto, Ontario M3Y 1W2			
	Tel: 391-0987			
Fairchild Insurance Corporation (Corporate Plans)	33 Richmond Rd. Toronto, Ontario M5T 1D2			
	Tel: 471-1019 Fax: 471-2211			

Vendor Name (Contact)	Address, Telephone & Fax	Invoice Date	Invoice Number	Outstanding Balance
Fine Furniture Designers (Jack Frame)	12 Cherry Drive Toronto, Ontario M8Y 1S3 Tel: 723-1234 Fax: 725-1912			
Kwik Air	121 Allenby Rd. Toronto, Ontario M4R 1J3 Tel: 483-9087			
Persia Carpets (Softu Foote)	34 Knots Landing Toronto, Ontario M8J 1Q9 Tel: 991-9876	Sep. 1/91 Sep. 2/91	PC-279 PC-287 Total	$3 200.00 $2 400.00 ———— $5 600.00
The Receiver General of Canada	Box 100, Station Q Toronto, Ontario M4T 2L7 Tel: 973-1000			
The Treasurer of Ontario	Box 620, 33 King Street W., Oshawa, Ontario L1H 8H5 Tel: 965-8470			
Toronto Hydro	14 Carlton St. Toronto, Ontario M5B 1K5 Tel: 599-0735			
Toronto Star	1 Yonge St. Toronto, Ontario M5E 1E6 Tel: 368-3611			
Vision Lighting Co. (Fluora Halogen)	1 Clearview Rd. Toronto, Ontario M6A 4E2 Tel: 767-1231			
Workers' Compensation Board	1033 Bay St. Toronto, Ontario M5T 1D3 Tel: 925-7176			
			GRAND TOTAL	$6 850.00

ARTISTIC INTERIORS
CUSTOMER INFORMATION

Customer Name (Contact)	Address Telephone & Fax	Credit Limit	Invoice Date	Invoice Number	Outstanding Balance
Axiom Real Estate (M. T. House)	151 Bloor St. Toronto, Ontario M5P 1A3	$20 000	Sep. 17/91	AI-95	$ 3 200.00
	Tel: 923-4536 Fax: 923-4560				
Baihai & Cello Investment (Les Munney)	77 Maitland Rd. North York, Ontario M2U 4P2	$ 5 000	Aug. 2/91	AI-67	$ 500.00
	Tel: 661-0981 Fax: 661-0980				
Dubhei Consulate (Ms. L. Forren)	33 Holly Avenue Toronto, Ontario M6Y 1A2	$20 000	Sep. 30/91	AI-99	$ 4 500.00
	Tel: 925-1231 Fax: 925-1100				
Dyle & Groen, Lawyers (Rick Groen)	2 Litigate Ave. Toronto, Ontario M4F 1X1	$10 000			
	Tel: 881-8901 Fax: 881-8900				
Faigaux Insurance Co. (Ho Le Covrage)	39 Jarvis St. Toronto, Ontario M7T 1M9	$15 000	Sep. 8/91	AI-84	$ 2 000.00
	Tel: 881-6754 Fax: 880-6700				
				GRAND TOTAL	$10 200.00

ARTISTIC INTERIORS
EMPLOYEE INFORMATION SHEET

Employee Number:	1	2	3
Position:	Salesperson	Manager/Sales	Shipper/Receiver
Social Insurance Number:	231 763 172	462 928 123	238 383 227
Employee Name:	Alvin Sweeney	Vivian Young	Marcos Zarkos
Address & Telephone:	89 Broomfield Ave. Toronto, Ontario M9K 1A2	12 Huron Street Toronto, Ontario M8J 2C3	46 Danforth Ave. Toronto, Ontario M5P 1C2
	416-393-0245	416-739-0987	416-922-4523
Date of Birth (dd-mm-yy):	14-12-45	12-09-48	3-07-61

Tax Exemptions:
(TD1-1991)

Basic Personal	$ 6 280.00	$6 280.00	$6 280.00
Spouse	$ 5 757.00		
Children	$406.00		
Disability			
Education & Tuition			
Other			
Total Exemptions	$12 443.00	$6 280.00	$6 280.00
Less: Family Allowance	$392.88		
Net Claim	$12 050.12	$6 280.00	$6 280.00

Employee Earnings:

Regular Wage Rate			$12.00/hour
Overtime Wage Rate			$18.00/hour
Regular Salary	$3 200.00/period	$3 800.00/period	
Commissions			
Vacation Pay	4% (retained)	4% (retained)	4% (retained)

Employee Deductions:

RRS-Plan *	$50.00/period	$50.00/period	$25.00/period
CSB-Plan **	$50.00/period	$50.00/period	$25.00/period
CPP	***	***	***
UI	***	***	***
Income Tax	***	***	***

*   Registered Retirement Savings Plan
**   Canada Savings Bond Plan
***   Calculations built into ACCPAC Simply Accounting program

Employee Profiles and TD-1 Information

1. Alvin Sweeney is the junior salesperson. He is married and fully supports his wife and a child aged 12 who have no income. Alvin will receive $392.88 in family allowances for 1991. His salary is $3 200 per pay period ($38 400 per year). He receives no company benefits.

2. Vivian Young is the senior salesperson and manager. Her duties are to delegate work and to handle the daily operations of the business, including the routine accounting tasks. Vivian is single and self-supporting. Her salary is $3 800 per pay period ($45 600 per year). She receives no company benefits.

3. Marcos Zarkos is the shipper/receiver. He handles all incoming and outgoing goods. Occasionally, he delivers to customers or picks up goods from suppliers using the business van. Marcos is single and self-supporting. He earns $12 per hour for regular work and $18 per hour for overtime. He receives no company benefits.

Additional Payroll Information

1. There are 12 pay periods for salaried employees. Salaried employees are paid on the 30th of each month or the last day in February.

2. There are 26 pay periods for the hourly employee. Payment is made on the last day of each pay period.

3. All employees have chosen to participate in the Registered Retirement Savings Plan administered by the Fairchild Insurance Corporation and the Canada Savings Bond Plan administered by the Equity Investment Corporation.

4. The RRS and CSB Plan deductions are withheld from the employees and remitted to the proper agencies monthly.

5. The employer's contributions include the following:
   - CPP contributions equal to employee contributions;
   - UI factor of 1.4;
   - WCB rate of 1.01;
   - EHT rate of .98.

ARTISTIC INTERIORS
HISTORICAL PAYROLL INFORMATION
Pay Period Ending September 30, 1991

Employee:	Alvin Sweeney	Vivian Young	Marcos Zarkos
Regular			$6 720.00
Overtime			252.00
Salary	$9 600.00	$11 400.00	
Commission			
Benefit			
Vacation Paid			
Gross	9 600.00	11 400.00	6 972.00
UI Ins. Earnings	9 600.00	11 400.00	6 972.00
UI	187.20	187.20	156.87
CPP	195.81	235.41	136.78
Income Tax	1 993.53	3 113.13	1 300.67
RRS-Plan	150.00	150.00	175.00
CSB-Plan	150.00	150.00	175.00
Withheld	2 676.54	3 835.74	1 944.32
Net Pay	6 923.46	7 564.26	5 027.68
Advance Paid			
Vacation Owed	384.00	456.00	278.88

ARTISTIC INTERIORS
INVENTORY INFORMATION

Item Number & Name	Unit Description	Selling Price	Quantity on Hand	Amount (cost)	Minimum Stock Level
11 Accessories:Prints	item(s)	$450.00	40	$ 8 000.00	20
12 Accessories:Sculptures	item(s)	$200.00	20	$ 2 500.00	10
13 Accessories:Vases	item(s)	$150.00	20	$800.00	10
				$11 300.00	
21 Carpets:Chinese Floral	item(s)	$1 200.00	6	$ 3 600.00	2
22 Carpets:Indian Floral	item(s)	$1 100.00	6	$ 3 300.00	2
23 Carpets:Isfahan	item(s)	$1 400.00	10	$ 8 000.00	4
24 Carpets:Kashan	item(s)	$2 200.00	10	$15 000.00	4
25 Carpets:Mashad	item(s)	$800.00	10	$ 5 000.00	4
26 Carpets:Qum	item(s)	$2 100.00	10	$16 000.00	2
27 Carpets:Tabriz	item(s)	$2 400.00	10	$18 000.00	4
				$68 900.00	
31 Chairs:Classic-armchair	item(s)	$350.00	10	$ 2 250.00	4
32 Chairs:Classic-highback	item(s)	$400.00	10	$ 2 500.00	4
33 Chairs:Exec-armchair	item(s)	$500.00	10	$ 3 000.00	4
34 Chairs:Exec-highback	item(s)	$550.00	10	$ 3 200.00	4
35 Chairs:Prof-lounger	item(s)	$250.00	10	$ 1 250.00	4
36 Chairs:Prof-swivel	item(s)	$300.00	10	$ 1 500.00	4
				$13 700.00	

Item Number & Name	Unit Description	Selling Price	Quantity on Hand	Amount (cost)	Minimum Stock Level
41 Lamps:Floor-brass	item(s)	$120.00	10	$700.00	4
42 Lamps:Floor-enamel	item(s)	$80.00	10	$400.00	4
43 Lamps:Spotlight-enamel	item(s)	$80.00	10	$400.00	4
44 Lamps:Table-brass	item(s)	$80.00	10	$400.00	4
45 Lamps:Wall-brass	item(s)	$100.00	10	$600.00	4
46 Lamps:Wall-enamel	item(s)	$60.00	10	$400.00	4
				$2 900.00	
51 Sofas:2 seater-fabric	item(s)	$500.00	8	$2 400.00	3
52 Sofas:2 seater-leather	item(s)	$1 000.00	8	$4 800.00	3
53 Sofas:3 seater-fabric	item(s)	$750.00	8	$4 000.00	3
54 Sofas:3 seater-leather	item(s)	$1 500.00	8	$8 000.00	3
				$19 200.00	
61 Tables:3 m -mahogany	item(s)	$1 000.00	6	$3 600.00	2
62 Tables:3 m -oak	item(s)	$800.00	6	$3 000.00	2
63 Tables:5 m -mahogany	item(s)	$1 800.00	6	$6 600.00	2
64 Tables:5 m -oak	item(s)	$1 500.00	6	$4 800.00	2
65 Tables:7 m -mahogany	item(s)	$2 800.00	6	$10 800.00	2
66 Tables:7 m -oak	item(s)	$2 500.00	6	$9 600.00	2
				$38 400.00	
71 Wall Units:Office-mhg.	item(s)	$1 800.00	10	$10 000.00	4
72 Wall Units:Office-oak	item(s)	$1 500.00	10	$9 000.00	4
				$19 000.00	

Accounting Procedures

1. **The Goods and Service Tax: Remittances**
   Artistic Interiors will use the **regular method** for remittance of the Goods and Services Tax. GST collected from customers will be recorded as a liability in the GST Charged on Sales account. GST paid to vendors will be recorded in the GST Paid on Purchases account as a decrease in liability to Revenue Canada. The balance to be remitted or the request for a refund will be sent to the Receiver General of Canada by the last day of the current month for the previous month.

   Only the GST transactions that were entered through the Receivables Ledger journals (Sales and Receipts) or the Payables Ledger journals (Purchases and Payments) will be included in the GST report available from the pull-down menu under **Report**. GST-related transactions completed in the General Journal will not be included. Therefore, the amounts shown in the GST report may

NOTES:
Only customers and vendors for whom the *Include in GST report* box was checked will be included in GST reports.

differ from the balances in the General Ledger GST accounts, which include all GST transactions. Use the General Ledger accounts to determine the balance owing (or refund due) and make adjustments manually to the report as necessary.

After the report is filed, clear the GST report by choosing **Clear GST Report** from the pull-down menu under **Setup**. Be sure to make a backup copy of your files before clearing the GST report.

NOTES:
Provincial taxes will be levied for all sales in this application. Bank and other financial institution services in this application are exempt from GST.

2. **Provincial Sales Tax (PST)**
Provincial sales tax of eight percent is applied to all cash and credit sales of goods in Ontario. This amount must be remitted monthly to the Provincial Treasurer. Provincial sales taxes to be remitted must be set up as a liability owing to the vendor, The Treasurer of Ontario, in the Payables Ledger. The PST Payable account for the ending date of the previous month will provide you with the total owing. You may display or print this account for reference. A four percent sales tax commission is earned for prompt payment. Remittance must be made by the 23rd of the current month for the previous month.

3. **The Employer Health Tax (EHT)**
The Employer Health Tax (EHT) replaced the Ontario Health Insurance Plan (OHIP) premium payment on January 1, 1990. The health tax is paid by all employers permanently established in the province of Ontario.

The EHT is based on the total annual remuneration paid to employees. The EHT rate ranges from 0.98 percent to 1.95 percent. The lowest rate (0.98) is based on total remuneration under $200 000. The highest rate (1.95) is based on total remuneration exceeding $400 000.

In this application EHT Payable will be remitted quarterly. The EHT Payable account must be set up as a liablity owing to the vendor, The Treasurer of Ontario. The account balance in the General Ledger for the last day of the previous three months will provide you with the liability owing to the treasurer.

4. **Sales Discounts**
Discounts may be offered to encourage customers to settle their accounts early. When earned by the customers, these discounts should be considered as negative invoices. They are handled in a similar way to cash sales transactions:

- Type "discount" or some other appropriate comment in the Description field.
- Enter GST **code 1** in the GST field to indicate that the discount is non-taxable.
- Enter a **negative** (-) amount in the Amount field for the discount.
- Enter the **Sales Discount** account number in the Account field.

- Leave the PST field blank to show that the discount is non-taxable.
- Leave the remaining fields blank because they pertain to the sale of inventory items.

5. **Purchase Discounts**

Artistic Interiors could take advantage of discounts from vendors by settling its accounts early. These discounts should be considered as negative invoices. Create a negative invoice by increasing the Purchase Discount revenue account for the amount of the discount. Make this entry in the Purchases Journal as a non-inventory purchase.

6. **Freight Expense**

When a business purchases inventory items, the cost of any freight that cannot be directly allocated to a specific item must be charged to the Freight Expense account. This amount will be regarded as an expense rather than being charged to the costs of any inventory asset account.

7. **Sales Invoices**

Sales invoices are prepared manually in this application; they are not generated by the ACCPAC Simply Accounting program. The user has the option of generating invoices through the software.

8. **Purchase Returns**

A business will sometimes return inventory items to vendors due to damage, poor quality or shipment of the wrong items. Usually a business records these returns after it receives a credit note from a vendor. The return of inventory is entered in the Purchases Journal as an inventory purchase:

- After selecting the appropriate item in the Item field, enter the quantity returned as a **negative** amount in the Quantity field. The program will automatically calculate a negative amount as a default in the Amount field.
- Accept the default amount and continue entering any other items returned to the vendor.
- When there are no further items, click on **the Freight field**. If there is any freight applicable, enter a **negative** amount in this field and press ⌨Tab .
- Click on **the GST** field and enter the amount of GST applicable to the returns as a **negative** amount and press ⌨Tab .

The program will create a negative invoice to reduce the balance owing to the vendor and will reduce the applicable inventory assets, the freight accounts, the GST Paid on Purchases account and the quantity of items in the Inventory Ledger database.

9. **Sales Returns**

Sometimes customers will return inventory items. Usually a business records the return after it has issued a credit note. The return is entered in the Sales Journal as an inventory sale:

- Select the appropriate item in the Item field.
- Enter the quantity returned as a **negative** amount in the Quantity field.
- The price of the item appears as a positive number in the Price field, and the Amount field is calculated automatically as a default which you can accept or change.
- Enter the applicable GST code, PST and the account number for Sales Returns and Allowances.

The program will create a negative invoice to reduce the balance owing by the customer, the Cost of Goods Sold account, the GST Charged on Sales account and the PST Payable account. The applicable inventory asset accounts and the quantity of items in the Inventory Ledger database will be increased.

10. **GST Adjustments for Bad Debt**

Most businesses set up an allowance for doubtful accounts or bad debts, knowing that some of their customers will fail to pay. When the allowance is set up, a bad debts expense account is debited. When a business is certain that a customer will not pay its account, the debt should be written off. In the past, the business would do this by crediting the Accounts Receivable account and debiting the Allowance for Bad Debts account. Now that GST has been introduced, an extra step is required. Part of the original sales invoice was entered as a credit (increase) to GST Charged on Sales. The amount of the GST liability can be reduced by the portion of the unpaid debt that was GST. A special GST account, **ITC Adjustments**, is used to record the GST for this transaction. The procedure for entering the transaction in ACCPAC Simply Accounting is to record the write-off of the debt in the Sales Journal using the following steps:

- Select the customer whose debt will not be paid.
- Enter a source document number to identify the transaction (e.g., memo from manager).
- Enter the amount of the unpaid invoice **minus GST** in the Amount field as a **negative** amount.
- Enter the *Allowance for Bad Debts* account number in the Account field.
- Advance to the next line of the invoice.
- Enter the amount of GST that was charged on the invoice in the Amount field as a **negative** amount.
- Enter the *ITC Adjustments* account number in the Account

Review the transaction. The Accounts Receivable account is credited (reduced) by the full amount of the invoice to remove the balance owing by this customer. The Allowance for Bad Debts account has been debited (reduced) by the amount of the invoice minus GST. The ITC Adjustments account has been debited for the portion of the invoice that was GST in order to reduce the liability to the Receiver General.

Manually you would complete the entry as follows:

Set up the Allowance for Bad Debts.

Date	Particulars	Ref.	Debit	Credit
xx/xx	Bad Debts Expense		1 000.00	
	Allowance for Bad Debts			1 000.00

Customer G. Bell declares bankruptcy. Write off outstanding balance, $214, including GST.

Date	Particulars	Ref.	Debit	Credit
xx/xx	Allowance for Bad Debts		200.00	
	ITC Adjustments		14.00	
	Accounts Receivable, G. Bell			214.00

Occasionally, a bad debt will be recovered after it has been written off. When this occurs, the above procedure is reversed and the GST liability must also be restored. Another special GST account, **GST Adjustments**, is used to record the increase in the liability to the Receiver General. The recovery is entered as a non-inventory sale in the Sales Journal using the following steps:

- Select the customer.
- Enter a source document invoice number.
- Type an appropriate comment such as "Debt recovered" in the Description field.
- Enter the amount of the invoice **minus GST** in the amount field as a **positive** amount.
- Enter the *Allowance for Bad Debts* account number in the account field.
- Advance to the next line of the invoice.
- Enter the amount of GST that was charged on the original invoice as a **positive** amount in the Amount field.
- Enter the *GST Adjustments* account number in the account field.

Review the transaction. You will see that the Accounts Receivable account has been debited for the full amount of the invoice. The Allowance for Bad Debts account has been credited for the amount of the invoice minus GST. The GST Adjustments account has been credited for the amount of the GST to record the increase in the liability to the Receiver General.

As the final step, record the customer's payment using the Payments Journal as you would record any other customer payment.

11. **Interior Decorating Contracts**

When a contract is made with a client, Artistic Interiors requires an advance of up to 40 percent as a downpayment. Consider the advance as a prepayment from the customer, and handle it in the Sales Journal as a non-inventory cash sale:

- Select the customer from the displayed list.
- Enter the cheque number instead of entering an invoice number.
- Enter an appropriate comment, such as "Advance on contract," in the Description field.
- Enter a **negative** amount in the Amount field for the amount of the cheque.
- Enter the **Cash in Bank** account number in the Account field.

Review the transaction. The Cash in Bank account has been debited and the Accounts Receivable account has been credited for the customer.

When the contract is completed, enter the full amount negotiated on the contract as another invoice in the Sales Journal. This time, credit the Revenue from Contracting account. The balance in the customer's account, when displayed or printed, will indicate the amount owing on the contract.

12. **Remittances**

The Receiver General of Canada:
Monthly UI, CPP and Income Tax deductions withheld from employees must be paid by the 15th of each month for the previous month.

Monthly GST owing or requests for refunds must be filed by the end of each month for the previous month. The GST clearing account, GST Owing (Refund), will provide you with the balance.

The Treasurer of Ontario:
Quarterly Employer Health Tax (EHT) deductions must be paid by the 15th of April, July, October and January for the previous quarter.

Monthly provincial sales taxes (PST) on Revenue from Sales must be paid by the 23rd of the month for the previous month. A four (4) percent sales tax commission is earned for prompt payment of PST.

The Fairchild Insurance Corporation:
Monthly Registered Retirement Savings Plan (RRS-Plan) deductions withheld from employees must be paid by the 15th of the month for the previous month.

The Equity Investment Corporation:
Monthly Canada Savings Bond Plan (CSB-Plan) deductions withheld from employees must be paid by the 15th of the month for the previous month.

The Workers' Compensation Board:
Quarterly Workers' Compensation Board (WCB) assessment for employees must be paid by the 15th of the month for the previous quarter.

Special Instructions

The **Data Disk** files for this application have been set up so that you can complete segments of the application rather than having to work through it entirely. Each file stands alone so you can omit any month at your discretion.

Stage	Period Covered	Filename on Data Disk
Transactions:	Oct. 1 - Oct. 31	art-oct.asc
Transactions:	Nov. 1 - Nov. 30	art-nov.asc
Transactions:	Dec. 1 - Dec. 30	art-dec.asc
Transactions:	Dec. 31	art-adj.asc

Instructions for Setup

Using the Chart of Accounts, Balance Sheet, Income Statement, Post-Closing Trial Balance, Vendor, Customer, Employee and Inventory Information provided above for September 30, 1991, set up the company accounts. Use the set-up input forms provided in Appendix A. Detailed instructions to assist you in setting up the company accounts follow.

NOTES:

Using subsequent versions of the ACCPAC Simply Accounting program may result in different screens and keystrokes from those described in this application.

NOTES:

When working through this application you should save your work frequently. You may do this by choosing Save from the pull-down menu under File. You will also save your work by finishing your session properly. You may finish your session at any time while completing the setup. Simply continue the next time from where you left off.

Keystrokes for Setup

There are four key stages in preparing the ACCPAC Simply Accounting program for use by a company:

1. creating company files;
2. preparing the system;
3. preparing the ledgers;
4. making the program ready.

The following keystroke instructions are written for a stand-alone IBM-PC or compatible with a hard disk system and single or dual floppy disk drives. The keystroke instructions provided in this application demonstrate one approach to setting up company accounts. Always refer to your ACCPAC Simply Accounting user's guide and DOS and Windows manuals for further details.

Creating Company Files

The following instructions assume that you have the ACCPAC Simply Accounting program correctly installed on your hard disk in drive C in the WINSIM directory.

ACCPAC Simply Accounting provides the user with a set of starter files to make it easier to create files for a new company. These starter files contain different sets of accounts that match the needs of different kinds of businesses. By starting with one of these starter files, you eliminate the need to create all of the accounts for your business from scratch. You should work with a copy of these files so that you can use the original starter files for future applications. ACCPAC Simply Accounting includes the following starter files:

- Construction;
- Integration Plus;
- Manufacturing;
- Retail;
- Service;
- Skeleton.

You will have to customize any of these starter files to your particular company. Rarely are accounts identical for any two businesses. The files that most closely match the Chart of Accounts for Artistic Interiors are the Integration Plus files (inteplus.asc).

The starter files are located in the subdirectory called SAMDATA under the WINSIM directory, which also contains your ACCPAC Simply Accounting program. These starter files were created when you installed the program.

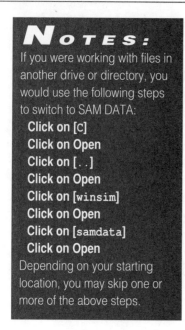
Start the ACCPAC Simply Accounting program.

If you were previously working with files in the WINSIM\DATA subdirectory,

Click on [..] to highlight it.

Click on Open to see the subdirectories under WINSIM.

Click on [samdata] to highlight it.

Click on Open to switch to this subdirectory.

You should now see the list of starter files as shown:

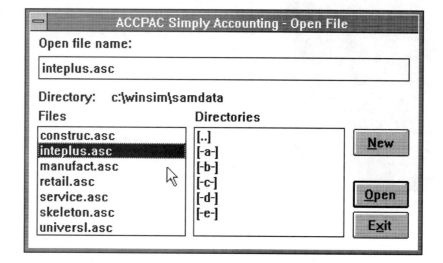

Click on inteplus.asc

Click on Open to access the Integration plus starter files.

The familiar Ledger/Journal company window appears. You are now ready to make a copy of these files to store your records for Artistic Interiors. Always work with a backup copy of the starter files so that you will have the original to use when creating other company records.

Choose Save As from the pull-down menu under **File** to display the following dialogue screen:

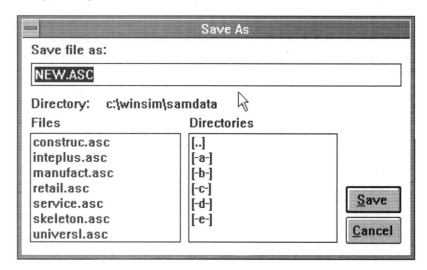

The file name is highlighted, ready for you to type in the name for the Artistic Interiors files.

Type: `c:\winsim\data\artistic.asc`

Click on Save

You have now created a copy of the Integration Plus starter files under the new name in the data subdirectory where you stored your other data files. Four files were created in this procedure, all of which are necessary to work in ACCPAC Simply Accounting. The .asc file is the only one displayed on your file list because it is the one that you open to get started. If the other three files are not in the same directory, you will not be able to access your data. Using the Save As command automatically puts all the necessary files together.

When you return to the Ledger/Journal company window, the name Artistic appears at the top of the window as shown:

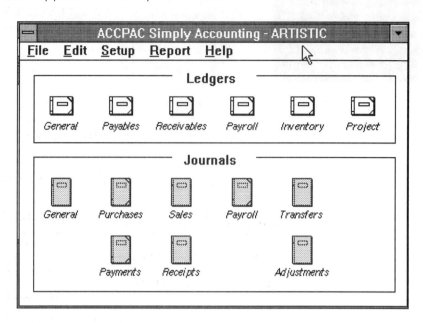

All of the journal icons are dimmed because the files are not ready for you to enter transactions. First you must enter all of the necessary company information.

Preparing the System

Before entering financial records for a new company, you must prepare the system for operation. This involves changing the defaults that were set up when Artistic Interiors' company files were created. These defaults include the Chart of Accounts and subsidiary ledger integration accounts that came with the Integration Plus files, names or titles, and functions. Some of these defaults will not be suitable for Artistic Interiors. You must also provide other information, such as the type of printer(s) that you will be using. This process of adding, deleting and modifying information is called *customizing the system*.

You should change the defaults to suit your own work environment if you have more than one printer or if you are using forms for cheques, invoices or statements. The keystroke instructions are given for computer-generated cheques, invoices and statements.

Set-Up Input Forms

You will need input forms to enter the information for setting up the company files. We will discuss each of the different set-up input forms as it is used.

The set-up input forms, Form SYS-1 and Form SYS-2, are used to enter changes to the defaults and computer equipment. Form SYS-1 profiles the company and gives information about Artistic Interiors' computer equipment. Form SYS-2 shows the defaults we have selected for Artistic Interiors for each of the accounting ledgers.

Changing Company Information

Form SYS-1 provides the information you need to complete this step.

Choose Company Information from the pull-down menu under **Setup** to display the following information screen:

Company Information	
Name: Your Company	**Fiscal start:** 1/1/91
Street: 123 Your St	**Fiscal end:** 12/31/91
City: Your Town	**Conversion:** 3/1/91
Province: Your Province	**Using:** 3/1/91
Postal: A0A 0A0	**Using tax table: MC55**
Employer no.:	
GST reg. no.:	OK Cancel

This window shows the company address and registration information. You must customize it for Artistic Interiors. The cursor is flashing in the Name field. Drag the cursor through "Your Company," the information that was entered by default, to highlight it. The field is now ready to be edited.

Type: Artistic Interiors

Press ⌈Tab⌉

The cursor advances to the Street field, with the default information highlighted.

Type: 22 Harridge Road

Press ⌈Tab⌉

The cursor moves to the City field, again highlighting the existing information.

SYSTEM PREPARATION

COMPANY INFORMATION

Name: Artistic Interiors

Street: 22 Harridge Road

City: Toronto

Province: Ontario

Postal Code: M4R 1J2

Employer #: AIC123456

GST Reg. #: R107165829

Fiscal Start: 07-01-91 (mm-dd-yy)

Fiscal End: 12-31-91 (mm-dd-yy)

Conversion: 09-30-91 (mm-dd-yy)

PAYROLL NAMES

Income A: Salary

Income B: Commission

Deduction A: RRS-Plan

Deduction B: CSB-Plan

Deduction C: N/A

Project Title: N/A

PRINTER NAMES

		Margins	
		TOP	LEFT
Reports:	Postscript	1.0	.50
Cheques:	N/A		
Invoices:	N/A		
Other Forms:	N/A		

		Number across page	Height	Width
Labels:	N/A			

SYSTEM PREPARATION

SETTINGS

Receivables

Aging: 3 0 , 6 0 , 9 0

Interest Charges: 0 %   Y __ , N ✔

GST Rate 1: 7 %

GST Rate 2: 0 %

PST Rate: 8 %

Apply PST to Freight: Y __ , N ✔

Apply PST to GST: Y __ , N ✔

Payables

Aging: 3 0 , 6 0 , 9 0

Payroll

Auto Payroll Deduction : Y ✔ , N __

Deduction A after Tax : Y __ , N ✔

Deduction B after Tax : Y ✔ , N __

Deduction C after Tax : Y __ , N __

UI Factor : 1 . 4

EHT Factor : 0 . 9 8

Payroll WCB

Province : Ontario

WCB Maximum Assessable Earnings: 4 2 0 0 0

SYSTEM PREPARATION

Forms

Next invoice number : N / A

Next payables cheque number : N / A

Next payroll cheque number : N / A

Confirm printing   for invoices : Y __ , N ✓

                       for cheques : Y __ , N ✓

Print company address on invoices : Y __ , N ✓

                       on statements : Y ✓ , N __

                       on cheques : Y __ , N ✓

Default invoice comment :

Inventory

Markup ____✓____   Margin _____   (Choose one only)

Distributions

Distribute General Journal by:
(Choose one only)

       Amount : _____

       Percent : _____

Distribute Payroll Journal by:
(Choose one only)

       Amount : _____

       Percent : _____

       Hours : _____

Warn if distribution is not complete: Y __ , N __

Report Font

Display Font : Helvetica-Narrow   Size : 8

Type: `Toronto`

Press [Tab]

The Province field information is now highlighted.

Type: `Ontario`

Press [Tab]

The Postal (code) field information can now be changed.

Type: `m4r1j2`

Press [Tab]

The postal code format has been corrected automatically and the cursor is flashing in the Employer number field. Revenue Canada assigns this number for payroll registration.

Type: `AIC123456`

Press [Tab]

The cursor advance to the GST registration number field. Revenue Canada assigns this number for the filing of GST returns by the company.

Type: `R107165829`

Press [Tab]

The fiscal start date is now highlighted. This is the date on which the business begins its fiscal year. For Artistic Interiors, the fiscal start date is the same as the starting date of the business. The format for dates is the same as for journal entries: month, day and year.

Type: `07-01-91`

Press [Tab]

The cursor advances and the program highlights the fiscal end date, the date on which the fiscal period ends and Artistic Interiors will close its books.

Type: `12-31-91`

Press [Tab]

The program now highlights the conversion date. This is the date on which the business is changing from a manual accounting system to a computerized accounting system.

Type: 09-30-91

Press ⌈Tab⌉

Check the information you have just entered. To correct any errors, return to the field with the error, drag the cursor through the incorrect information and type the correct information.

Click on OK to save the new information and return to the main Ledger/Journal company window.

You can return to the Company Information screen at any time to make changes. For example, the company may move or change its name or you may want to correct typing errors. The program will automatically set up defaults for the using date and for the city and province fields for customers, vendors and employees based on the information you have just entered.

Changing the Defaults

Form SYS-1 on page 236 provides the information to complete this next step.

Choose Names from the pull-down menu under **Setup** to display the following screen showing the preset payroll field names:

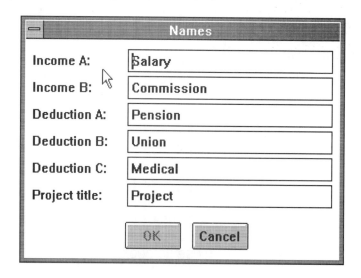

Some of these fields are already correct so you do not need to redefine them. You can leave Income A and B, labelled "Salary" and "Commission," as they are because Artistic Interiors uses both methods to pay its employees.

Press ⌈Tab⌋ twice to advance to the Deduction A field. Artistic Interiors will use this field for Registered Retired Savings Plan contributions.

Type: `RRS-Plan`

Press ⌈Tab⌋ to advance to the next field.

The Deduction B field will be used for the Canada Savings Bond Plan that Artistic offers its employees.

Type: `CSB-Plan`

Press ⌈Tab⌋

You can ignore the Medical field and Project title fields because Artistic Interiors does not use them. To indicate that these fields are not applicable,

Type: `N/A` to replace the default title "Medical."

Press ⌈Tab⌋

Type: `N/A` in the Project title field.

Press ⌈Tab⌋

Click on OK to save the new name settings and to return to the main Ledger/Journal company window.

Form SYS-1 provides the information about printers.

Choose Printers from the pull-down menu under **Setup** to display the following dialogue box:

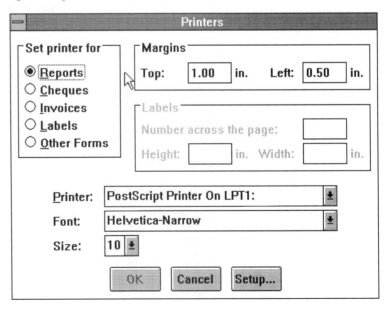

ACCPAC Simply Accounting allows you to use several printers for printing the various reports, cheques, invoices and labels. In order to take full advantage of this printing capability, you should have the appropriate forms. For tutorial purposes, however, you can use plain paper.

The printer setting options for reports are given. Change the margins if necessary. Choose the printer you will be using for reports from the list provided using the arrow beside the field. All printers that are attached to your computer and were installed under Windows should be on the list. Choose a font and type size from the lists available when you click on the arrows beside these fields. You may have to experiment with fonts and type sizes to find the combination that will fit the reports neatly on the page.

Click on Setup to set the options for your particular printer. The following screen shows the options for a postscript printer:

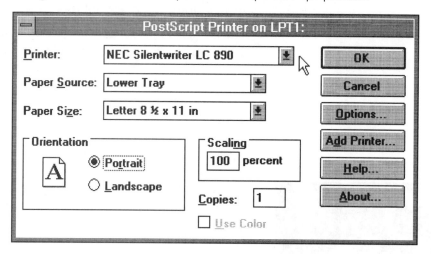

You may need to change these options according to the printers and paper you are using.

Click on OK to save your settings and return to the previous Printers setting screen.

To set the printer options for cheques, invoices or other forms,

Click on the circle beside the one you need to set.

As you did for reports, set the margins and select the printer, font and type size to match the forms you are using.

Click on Setup and complete the setting of options if necessary.

Click on OK to save the information.

For printing labels, you need to include the size of your labels and the number that are placed across the page. This box will be darkened and available when you click on the circle beside Labels.

Click on OK to save the information when all the settings are correct and to return to the Ledger/Journal company window. You can change the printer settings at any time.

Form SYS-2 on pages 237 and 238 provides information about the remaining default settings.

Choose Settings from the pull-down menu under **Setup** to display the following default settings for the Receivables Ledger:

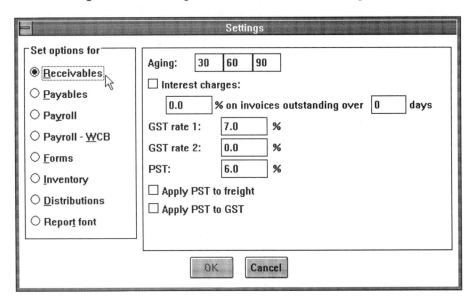

Many of the default settings are correct and you do not need to change them. Artistic Interiors uses the periods of 30, 60 and 90 days to age its accounts and it does not yet charge interest on overdue accounts. The GST rate 1 set at 7.0% is also correct. The GST rate 2 field might be used in the future if different tax rates were applied to different types of goods or services. At present, however, there is no second rate for GST, so you can leave 0.0% unchanged. You must change the PST rate.

Click on the PST field to highlight the contents.

Type: 8

Press ⌈Tab⌉

The final two options concern the application of PST. Leave the boxes unchecked for Artistic Interiors because PST is not applied to freight charges or on top of GST in Ontario. For Quebec and the eastern provinces, you would check this last box. If at any time the regulations in Ontario or your own province changed, you could return to this field and click on the appropriate box to change the setting.

Click on Payables from the list on the left side of the screen to display its default settings as follows:

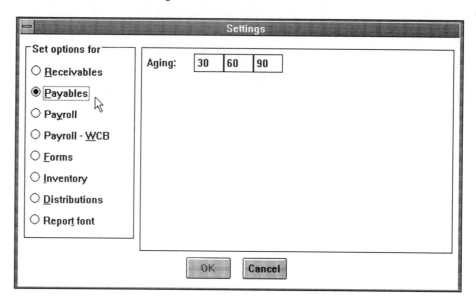

The only option for the Payables Ledger concerns the aging of accounts, and the 30, 60 and 90 day setting is correct.

Click on Payroll from the list on the left side of the screen to display its options:

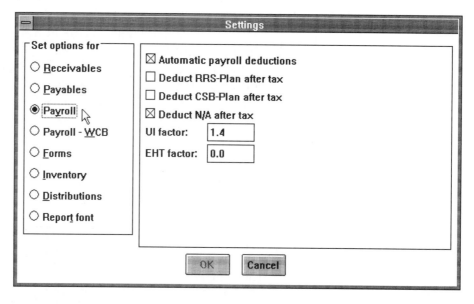

Notice that the deduction names you entered earlier now appear on the screen. Again, most of the information is correct. We want payroll deductions to be calculated automatically so leave this box checked.

The three deductions are set by default as either pretax or after tax. The RRS-Plan deduction is already set correctly as a pretax deduction (after tax is not turned on). This means that it will be subtracted from gross income before income tax is calculated.

CSB-Plan is an after-tax deduction, meaning that it is subtracted from income after income tax has been deducted.

Click on the box beside Deduct CSB-Plan after tax to change the setting.

The third deduction field is not used so you can leave it as it is. You can see that it is set as an after-tax deduction by default.

The next two fields refer to the rate at which employer tax obligations are calculated. The rate for Unemployment Insurance (UI) is correct at 1.4. The employer's contribution is set at 1.4 times the employee's contribution.

Click on the EHT factor field. This field shows the percentage of payroll costs that the employer contributes to the provincial health plan. Based on the total payroll costs per year, the percentage for Artistic Interiors is 0.98 percent.

Type: .98

Press [Tab]

You have now finished setting the Payroll defaults.

Click on Payroll-WCB from the list on the left side of the screen to display its options:

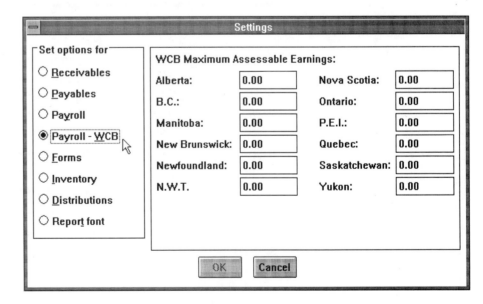

Since all Artistic Interiors' employees work in Ontario, you need only enter the maximum assessable earnings amount for Ontario. This is the maximum salary on which the Workers' Compensation Board deduction is calculated and on which any benefits are based.

Click on the Ontario field to move the cursor.

Type: 42000

Press ⌈Tab⌉

Click on Forms from the list on the left side of the screen to display its options:

```
┌─────────────────────────────────────────────────────────────────┐
│ ─                          Settings                               │
├─────────────────────────────────────────────────────────────────┤
│ ┌─Set options for──────┐  ┌──────────────────────────────────┐  │
│ │                      │   Next invoice number:        [1   ] │  │
│ │  ○ Receivables       │                                      │  │
│ │                      │   Next payables cheque number: [1  ] │  │
│ │  ○ Payables          │                                      │  │
│ │                      │   Next payroll cheque number:  [1  ] │  │
│ │  ○ Payroll           │                                      │  │
│ │                      │   □ Confirm printing for invoices    │  │
│ │  ○ Payroll - WCB     │   □ Confirm printing for cheques     │  │
│ │  ◉ Forms             │   □ Print company address on invoices│  │
│ │  ○ Inventory         │   □ Print company address on statements│ │
│ │                      │   □ Print company address on cheques │  │
│ │  ○ Distributions     │   Default invoice comment:           │  │
│ │  ○ Report font       │   [                               ]  │  │
│ └──────────────────────┘                                      │  │
│                             [  OK  ]  [ Cancel ]                  │
└─────────────────────────────────────────────────────────────────┘
```

These settings refer to the automatic numbering and printing of all cheques and invoices. They apply only to numerical invoices. Although Artistic Interiors does not use these options, they are very useful for most businesses. Alphanumeric invoice numbers cannot be increased automatically by the computer.

If you want to use automatic invoice numbering, type in the next number so the automatic numbering sytem can take over from the manual system. Notice that separate ledgers can have separate bank accounts and cheque numbering.

If you are printing invoices and cheques through the computer, you should turn on the option to confirm printing. The program will then warn you to print before posting a transacion. Remember that if a cheque is printed in error, an appropriate entry or comment should be recorded to explain the missing cheque number for the discarded cheque.

Click on the appropriate boxes to receive the warning.

When printing invoices, statements or cheques, it is good practice to include the company address.

Click on the appropriate boxes to add this feature.

The final option is to add the same comment or notice to all of your invoices. You could use this feature to include payment terms, a company motto or notice of an upcoming sale. Remember that you can change the default message any time you want. You can also edit it for a particular invoice when you are completing the invoice.

Type in the comment you want to see on all your customer invoices.

Click on Inventory from the list on the left side of the screen to see the options for this ledger:

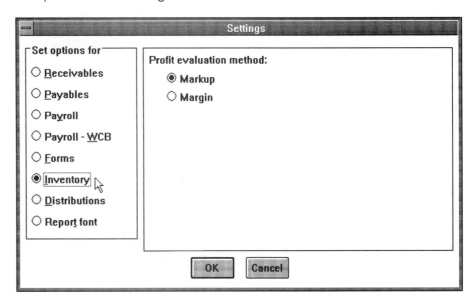

The default setting for the Markup method of evaluating the profit on inventory sales is the correct one for Artistic Interiors. Markup is calculated as follows:

Markup = (Selling Price - Cost Price)/ Cost Price

Click on Distributions from the list on the left side of the screen to display its options:

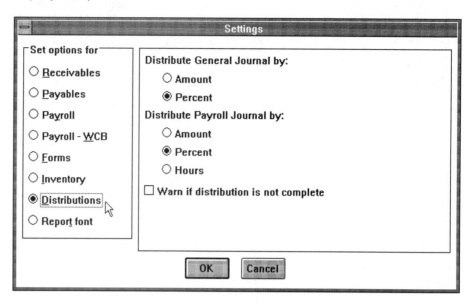

Since Artistic Interiors does not use job costing, you do not need to change these settings. You can see that the alternative ways of allocating costs are by percentage (as used for payroll in the Melody Music Centre application) and by amount. For payroll, the costs may also be distributed according to the number of hours worked. If you are using job costing distributions, you should turn on the warning for incomplete distributions by clicking on its box.

Click on Report font from the list on the left side of the screen to display its options:

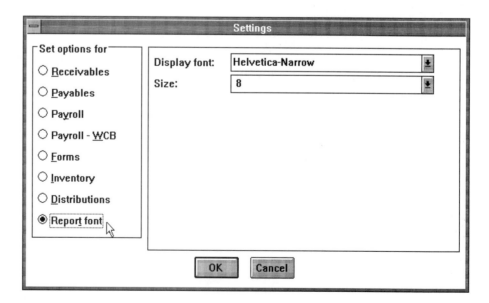

Using this screen, you can set the fonts and type sizes for the reports you display on the screen. Display the available fonts and sizes by clicking on the arrows beside these fields.

You have now entered all of the default settings for Artistic Interiors. As you work through the transactions, the program will use these defaults for automatic calculations, field names and contents.

Click on OK to save your new settings and to return to the Ledger/Journal company window.

Setting the Security for the System

ACCPAC Simply Accounting allows you to set up as many as four passwords. One password controls access to the system or program. The other three control viewing and editing privileges for different ledgers. For example, if different employees worked with different accounting records, they could be given different passwords.

We strongly advise you not to set passwords for applications used for tutorial purposes. If you set them and forget them, you will be locked out of your data files.

If you want to set passwords,

Choose Set Security from the pull-down menu under Setup to display the following screen:

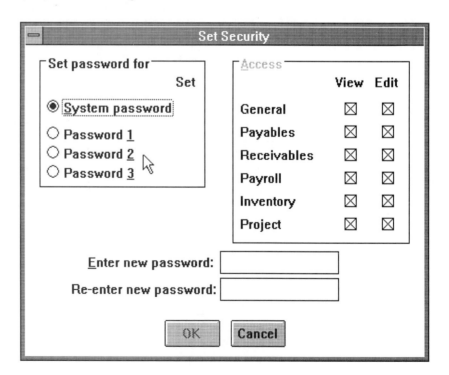

On this screen, indicate what part of the system you are setting the password for and what access privileges you want associated with this password. Then, enter the password itself. Consult your ACCPAC Simply Accounting user's guide if you need further assistance or if you wish to remove or change passwords.

Preparing the Ledgers

The third stage in setting up an accounting system involves preparing each ledger for operation. This is the most important stage since it involves the following steps:

1. organizing all accounting reports and records (this step has already been completed for you);
2. modifying some existing accounts;
3. removing some existing accounts;
4. creating new accounts;
5. inserting vendor, customer, employee and inventory information;
6. entering historical startup information.

Defining the Integration Plus Starter Files

When you created the company files for Artistic Interiors in stage one, creating company files, a list of preset startup accounts was provided in the Integration Plus files. You can find a complete list of these accounts and their descriptions in Chapter 5 of the ACCPAC Simply Accounting user's guide and the print-out requested earlier. You can also see these accounts on the input forms (see Form INT-1 on pages 257-259).

Form INT-1 lists both integration accounts and other accounts for the various ledgers. The integration accounts are shown in boldface type. The accounts are organized by section, including Assets, Liabilities, Equity, Revenue and Expense. The form also shows the account type, such as Heading (H), Subtotal (S), Total (T), Left Column (L), Right Column (R) and Current Earnings (X). Account type is a method of classifying and organizing accounts within a section or subsection of a report.

Form INT-1 also provides the Initial Account Number for each account on the list. The accounts are numbered as follows:

• 1000 - 1999   Assets
• 2000 - 2999   Liabilities
• 3000 - 3999   Equity
• 4000 - 4999   Revenue
• 5000 - 5999   Expense

The Chart of Accounts for Artistic Interiors follows these sectional boundaries.

The Format of Financial Statements

When setting up the complete Chart of Accounts for Artistic Interiors, it is important that you understand the composition and format of financial statements that ACCPAC Simply Accounting will accept.

The Balance Sheet is organized and divided into three sections, each with headings: Assets, Liabilities and Equity. The Income Statement is divided into two sections, each with headings: Revenue and Expense.

Each section of the financial statements can be further subdivided into blocks. Assets can be divided into blocks titled CURRENT ASSETS, INVENTORY ASSETS and PLANT AND EQUIPMENT. Liabilities can be divided into blocks titled CURRENT LIABILITIES and LONG TERM DEBT. Equity, Revenue and Expense sections can also be divided.

ACCPAC Simply Accounting requires that all accounts, including block headings, subtotals and block totals, be assigned numbers. This is quite different from a manual accounting system, in which numbers are assigned only to postable accounts. Predefined section headings and section totals (e.g., ASSETS, TOTAL ASSETS and LIABILITIES), however, are not assigned numbers by the program.

The following are the ACCPAC Simply Accounting rules concerning financial statement **blocks**:

1. Each block must contain a block heading (H), which will be printed in boldface type. A heading is not considered a postable account, cannot be debited or credited through transaction entries, and cannot have an amount assigned to it.

2. Each block must contain at least one, and possibly more, postable accounts. Postable accounts are those that can be debited or credited through transaction entries. Postable accounts may have an opening balance.

3. Postable accounts can appear in the left (L) or the right (R) column.

4. Postable accounts in the left column must be followed by a subtotal (S) account. A subtotal is not a postable account and cannot be given an opening balance. The program automatically calculates a subtotal by adding left postable account balances. Subtotal balances always appear in the right column.

5. Each block must contain a block total (T). All accounts in the right column, both postable and subtotal accounts, are added together to form the block total. A block total is not a postable account. The program automatically calculates it and prints it in boldface type.

The following are the ACCPAC Simply Accounting rules concerning financial statement **sections**:

1. Each of the financial statement sections described above must have a total. A section total is the total of the individual block totals within that section. The five section totals are:

    TOTAL ASSETS;
    TOTAL LIABILITIES;
    TOTAL EQUITY;
    TOTAL REVENUE;
    TOTAL EXPENSE.

    The user cannot change the titles of the section totals; the program will automatically print them in the financial statement reports.

2. The Liabilities and Equity section totals are also automatically added together. LIABILITIES AND EQUITY is the sum of TOTAL LIABILITIES and TOTAL EQUITY. The user cannot change this title.

3. In the Income Statement, the difference between TOTAL REVENUE and TOTAL EXPENSE is automatically calculated as NET INCOME and listed under TOTAL EXPENSE. The user cannot change this title.

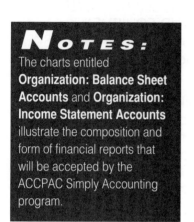

The Current Earnings (X) Account

The Current Earnings account appears under the EQUITY section in the Balance Sheet. It is easy to identify because it is the only account in the Chart of Accounts whose type is X. This account is calculated as follows:

Current Earnings = Total Revenue - Total Expense

The Current Earnings account is not a postable account and only appears in the right (R) column of the block. It cannot be removed, but its title can be modified. The Current Earnings account is updated from any transaction changes in revenue and expense accounts. At the end of the fiscal period when closing routines are performed, the balance of this account is added to the Retained Earnings account (or a renamed account for Retained Earnings) and then it is reset to zero.

For Artistic Interiors, a sole proprietorship, the Retained Earnings account will be renamed "J. Klassen, Capital." The Current Earnings account will be renamed "Net Income."

ORGANIZATION: BALANCE SHEET ACCOUNTS

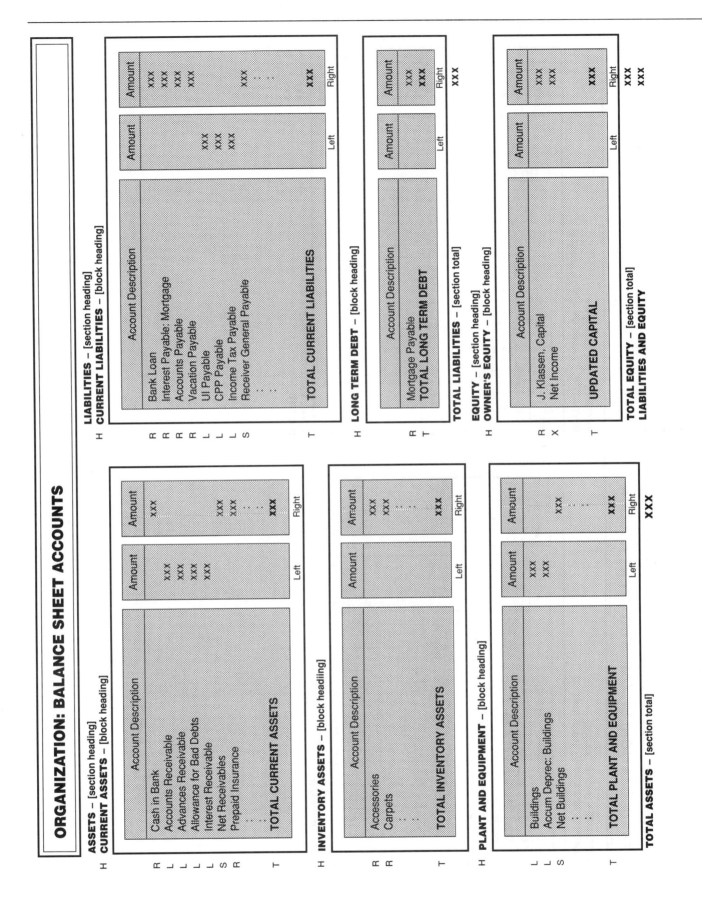

ASSETS – [section heading]
H **CURRENT ASSETS** – [block heading]

	Account Description	Amount	Amount
R	Cash in Bank		xxx
L	Accounts Receivable	xxx	
L	Advances Receivable	xxx	
L	Allowance for Bad Debts	xxx	
L	Interest Receivable	xxx	
S	Net Receivables		xxx
R	Prepaid Insurance		xxx
T	**TOTAL CURRENT ASSETS**	Left	**xxx** Right

H **INVENTORY ASSETS** – [block heading]

	Account Description	Amount	Amount
R	Accessories		xxx
R	Carpets		xxx
T	**TOTAL INVENTORY ASSETS**	Left	**xxx** Right

H **PLANT AND EQUIPMENT** – [block heading]

	Account Description	Amount	Amount
L	Buildings	xxx	
L	Accum Deprec: Buildings	xxx	
S	Net Buildings		xxx
T	**TOTAL PLANT AND EQUIPMENT**	Left	**xxx** Right

TOTAL ASSETS – [section total]   **XXX**

LIABILITIES – [section heading]
H **CURRENT LIABILITIES** – [block heading]

	Account Description	Amount	Amount
R	Bank Loan		xxx
R	Interest Payable: Mortgage		xxx
R	Accounts Payable		xxx
R	Vacation Payable		xxx
L	UI Payable	xxx	
L	CPP Payable	xxx	
L	Income Tax Payable	xxx	
S	Receiver General Payable		xxx
T	**TOTAL CURRENT LIABILITIES**	Left	**xxx** Right

H **LONG TERM DEBT** – [block heading]

	Account Description	Amount	Amount
R	Mortgage Payable		xxx
T	**TOTAL LONG TERM DEBT**	Left	**xxx** Right

TOTAL LIABILITIES – [section total]   **XXX**

EQUITY – [section heading]
H **OWNER'S EQUITY** – [block heading]

	Account Description	Amount	Amount
R	J. Klassen, Capital		xxx
X	Net Income		xxx
T	**UPDATED CAPITAL**	Left	**xxx** Right

TOTAL EQUITY – [section total]   **XXX**
LIABILITIES AND EQUITY   **XXX**

ORGANIZATION: INCOME STATEMENT ACCOUNTS

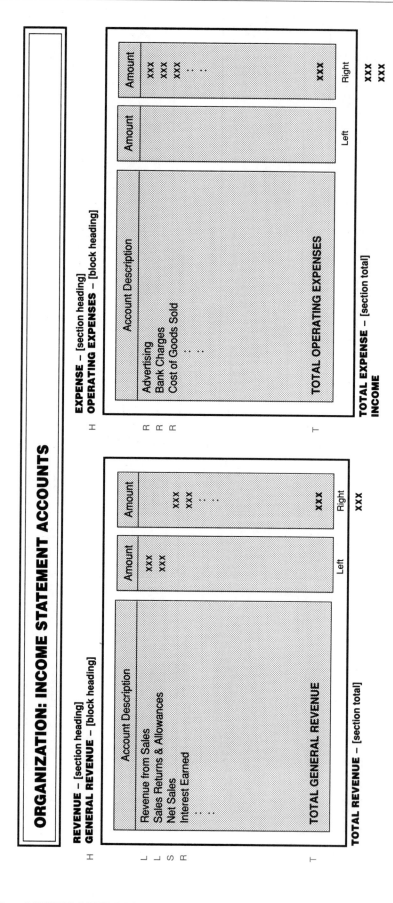

REVENUE – [section heading]

H **GENERAL REVENUE** – [block heading]

Account Description	Amount	Amount
	Left	Right
Revenue from Sales	xxx	
Sales Returns & Allowances	xxx	
Net Sales		xxx
Interest Earned		xxx
. . . . .		. . . .
TOTAL GENERAL REVENUE		xxx

L
L
S
R

T

TOTAL REVENUE – [section total]   xxx

EXPENSE – [section heading]

H **OPERATING EXPENSES** – [block heading]

Account Description	Amount	Amount
	Left	Right
Advertising		xxx
Bank Charges		xxx
Cost of Goods Sold		xxx
. . . . .		. . . .
TOTAL OPERATING EXPENSES		xxx

R
R
R

T

TOTAL EXPENSE – [section total]   xxx
INCOME   xxx

Integration Accounts

Integration Accounts are accounts in the General Ledger that are affected by changes resulting from entries in other journals. For example, an entry to record a credit sale of an inventory item in the Sales Journal will cause automatic changes in the Inventory Ledger as well as in several General Ledger accounts. In the General Ledger, the Accounts Receivable [+], Inventory Asset [-], Revenue from Sales [+], GST Charged on Sales [+], PST Payable [+] and Cost of Goods Sold [+] accounts will all be affected by the sale. The type of change, increase (+) or decrease (-), is indicated in the brackets. In the Inventory Ledger, the sale will cause an automatic decrease in the inventory on hand for the items sold. The program must know which account numbers are to be used for posting journal entries in any of the journals. It is this interconnection of account numbers and information between ledgers that makes ACCPAC Simply Accounting fully integrated.

Suppressing Zero Account Balances

At certain times, it may be appropriate to print an account with a zero balance, although usually zero balance accounts do not need to be printed. The user has the option in ACCPAC Simply Accounting to suppress the printing of accounts with zero balances. You may select this option in the General Ledger.

Preparing the General Ledger

Compare the Integration Plus Chart of Accounts you have printed out with the Artistic Interiors' Chart of Accounts, Balance Sheet and Income Statement provided in this application. You will see that some of the accounts are the same, some of the accounts you need are not yet in the program, and others that appear on the computer list are not needed for Artistic Interiors. You have to customize the accounts specifically for Artistic Interiors.

Changing Integration Plus Accounts

The first step, that of identifying the changes needed in the Integration Plus preset accounts to match the accounts needed for Artistic Interiors, is a very important one. Form INT-1, which follows, shows the changes that must be made to these preset accounts. On Form INT-1, the following steps have been done for you:

1. The Integration Plus accounts provided by the program that require no changes have been marked with an asterisk (*). The account title, the initial account number and the account type are the same as those given in the financial statements. Those accounts not requiring changes follow:

CURRENT ASSETS	1000
TOTAL CURRENT ASSETS	1390
CURRENT LIABILITIES	2000
Accounts Payable	2200
Vacation Payable	2300
UI Payable	2310
CPP Payable	2320
Income Tax Payable	2330
Receiver General Payable	2340
EHT Payable	2390
WCB Payable	2460
PST Payable	2640
GST Charged on Sales	2650
GST Paid on Purchases	2670
GST Adjustments	2710
ITC Adjustments	2730
GST Owing (Refund)	2750
TOTAL CURRENT LIABILITIES	2800
Wages	5300
UI Expense	5310
CPP Expense	5320
WCB Expense	5330
EHT Expense	5360

INTEGRATION PLUS ACCOUNTS - MAINTENANCE

Account Title [Initial]	SECTION	TYPE	Module [used by]	Initial Account Number	CODE	Account Title [New]	TYPE	New Account Number
CURRENT ASSETS	A	H	—	1 0 0 0	*			
Bank A - Payable	A	L	A P	1 0 6 0	R			
Bank B - Receivable	A	L	A R	1 0 8 0	M	Cash in Bank	R	1 0 8 0
Bank C - Payroll	A	L	P R	1 1 0 0	R			
Cash - Total	A	S	—	1 1 2 0	M			
Accounts Receivable	A	R	A R	1 2 0 0	M	Accounts Receivable	L	1 2 0 0
Advances Receivable	A	R	A R	1 2 4 0	M	Advances Receivable	L	1 2 4 0
Inventory	A	R	—	1 2 6 0	M	Interest Receivable	L	1 2 6 0
TOTAL CURRENT ASSETS	A	T	—	1 3 9 0	*			
CURRENT LIABILITIES	L	H	—	2 0 0 0	*			
Accounts Payable	L	R	A P	2 2 0 0	*			
Vacation Payable	L	R	P R	2 3 0 0	*			
UI Payable	L	L	P R	2 3 1 0	*			
CPP Payable	L	L	P R	2 3 2 0	*			
Income Tax Payable	L	L	P R	2 3 3 0	*			
Receiver General Payable	L	S	—	2 3 4 0	*			

SECTION:
A = ASSETS
L = LIABILITIES
E = EQUITY
R = REVENUE
X = EXPENSE

TYPE:
H = Heading
R = Right
L = Left
S = Subtotal
X = Current Earnings
T - Total

MODULE:
GL = GENERAL
AP = PAYABLE
AR = RECEIVABLE
PR = PAYROLL
IN = INVENTORY

CODE:
R = Remove
M = Modify
* = no change

INTEGRATION PLUS ACCOUNTS - MAINTENANCE

Account Title [Initial]	SECTION	TYPE	Module [used by]	Initial Account Number	Account Title [New]	CODE	TYPE	New Account Number
QPP Payable	L	L	P R	2 3 5 0		R		
Que. Income Tax Payable	L	L	P R	2 3 6 0		R		
QHIP Payable	L	L	P R	2 3 7 0		R		1 0 8 0
Que. Minister of Finance	L	S	—	2 3 8 0		R		
EHT Payable	L	R	P R	2 3 9 0		*		
Deduction A Payable	L	R	P R	2 4 0 0	RRS–Plan Payable	M	R	2 4 0 0
Deduction B Payable	L	R	P R	2 4 2 0	CSB–Plan Payable	M	R	2 4 2 0
Deduction C Payable	L	R	P R	2 4 4 0		R		
WCB Payable	L	R	P R	2 4 6 0		*		
PST Payable	L	R	A R	2 6 4 0		*		
GST Charged on Sales	L	L	A R	2 6 5 0		*		
GST Paid on Purchases	L	L	A P	2 6 7 0		*		
GST Payroll Deductions	L	L	T	2 6 9 0		R		
GST Adjustments	L	L	T	2 7 1 0		*		
ITC Adjustments	L	L	T	2 7 3 0		*		
GST Owing (Refund)	L	S	T	2 7 5 0		*		
TOTAL CURRENT LIABILITIES	L	T	T	2 8 0 0		*		
EARNINGS	E	H		3 0 0 0	OWNER'S EQUITY	M	H	3 0 0 0
Retained Earnings	E	R		3 5 6 0	J. Klassen, Capital	M	R	3 5 6 0
Current Earnings	E	X		3 6 0 0	Net Income	M	X	3 6 0 0
TOTAL EARNINGS	E	T		3 6 9 0	UPDATED CAPITAL	M	T	3 6 9 0

SECTION:
A = ASSETS
L = LIABILITIES
E = EQUITY
R = REVENUE
X = EXPENSE

TYPE:
H = Heading
R = Right
L = Left
S = Subtotal
X = Current Earnings
T - Total

MODULE:
GL = GENERAL
AP = PAYABLE
AR = RECEIVABLE
PR = PAYROLL
IN = INVENTORY

CODE:
R = Remove
M = Modify
* = no change

INTEGRATION PLUS ACCOUNTS - MAINTENANCE

Initial

Account Title [Initial]	SECTION	TYPE	Module [used by]	Initial Account Number
REVENUE	R	H	—	4 0 0 0
General Revenue	R	R	—	4 0 2 0
Freight Revenue	R	R	A R	4 2 0
TOTAL REVENUE	R	T	—	4 3 9 0
ADMINISTRATION	X	H	—	5 0 0 0
General Expense	X	R	—	5 0 2 0
Adjustment Write-off	X	R	I N	5 0 3 0
Transfer Costs	X	R	I N	5 0 4 0
Freight Expense	X	R	A P	5 2 0
Wages	X	R	P R	5 3 0 0
UI Expense	X	R	P R	5 3 1 0
CPP Expense	X	R	P R	5 3 2 0
WCB Expense	X	R	P R	5 3 3 0
QPP Expense	X	R	P R	5 3 4 0
QHIP Expense	X	R	P R	5 3 5 0
EHT Expense	X	R	P R	5 3 6 0
TOTAL ADMINSTRATION	X	T	—	5 3 9 0

New

CODE	Account Title [New]	TYPE	New Account Number
M	GENERAL REVENUE	H	4 0 0 0
M	Revenue from Sales	L	4 0 2 0
R			
M	TOTAL GENERAL REVENUE	T	4 3 9 0
M	OPERATING EXPENSES	H	5 0 0 0
M	Advertising	R	5 0 2 0
M	Adjustment Write-off	R	5 0 7 0
R			
M	Freight Expense	R	5 1 5 0
*			
*			
*			
*			
R			
R			
*			
M	TOTAL OPERATING EXPENSES	T	5 3 9 0

SECTION:
A = ASSETS
L = LIABILITIES
E = EQUITY
R = REVENUE
X = EXPENSE

TYPE:
H = Heading
R = Right
L = Left
S = Subtotal
X = Current Earnings
T - Total

MODULE:
GL = GENERAL
AP = PAYABLE
AR = RECEIVABLE
PR = PAYROLL
IN = INVENTORY

CODE:
R = Remove
M = Modify
* = no change

2. Account **1080 Cash in Bank** has been identified as the only integrated bank account for the Payables, Receivables and Payroll ledgers. These account titles, types, and initial account numbers have been removed (R) or modified (M) on Form INT-1. These include:

Bank A - Payable	1060	remove (R)
Bank B - Receivable	1080	modify (M)
Bank C - Payroll	1100	remove (R)

3. The accounts for which only the account type needs to be changed have been identified and modified (M) on Form INT-1. These accounts, for which the initial account numbers and titles are correct but the type is different, include:

Accounts Receivable	1200
Advances Receivable	1240

4. The accounts for which only the account number needs to be changed have been identified and modified (M) on Form INT-1. These accounts, for which the initial account titles and type are correct but the account number is different, include:

Adjustment Write-off	5030
Freight Expense	5200

5. The accounts for which the account titles and possibly the account type need to be changed have been identified and modified (M) on Form INT-1. These accounts, for which the initial account numbers are correct but the account titles are different, include:

Inventory	1260
Deduction A Payable	2400
Deduction B Payable	2420
EARNINGS	3000
Retained Earnings	3560
Current Earnings	3600
TOTAL EARNINGS	3690
REVENUE	4000
General Revenue	4020
TOTAL REVENUE	4390
ADMINISTRATION	5000
General Expense	5020
TOTAL ADMINISTRATION	5390

7. Form INT-1 identifies all the accounts that are going to be removed (R) because they are not required for Artistic Interiors:

Cash - Total	1120
QPP Payable	2350
Quebec Income Tax Payable	2360
QHIP Payable	2370
Quebec Minister of Finance	2380
Deduction C Payable	2440
GST Payroll Deductions	2690
Freight Revenue	4200
Transfer Costs	5040
QPP Expense	5340
QHIP Expense	5350

Creating New Accounts

After identifying the modifications that must be made to the Integration Plus accounts and the accounts that must be removed, the next step is to identify the accounts that you will need to create or add to the preset accounts in the computer. Again, you need to refer to the company Chart of Accounts, Balance Sheet and Income Statement in this application to complete this step.

The Chart of Accounts Maintenance input form (Form CHA-1) that follows, shows the Assets section accounts that you will need to create for Artistic Interiors. The chart includes account titles, account numbers, account types and the option to suppress printing zero balances. It lists both postable accounts and non-postable accounts (block headings, subtotals and block totals).

The remaining accounts to be created (accounts from the Liabilities, Equity, Revenue and Expense sections, including non-postable accounts) are identified below. You should insert (create) each of these accounts on Form CHA-1 provided in Appendix A. Remember to add the type of account and whether you wish to suppress the printing of zero balances:

Bank Loan	2100
Interest Payable:Mortgage	2120
LONG TERM DEBT	2820
Mortgage Payable	2850
TOTAL LONG TERM DEBT	2900
Sales Returns & Allowances	4040
Net Sales	4060
Interest Earned	4100
Purchases Discount	4120
Sales Tax Commission	4160
Bad Debts Expense	5030
Bank Charges	5040
Cost of Goods Sold	5060
Depreciation: Buildings	5080
Depreciation: Computers	5100
Depreciation: Van	5120
Delivery Expense	5140
Hydro Expense	5160
Insurance Expense	5170
Interest: Mortgage	5190
Maintenance & Repairs	5220
Property Taxes	5230
Supplies Used:Computers	5260
Supplies Used:Office	5280
Telephone Expense	5290

NOTES:

If you wish to include the additional accounts listed on page 213 for Artistic Interiors, include these accounts on Form CHA-1 at this stage as well.

You are now ready to enter the account information into the company files.

CHART OF ACCOUNTS MAINTENANCE

Code: M = Modify   Type: H = Heading   S = Subtotal   Suppress: Y = Yes
        C = Create   R = Right   X = Current Earnings   N = No
        R = Remove   L = Left   T = Total

Code	Account Title (Maximum 26 Characters)	Account No.	Type	Sup-press
C	Allowance for Bad Debts	1220	L	Y
C	Net Receivables	1280	S	N
C	Prepaid Insurance	1300	R	Y
C	Supplies: Computer	1320	R	Y
C	Supplies: Office	1360	R	Y
C	INVENTORY ASSETS	1450	H	N
C	Accessories	1500	R	N
C	Carpets	1520	R	N
C	Chairs	1540	R	N
C	Lamps	1560	R	N
C	Sofas	1580	R	N
C	Tables	1600	R	N
C	Wall Units	1620	R	N
C	TOTAL INVENTORY ASSETS	1640	T	N
C	PLANT AND EQUIPMENT	1650	H	N
C	Buildings	1700	L	N
C	Accum Deprec: Building	1720	L	N
C	Net Buildings	1740	S	N
C	Computers	1760	L	N
C	Accum Deprec: Computers	1780	L	N
C	Net Computers	1800	S	N
C	Land	1820	R	N
C	Van	1840	L	N
C	Accum Deprec: Van	1860	L	N
C	Net Van	1880	S	N
C	TOTAL PLANT AND EQUIPMENT	1900	T	N

Modifying Integration Account Settings

Artistic Interiors has only a single bank account **Cash in Bank**. This account has to be integrated to each of the subsidiary ledgers: Payables, Receivables and Payroll. When the company files were created, ACCPAC Simply Accounting established three default bank integration accounts (see Form INT-1 on page 257). Access the Artistic Interiors files so you can modify the intregration accounts.

Modifying the Payables Integration settings

To modify the Payables Ledger integration accounts,

Click on the Payables Ledger icon in the Ledger/Journal company window to highlight it.

Choose Payables Integration Accounts from the pull-down menu under **Setup**. This option will appear only when the Payables icon is darkened or selected. The following screen appears with the Payables bank account field highlighted and ready to be changed:

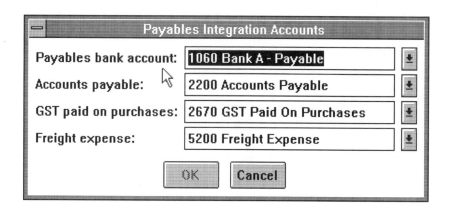

Type: 1080

Press `Tab` to enter the new account number.

Cash transactions in the Payments Journal will automatically be posted to this General Ledger account when journal entries are made. You will modify the name of the account later.

The default integration account in the General Ledger, **Bank A - Payable**, can now be removed since it is no longer integrated to any ledger. (See the section Removing Accounts in the General Ledger on page 267.)

Click on OK to save the new integration account setting and exit to the Ledger/Journal company window.

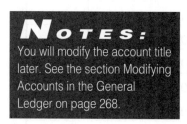

NOTES:
You will modify the account title later. See the section Modifying Accounts in the General Ledger on page 268.

Modifying the Payroll Integration Settings

Click on the Payroll Ledger icon to highlight it.

Choose Payroll Integration Accounts from the pull-down menu under **Setup** to display the following screen:

```
┌──────────────────────────────────────────────────────────────┐
│ ▭              Payroll Integration Accounts                   │
├──────────────────────────────────────────────────────────────┤
│                                                              │
│  Bank:  [1100 Bank C - Payroll ▼]   Advances: [1240 Advances Receivabl ▼] │
│                                                              │
│  ┌Payables──────────────────────────────────────────────┐   │
│  Vacation: [2300 Vacation Payable ▼]  QTax:   [2360 Quebec Income Tax ▼] │
│  UI:       [2310 UI Payable ▼]        QPP:    [2350 QPP Payable ▼]       │
│  CPP:      [2320 CPP Payable ▼]       QHIP:   [2370 QHIP Payable ▼]      │
│  Tax:      [2330 Income Tax Payable ▼] RRS-Plan: [2400 Deduction A Payabl ▼] │
│  WCB:      [2460 WCB Payable ▼]       CSB-Plan: [2420 Deduction B Payabl ▼] │
│  EHT:      [2390 EHT Payable ▼]       N/A:    [2440 Deduction C Payabl ▼] │
│  └──────────────────────────────────────────────────────┘   │
│                                                              │
│  ┌Expenses──────────────────────────────────────────────┐   │
│  Wage:  [5300 Wages ▼]                EHT:  [5360 EHT Expense ▼]  │
│  UI:    [5310 UI Expense ▼]           QPP:  [5340 QPP Expense ▼]  │
│  CPP:   [5320 CPP Expense ▼]          QHIP: [5350 QHIP Expense ▼] │
│  WCB:   [5330 WCB Expense ▼]                                     │
│  └──────────────────────────────────────────────────────┘   │
│                                                              │
│                    [  OK  ]   [ Cancel ]                      │
└──────────────────────────────────────────────────────────────┘
```

The Bank field is highlighted, ready for you to enter the new account number.

Type: 1080

Press [Tab]

Cash transactions in the Payroll Journal will automatically be posted to this General Ledger account when journal entries are made.

The default integration account in the General Ledger, **Bank C - Payroll**, can now be removed since it is no longer integrated to any other ledger. (See the section Removing Accounts in the General Ledger on page 267.)

The title of the default integration account in the General Ledger, **Bank B - Receivable**, can now be modified to **Cash in Bank.** (See the section Modifying Accounts in the General Ledger on page 268.)

Preparing Integration Accounts for Removal

Removing integration accounts in ACCPAC Simply Accounting involves two stages. The first stage is to turn the integration function off for the account from the Setup menu. This action breaks the integration link between General Ledger accounts and the subsidiary ledgers. The second stage involves removing (deleting) the account itself from the Chart of Accounts in the General Ledger. An analogous situation is turning off a circuit breaker or fuse before removing the electrical wiring or connectors.

The following integration accounts are identified on Form INT-1 for removal:

Payroll Integration Accounts
2360   Quebec Income Tax Payable
2350   QPP Payable
2370   QHIP Payable
2440   Deduction C Payable
5340   QPP Expense
5350   QHIP Expense

Receivables Integration Accounts
4200   Freight Revenue

Inventory Integration Accounts
5040   Transfer Costs

The following keystrokes will prepare the Quebec Income Tax Payable integration account for removal. You should still be in the Payroll Integration Accounts dialogue screen.

Click on the QTax field. Be sure it is highlighted.

Press the Delete key or the Backspace (<—) key to clear the entry. You have now turned off the integration function for this account.

Press ⌈Tab⌋ to advance and to highlight the next field that should be deleted. Repeat this procedure for all other integration accounts identified for removal in the Payroll Ledger.

Click on OK to save the integration account settings and return to the Ledger/Journal company window.

You should now turn off the integration function for the integration accounts identified for removal in the Receivables and Inventory ledgers. Highlight the appropriate ledger icon, then choose **Integration Accounts** for this ledger from the pull-down menu under **Settings. Do not forget to complete this step before continuing on**.

Removing Accounts in the General Ledger

The following keystrokes will remove the Quebec Income Tax Payable integration account in the General Ledger.

Open the General Ledger to display the account information for 1000, the first account in the preset Chart of Accounts.

Choose Find from the pull-down menu under **Edit**. Scroll through the list of accounts to *2360 Quebec Income Tax Payable*.

Click on 2360 Qubec Income Tax Payable to highlight it.

Click on Find to display the information for this account.

Choose Remove from the pull-down menu under **Report**. The following warning message appears, asking for confirmation before the account is removed:

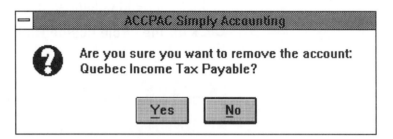

If you have chosen the wrong account, click on **No**. If you have chosen the correct account,

Click on Yes to remove the account and to display the next account on the Chart of Accounts.

You can use the **Find** option from any account displayed to repeat the procedure for other accounts marked for removal based on Form INT-1. Remember to remove accounts **1060 Bank A - Payable** and **1100 Bank C - Payroll**, which are no longer integrated.

After you have finished removing the designated accounts, you may close the account window and exit to the Ledger/Journal company window or you may continue directly to the next step, modifying accounts.

Modifying Accounts in the General Ledger

The following keystrokes will modify the **Bank B - Receivable** account in the General Ledger as directed on Form INT-1.

With the General Ledger open and any account on display,

Choose Find from the pull-down menu under **Edit.**

Click on 1080 Bank B - Receivable to highlight it.

Click on Find to display it.

Press `Tab` to advance to the Account name field and highlight it.

Type: `Cash in Bank`

You must now indicate that the balance of this account should appear in the right-hand column of the Current Assets block.

Click on the circle beside Right Column to change the account type.

CORRECTING AN ACCOUNT MODIFICATION

Highlight the field that contains the error. **Type** in the correct information.

To correct the account type, **click on** the appropriate circle.

Repeat this procedure to modify other accounts, changing the account title, type and account number according to Form INT-1.

Close the account window to return to the main Ledger/Journal company window unless you want to continue on to the next step, which also involves working in the General Ledger.

Creating New Accounts in the General Ledger

The following keystrokes will create the new account **Allowance for Bad Debts** in the General Ledger as directed on Form CHA-1.

With any General Ledger account on display,

Choose Create from the pull-down menu under **Edit** to display the following input screen:

```
┌─────────────────────────────────────────────────────────────┐
│─                        General Ledger                       │
├─────────────────────────────────────────────────────────────┤
│  E̲dit   R̲eport   Help                                        │
│                                                              │
│  Account:  ┌──────┐ ┌────────────────────────────────────┐   │
│            │      │ │ New Account                        │   │
│            └──────┘ └────────────────────────────────────┘   │
│  Balance: ┌──────────────┐   Account type:  ○ B̲lock heading  │
│           │ 0.00         │                  ○ L̲eft column    │
│           └──────────────┘                  ◉ R̲ight column   │
│  ☐ Suppress p̲rinting if balance is zero.    ○ S̲ubtotal       │
│                                             ○ Block t̲otal    │
│                                                              │
│                          ┌─────────┐                         │
│                          │ Create  │                         │
│                          └─────────┘                         │
│                                                              │
├─────────────────────────────────────────────────────────────┤
│ ←                                                        ■  → │
└─────────────────────────────────────────────────────────────┘
```

The cursor is in the Account field, ready for you to enter the account number. Remember, you cannot use duplicate account numbers.

Type: 1220

Press [Tab]

The cursor advances to the Account title field.

Type: Allowance for Bad Debts

Press [Tab]

The cursor advances to the Balance field. Ignore this field for now; you will enter the account balances in the next stage.

You need to select Left column as the Account type so that the balance for this account will appear on the left column side in the Current Assets block.

Click on the circle beside Left column

Now you must indicate whether you want to suppress this account if its balance is zero.

Click on the box beside Suppress printing if balance is zero to turn on this option.

CORRECTING NEW ACCOUNTS

Highlight the field containing the mistake. **Type** the correct information.

Correct the account type or the *Suppress printing* option by **clicking on** the appropriate circle or box.

When all the information is entered correctly, you must save your account.

Click on Create to save the new account and advance to the next blank account window.

Repeat these procedures to create the other accounts marked for creation on Form CHA-1.

Close the account window to return to the Ledger/Journal company window when you have entered all of the accounts or when you want to end your session.

You may wish to finish your session.

NOTES:
You may wish to display or print your updated Chart of Accounts at this stage to check for accuracy.

Entering Historical Account Balances

The opening historical balances for Artistic Interiors can be found in the Post-Closing Trial Balance dated September 30, 1991. There are zero balances for Income Statement accounts because the books were closed at the end of the first quarter. Do not enter balances for headings, totals or subtotals (i.e., for the non-postable accounts).

The following keystrokes will enter the historical balance for the **Cash in Bank** account as of the conversion date, September 30, 1991.

Open the General Ledger to see the first account displayed.

Choose Find from the pull-down menu under **Edit.** Scroll through the accounts. **Click on 1080 Cash in Bank** to highlight it.

Click on Find to display this account.

NOTES:
Accounts that decrease the total in a block or section (e.g., Allowance for Bad Debts, Accumulated Depreciation or Drawings) must be entered as negative numbers. These account balances are indicated with a (-) minus sign in the Balance Sheet.

Press [Tab] until you advance to the Amount field and highlight its contents.

Type: 23964.68

Press [Tab]

Correct the information if necessary by repeating the above steps.

Repeat the above procedures to enter the balances for the remaining accounts as indicated in the Post-Closing Trial Balance.

Close the account window when you want to finish your session and return to the Ledger/Journal company window.

NOTES:
You may wish to display or print your Balance Sheet, Income Statement and Trial Balance at this stage to check them for accuracy.

Preparing the Payables Ledger

Using Artistic Interiors' Vendor Information and forms VEN-1 and VEN-2 provided in Appendix A, you should complete the following steps:

1. Complete the Vendor Maintenance form, Form VEN-1. Form VEN-1 profiles the vendor. For the first vendor, the form is completed as follows:

VENDOR MAINTENANCE

PAYABLES LEDGER
Form VEN-1
Page 1 of ___

Code	C	Code : M = Modify C = Create R = Remove
Vendor Name	Artworks Inc.	
Contact	Joan Miro	
Street Address	33 Granite Rd.	
City	Toronto	
Province	Ontario	
Postal Code	M5T 1A2	Yes/No
Phone Number	476-2234	Clear Invoices when paid — N
Fax Number	476-2290	Include in GST Report — Y

2. Next you should complete the Vendor Transactions (Historical) form, Form VEN-2. Form VEN-2 records all transactions with a vendor prior to conversion. The first vendor's transactions are completed as follows:

VENDOR TRANSACTIONS (HISTORICAL)

PAYABLES LEDGER
Form VEN-2
Page 1 of ___

Code: 1 = Purchase 2 = Payment

Code	Vendor	Invoice	Date (mm-dd-yy)	Amount	Cheque
1	Artworks Inc.	AW – 121	09-16-91	500.00	
1	Artworks Inc.	AW – 130	09-18-91	500.00	

Entering Vendor Accounts

The following keystrokes will enter the information for a vendor of Artistic Interiors, **Artworks Inc.**, using Form VEN-1.

Open the Payables Ledger from the Ledger/Journal company window to display the following input screen:

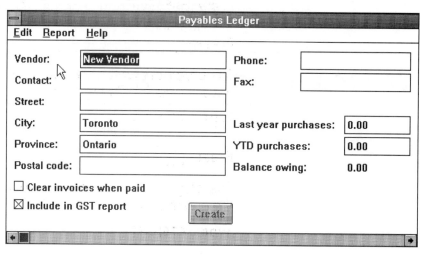

The Vendor field is highlighted, ready for you to enter information.

Type: `Artworks Inc.`

Press `Tab`

The cursor advances to the Contact field. Here you should enter the name of the person (or department) at Artworks with whom Artistic Interiors will be dealing. This information will enable a company to make enquiries more professionally and effectively. For a small business, the owner's name may appear in this field.

Type: `Joan Miro`

Press `Tab`

The cursor advances to the Street field.

Type: `33 Granite Rd.`

Press `Tab`

The cursor advances to the City field. Toronto has been entered by default because it is the city in which Artistic Interiors is located. Since it is correct, you can accept it.

Press `Tab`

The cursor advances to the Province field. Again, the default information is correct.

Press [Tab]

The cursor advances to the Postal code field.

Type: m5t1a2

Press [Tab]

The program corrects the format of the previous field, and the cursor advances to the Phone field.

Type: 4762234

Press [Tab]

The program corrects the format of the previous field, and advances the cursor to the Fax field.

Type: 4762290

Press [Tab]

Indicate that you want to retain all invoices for this vendor by leaving the box beside "Clear invoices when paid" unchecked.

Indicate that purchases from this vendor are eligible for GST input credits and should be included in GST reports by leaving this box checked. Vendors such as the Receiver General of Canada, Equity Investment Corporation and others who do not supply goods or services eligible for input tax credits, should not be included in GST reports.

The remaining fields refer to previous purchases and will be completed automatically by the program once you have entered historical information in the following section.

Correct any errors by returning to the field with the mistake, highlighting the errors and entering the correct information.

When all the information is entered correctly, you must save your vendor information.

Click on Create to save the vendor information and display a blank new vendor screen.

Repeat these procedures to enter the remaining vendors.

Entering Historical Vendor Information

The following keystrokes will enter the historical information for **Artworks Inc**. using Form VEN-2.

With the Payables Ledger open, and a vendor or new vendor form displayed,

Choose Find from the pull-down menu under **Edit**.

Click on Artworks Inc. to highlight it.

Click on Find to enter this vendor and display the following screen:

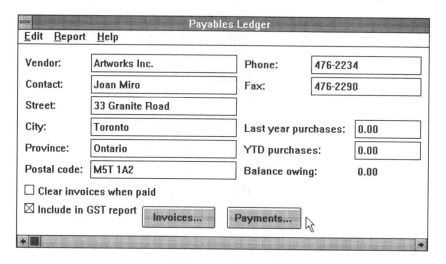

Notice that the screen now shows two additional options: *Invoices* and *Payments*. You should select the **Invoices** option in order to record the outstanding invoices. The **Payments** option could be used to record prior payments that you wanted to keep on record after entering the invoices.

Click on Invoices to see the following input screen:

Historical Invoices

Vendor:	Artworks Inc.
Number:	
Date:	9/30/91
Amount:	

Record   Done

The cursor is in the Number field so you can enter the first invoice number from Form VEN-2.

Type: AW-121

Press [Tab]

The cursor advances to the Date field. Enter the invoice date for the first invoice on Form VEN-2 to replace the default information (the using date).

Type: 09-16-91

The cursor advances to the Amount field, where you should enter the amount for the first invoice on Form VEN-2.

Type: 500

You may correct any errors by using [Tab] to return to the field with the error and highlight it. Then, enter the correct information.

When all the information is entered correctly, you must save your vendor account balance.

Click on Record to save the information and to display another blank invoice for this vendor.

Repeat these procedures to enter the remaining invoices for the vendor.

When you have recorded all outstanding invoices for a vendor,

Click on Done to return to the vendor information form. Notice that the invoices you have just entered have been added to the balance fields.

Repeat these procedures to enter historical transactions for other vendors.

Close the vendor display to return to the main Ledger/Journal company window.

Preparing the Receivables Ledger

Using Artistic Interiors' Customer Information Chart and forms CUS-1 and CUS-2 provided in Appendix A, you should complete the following steps:

1. Complete the Customer Maintenance form, Form CUS-1. Form CUS-1 profiles Artistic Interiors' customers. For the first customer, the form is completed as follows:

CUSTOMER MAINTENANCE	RECEIVABLES LEDGER
	Form CUS-1
	Page 1 of ___

Code	C	Code : **M** = Modify **C** = Create **R** = Remove	
Customer Name	Axiom Real Estate		
Contact	M.T. House		
Street Address	151 Bloor St.		
City	Toronto		
Province	Ontario		
Postal Code	M5P 1A3		
			Yes/No
Phone Number	923-4536	Clear Invoices when paid	N
Fax Number	923-4560	Include in GST Report	Y
Credit Limit	20 000	Print Statement for customer	Y

2. Next, you should complete the Customer Transactions (Historical) form, Form CUS-2. Form CUS-2 records all transactions with a customer prior to conversion. The first customer's transaction follows:

CUSTOMER TRANSACTIONS (HISTORICAL)	RECEIVABLES LEDGER
	Form CUS-2
	Page 1 of ___

Code: 1 = Sale 2 = Receipt

Code	Customer	Invoice	Date (mm-dd-yy)	Amount	Cheque
1	Axiom Real Estate	AI – 95	09-17-91	3 200.00	

Entering Customer Accounts

The following keystrokes will enter the information for **Axiom Real Estate**, a customer of Artistic Interiors, using Form CUS-1.

Open the Receivables Ledger from the Ledger/Journal company window to display the following input screen:

```
┌──────────────────────────────────────────────────────────────┐
│ ─                     Receivables Ledger                       │
├──────────────────────────────────────────────────────────────┤
│  Edit   Report   Help                                          │
│                                                                │
│  Customer:    │New Customer│      Phone:    │            │     │
│  Contact:  ⌖  │            │      Fax:      │            │     │
│  Street:      │            │      Credit limit:  │      │      │
│  City:        │Toronto     │      Last year sales: │0.00│      │
│  Province:    │Ontario     │      YTD sales:       │0.00│      │
│  Postal code: │            │      Balance owing:    0.00       │
│  ☐ Clear invoices when paid                                    │
│  ☒ Include in GST report                                       │
│  ☒ Print statements for this customer                          │
│                              │ Create │                        │
├──────────────────────────────────────────────────────────────┤
│ ← ■                                                          → │
└──────────────────────────────────────────────────────────────┘
```

The Customer field is highlighted, ready for you to enter information.

Type: `Axiom Real Estate`

Press ⌷ Tab ⌷

The cursor advances to the Contact field. Enter the name of the primary person or department who should be contacted by Artistic Interiors about any sale.

Type: `M. T. House`

Press ⌷ Tab ⌷

The cursor advances to the Street field.

Type: `151 Bloor St.`

Press ⌷ Tab ⌷

The cursor advances to the City field, where Toronto is entered by default because it is the city in which Artistic Interiors is situated. You should accept this entry.

Press ⌷ Tab ⌷

The cursor advances to the Province field. Again, the default entry is correct.

Press [Tab]

The cursor advances to the Postal code field.

Type: m5p1a3

Press [Tab]

The program corrects the format of the previous field and advances the cursor to the Phone number (Phone) field.

Type: 9234536

Press [Tab]

The program corrects the format of the previous field and advances the cursor to the Fax field. You should enter the customer's fax number (or skip this field if there is none).

Type: 9234560

Press [Tab]

The cursor is now in the Credit limit field. You should type in the amount that the customer can purchase on account before payments are required. If the customer goes beyond its credit limit, the program will issue a warning before accepting an invoice.

Type: 20000

Press [Tab]

Indicate that you want to retain all invoices by leaving the Clear invoices when paid box unchecked.

Indicate that this customer should be included in GST reports by leaving this box checked. The GST charged on sales to this customer will now automatically be included in the detailed GST reports.

Indicate that you want a statement to be printed for this customer by leaving this box checked.

You may correct any errors by returning to the field with the error, highlighting the error and entering the correct information. When all the information is entered correctly, you must save your customer information.

Balances will be included automatically once you have provided the outstanding invoice information.

Click on Create to save the information and advance to the next new customer input screen.

Repeat these procedures to enter the remaining customers.

Entering Historical Customer Information

The following keystrokes will enter the historical information for **Axiom Real Estate** using Form CUS-2.

With any customer information form displayed,

Choose Find from the pull-down menu under **Edit.**

Click on Axiom Real Estate to highlight it.

Click on Find to display the information for this customer as follows:

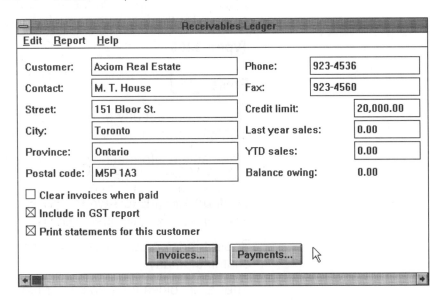

Notice that two new options are available: *Invoices* and *Payments*. You could use the *Payments* option to record any payments against previous invoices that you wanted to keep on record. However, for Artistic Interiors you will record only the outstanding invoices.

Click on Invoices to display the following input form:

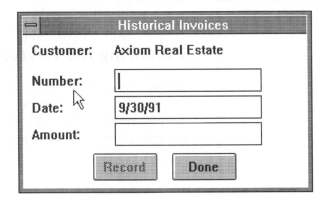

The cursor is in the Invoice (Number) field so you can enter the first invoice number on Form CUS-2.

Type: AI-95

Press Tab

The cursor advances to the Date field, ready for you to replace the using date with the date for the first invoice on Form CUS-2.

Type: 09-17-91

Press Tab

The cursor advances to the Amount field, so you can enter the amount for the first invoice on Form CUS-2.

Type: 3200

Press Tab

You may correct any errors by returning to the field with the error, highlighting the error and entering the correct, information.

When all the information is entered correctly you must save your customer account balance.

Click on Record to save the invoice and to display the next blank invoice form for this customer.

Repeat these procedures to enter the remaining invoices for this customer, if any.

After all invoices for a customer have been entered,

Click on Done to return to the customer information window. Notice that the program has added the customer's balance.

Repeat these procedures to enter historical transactions for other customers.

Close the customer display to return to the main Ledger/Journal company window.

Preparing the Payroll Ledger

Using Artistic Interiors' Employee Information Sheet, Employee Profiles, Additional Payroll Information, Historical Payroll Information and forms EMP-1 and EMP-2 provided in Appendix A, you should complete the following steps:

NOTES:
You may wish to display or print a Customer Detail Report to check it for accuracy.

1. Complete the Employee Maintenance form, Form EMP-1. Form EMP-1 provides basic personal and tax information about employees. For the first employee, the form is completed as follows:

EMPLOYEE MAINTENANCE

Code	C Code : M = Modify C = Create R = Remove
Employee Name	Sweeney, Alvin
Street Address	89 Broomfield Ave.
City	Toronto
Province	Ontario
Postal Code	M9K 1A2
Phone Number	4163930245
Soc. Ins. Number	231763172
Birth Date	12 - 14 - 45 (mm-dd-yy)
Tax Table	Ontario
Federal Claim	12050.12 dollar amount [TDI – TPD1]
Pay Periods per Year	12
WCB Rate	1.01 (%) WCB = Workers' Compensation Board
UI Eligibility	Y Y = Yes N = No
UI Premium Factor	1.4 (normally 1.4)
Vacation Pay Rate	4 (%)
Retain Vacation Pay	Y Y = Yes N = No
Regular Wage Rate	dollars / hour
Overtime Wage Rate	dollars / hour
Salary per Period	3200.00 dollars
Hire Date	07 - 01 - 91 (mm-dd-yy)

2. Next you should complete the Employee Records (Historical) form, Form EMP-2. Form EMP-2 is a record of the cumulative year-to-date earnings and deductions for employees. The first employee's record appears as follows:

EMPLOYEE RECORDS (HISTORICAL)

Employee Number	1
Regular Wages	
Overtime Wages	
Salary	9,600.00
Commissions	
Taxable Benefits	
Vacation Pay Paid Out	
CPP Contributions	195.81
QPP Contributions	N/A
UI Ins. Earnings	9,600.00
UI Premiums	187.20
Income Tax	1,993.53
Quebec Income Tax	N/A
RRS-Plan	150.00
CSB-Plan	150.00
N/A	
Net Earnings	6,923.46
Advances Paid	
Vacation Pay Owed	384.00

Entering Employee Records

The following keystrokes will enter the information for Artistic Interiors' employee, **Alvin Sweeney**, using Form EMP-1.

Open the Payroll Ledger from the Ledger/Journal company window to display the following new employee information form:

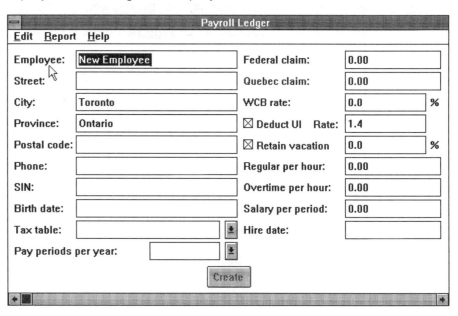

The Employee field is highlighted, ready for you to enter information.

Type: `Sweeney, Alvin`

Press [Tab]

The cursor advances to the Street field.

Type: `89 Broomfield Ave.`

Press [Tab]

The cursor advances to the City field, where you should accept the default entry.

Press [Tab]

The cursor advances to the Province field. Ontario is the correct entry.

Press [Tab]

The cursor advances to the Postal code field.

Type: `m9k1a2`

Press `Tab`

The program corrects the postal code format, and advances the cursor to the Phone field.

Type: `4163930245`

Press `Tab`

The program corrects the telephone number format, and advances the cursor to the Social Insurance Number (SIN) field.

Type: `231763172`

Press `Tab`

The cursor advances to the Birth date field. Enter the month, day and year separated by hyphens.

Type: `12-14-45`

Press `Tab`

The cursor advances to the Tax table field. A list of provinces appears on the screen when you click on the arrow beside this field.

Click on `Ontario`, the province of taxation for Artistic Interiors.

Press `Tab`

The cursor advances to the Pay periods per year field. Choose 12 from the list provided when you click on the arrow beside the field, or

Type: `12`

Press `Tab`

The cursor advances to the Federal claim field, which holds the total claim for personal tax credits.

Type: `12050.12`

Press `Tab`

The cursor skips over the QClaim field because you entered Ontario as the province of taxation. It advances to the WCB rate field. Here you should enter the applicable Workers' Compensation Board (WCB) rate.

Type: 1.01

Press [Tab]

The cursor advances to the Deduct UI field. If an employee is insurable by UI, you must leave the box checked. Then you should enter the UI contribution factor for Artistic Interiors by accepting the default 1.4.

Press [Tab]

The cursor advances to the Retain vacation field. Leave the box checked to retain vacation pay for this employee. You will turn this option off when an employee receives the vacation pay, either when taking a vacation or when leaving the company. Next, enter the vacation pay rate for this employee.

Type: 4

Press [Tab]

The cursor advances to the Regular per hour field where you could enter the regular per-hour wage for this employee. This is a salaried employee. Ignore this field.

Press [Tab]

The cursor advances to the Overtime per hour field. Enter the per-hour overtime earnings for the employee. Since Sweeney is a salaried employee, ignore this field.

Press [Tab]

The cursor advances to the Salary per period field where you can enter the salary Alvin receives every pay period.

Type: 3200

Press [Tab]

The cursor moves to the Hire date field, which should contain the date when the employee began working for Artistic.

Type: 07-01-91

Press [Tab]

You may correct any errors by returning to the field with the error, highlighting the error and entering the correct information.

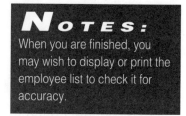
When all the information is entered correctly, you must save your employee record.

Click on Create to save the record and to move to a new blank employee information form.

Repeat these procedures to enter other employee records.

Entering Historical Employee Information

The following keystrokes will enter the historical information for **Alvin Sweeney** using Form EMP-2.

With any employee information screen displayed,

Choose Find from the pull-down menu under **Edit**.

Click on Alvin Sweeney to highlight his name.

Click on Find to display the information for this employee. Notice that a YTD (Year To Date) Totals option has been added for entering payroll information up to the conversion date.

Click on YTD Totals to display the following input screen:

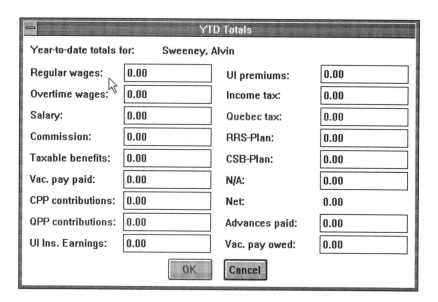

YTD Totals	
Year-to-date totals for: Sweeney, Alvin	
Regular wages: 0.00	UI premiums: 0.00
Overtime wages: 0.00	Income tax: 0.00
Salary: 0.00	Quebec tax: 0.00
Commission: 0.00	RRS-Plan: 0.00
Taxable benefits: 0.00	CSB-Plan: 0.00
Vac. pay paid: 0.00	N/A: 0.00
CPP contributions: 0.00	Net: 0.00
QPP contributions: 0.00	Advances paid: 0.00
UI Ins. Earnings: 0.00	Vac. pay owed: 0.00
OK Cancel	

Press ⌈Tab⌋ to highlight the Regular wages field. Ignore this field as well as the following Overtime wages field because Sweeney is a salaried employee.

Press [Tab]

Press [Tab]

The cursor advances to the Salary field.

Type: 9600

Press [Tab]

The cursor advances to the Commission field. You can ignore this field and the next two for this employee because they are not applicable. Sweeney is not paid a sales commission and he receives no company benefits. He has not received any vacation pay to date.

Press [Tab] until you are in the CPP contributions field.

Type: 195.81

Press [Tab]

The cursor advances to the UI insurable earnings field, ready for you to enter the total salary received to date that is UI insurable. The program will update this total every time you make payroll entries until the maximum salary on which UI is calculated has been reached. At that time, no further UI premiums will be deducted.

Type: 9600

Press [Tab]

The cursor advances to the UI premiums field.

Type: 187.20

Press [Tab]

The cursor advances to the Income tax field.

Type: 1993.53

Press [Tab]

The cursor advances to the RRS-Plan field.

Type: 150

Press [Tab]

The cursor advances to the CSB-Plan field.

Type: 150

Press Tab

The cursor advances to the N/A field. Ignore this field.

Press Tab

The cursor advances to the Advances paid field. Since Sweeney has not received any pay advances, you should skip this field.

Press Tab

The cursor advances to the Vacation pay owed field, so you can enter the amount of vacation pay owing to Sweeney.

Type: 384

Press Tab

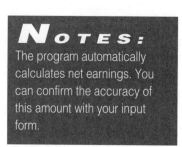

NOTES:
The program automatically calculates net earnings. You can confirm the accuracy of this amount with your input form.

You may correct any errors by returning to the field with the error, highlighting the incorrect entry and entering the correct information.

When all the information is entered correctly, you must save your employee information.

Click on OK

NOTES:
You may wish to display or print the Employee Records to check them for accuracy.

Repeat these procedures to enter historical payroll information for other employees.

Close the employee information screen to return to the Ledger/Journal company window.

Preparing the Inventory Ledger

Using Artistic Interiors' Inventory Information chart and Form INV-1 provided in Appendix A, you should complete the Inventory Maintenance form, Form INV-1. Form INV-1 records details about the inventory items on hand. The first inventory item is completed as follows:

INVENTORY MAINTENANCE

INVENTORY LEDGER
Form INV-1
Page 1 of ___

Code: **M = Modify** **C = Create** **R = Remove**

Code	Item No. Description	Asset Acct.	Rev. Acct.	Exp. Acct.	Unit of Sale	Price/ Unit (Sell)	Min. Stk. Lev.	Qty on hand	Total Value (Cost)
C	11 Accessories: Prints	1500	4020	5060	Item(s)	450.00	20	40	8 000.00

Entering Inventory Records

The following keystrokes will enter the information for Artistic Interiors' first inventory item, **Accessories:Prints**, using Form INV-1.

Open the Inventory Ledger from the Ledger/Journal company window to display the following new inventory item input screen:

```
┌─────────────────────── Inventory Ledger ───────────────────────┐
│ Edit   Report   Help                                           │
│                                                                │
│   Item:      │              New Item                          │
│                                                                │
│   Unit:      Each                                              │
│                                                                │
│   Unit price:  0.00        Quantity on hand:  0               │
│                                                                │
│   Min. level:  0           Total value:       0.00            │
│                                                                │
│   Asset:                                               ⬇       │
│                                                                │
│   Revenue:                                             ⬇       │
│                                                                │
│   Expense:                                             ⬇       │
│                                                                │
│                         Create                                 │
└────────────────────────────────────────────────────────────────┘
```

The cursor is on the Item field, where you should enter the inventory number and description for the first item.

Type: `11`

Press `Tab`

Type: `Accessories: Prints`

Press `Tab`

The cursor advances to the Unit field. Here you should enter the unit of sale for this item to replace the default entry.

Type: `Item(s)`

Press `Tab`

The cursor advances to the Unit price field. Here you should enter the selling price for this inventory item.

Type: `450`

Press `Tab`

The cursor advances to the Minimum level field. Here you should enter the minimum stock level or reorder point for this inventory item.

Type: `20`

Press `Tab`

The cursor advances to the Asset field. Here you must enter the asset account associated with the sale or purchase of this inventory item. You can review the list of asset accounts by clicking on the arrow beside the field.

Click on 1500

The cursor advances to the Revenue field. Here you must enter the revenue account that will be credited with the sale of this inventory item. Again, you can display the list of revenue accounts by using the arrow.

Click on 4020

The cursor advances to the Expense field. Here you must enter the expense account to be debited with the sale of this inventory item, normally the Cost of Goods Sold account. If a company wanted to keep track of each inventory category separately, it could set up different expense accounts for each category and enter them in this field. The appropriate expense account would then be updated automatically when an inventory item was sold. Use the arrow beside the field to display the list of available expense accounts.

Click on 5060

Press `Tab`

The cursor moves to the Quantity on hand field, ready for you to enter the opening level of inventory, the actual number of items available for sale.

Type: 40

Press `Tab`

The cursor advances to the Total value field, where you should enter the actual cost of the inventory on hand.

Type: 8000

Correct any errors by returning to the field with the mistake. Highlight the error and enter the correct information.

When all the information is entered correctly, you must save your inventory record.

Click on Create to save the record and advance to a new input screen.

Repeat these procedures to enter other inventory records.

Close the inventory information window to return to the Ledger/Journal company window.

Making the Program Ready

The last stage in setting up the accounting system involves making each ledger "Ready." You must complete this final sequence of steps before you can proceed with journalizing transactions. The status of each ledger must be changed from a Not Ready to a Ready state.

Making a Backup of the Company Files

Open the Artistic Interiors files. Place a blank formatted disk labelled Data Disk [backup] in drive A.

Choose Save As from the pull-down menu under **File**.

Type: `a:\nrartist.asc`

Click on Save

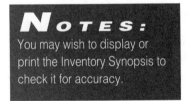

NOTES:
You may wish to display or print the Inventory Synopsis to check it for accuracy.

WARNING

Before you start making the ledgers Ready, make a backup copy of Artistic Interiors' company files. This is necessary if you decide later that you wish to change some of the historical information. Remember, once a ledger is set to Ready, you cannot change it back.

This command will create a copy of the four files for Artistic Interiors. The "NR" designates files as not ready to distinguish them from the ones you will work with to enter journal transactions. Put this backup disk in a safe place.

Changing the Status of the Ledgers

Each ledger must be set to Ready before you can begin to enter journal transactions.

Click on the General ledger icon on the Ledger/Journal company window.

Choose Set General Ready from the pull-down menu under **Setup** to display the following warning:

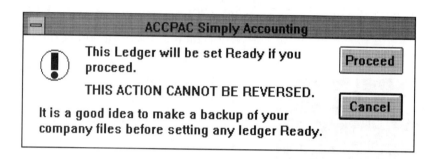

Click on OK to proceed if you have already backed up your files.

Repeat this procedure for the Payables, Receivables, Payroll and Inventory ledgers, highlighting each ledger in turn and choosing the corresponding Set Ready command.

When the program is Ready, all your ledgers are integrated and any journal entry you make henceforth will change the General Ledger accounts. Certain restrictions, outlined in the ACCPAC Simply Accounting user's guide, apply when you are operating the program in its Ready state. Please be aware of these restrictions.

The Artistic Interiors' files are now ready for you to enter transactions. Notice that the journal icons on the main Ledger/Journal company window are no longer dimmed.

Finish your session in order to save your work before entering transactions. This gives you the opportunity to advance the using date.

Exporting Reports

ACCPAC Simply Accounting allows you to export files to a specified drive and path. The files created by the program may then be used by a spreadsheet or wordprocessing program. File formats available for export purposes include Text for a wordprocessing format file, Lotus versions 1 and 2, Symphony, Excel, Supercalc and Comma separated.

Exporting files will allow you to manipulate and interpret data for reporting purposes. This process of integrating ACCPAC Simply Accounting files with other software is the final step in making the accounting process meaningful.

The following keystrokes will export the opening Balance Sheet for Artistic Interiors to a Lotus Version 2 file.

Display the Balance Sheet.

Choose Export from the pull-down menu under **File** to display the following options:

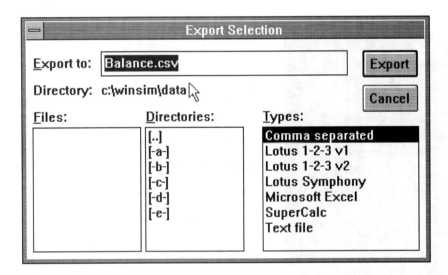

Insert a formatted disk in drive A.

Click on Lotus 1-2-3 v2 as the type for the Balance Sheet.

Click on [-a-] for drive A as the directory in which you want to store your file.

Accept the default filename, or type in the name you want for your file. Leave the extension of the filename as given by the program.

Click on Export

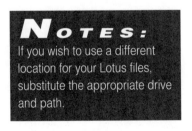

NOTES:
If you wish to use a different location for your Lotus files, substitute the appropriate drive and path.

Using Lotus on Exported Files

Finish the session using ACCPAC Simply Accounting.

Your Lotus system disk should have the default startup directory assigned to drive A. This is the directory where Lotus 1-2-3 saves your data files.

To access the Lotus system files, at the C>

Type: `cd\123`

At the C:\123> prompt,

Type: `123`

Press [Enter]

A blank 1-2-3 spreadsheet appears on your monitor. To call up the command menu,

Type: `/`

To invoke the file menu,

Type: `f`

To invoke the Retrieve command,

Type: `r`

Select the name of the file by moving the menu pointer to the file **balance.wk1** and **pressing** [Enter] , or you may type in the file name and press [Enter] .

The worksheet will contain the exported Balance Sheet for Artistic Interiors.

Instructions

Instructions for October

1. Using the Chart of Accounts and other information provided, enter the transactions for the month of October.

2. Print the following reports:

   a. the General Journal entries for the month of October;

   b. the Accounts Receivable Detail report for all customers for the month of October;

   c. the following General Ledger accounts:
      - Cash in Bank;
      - Allowance for Bad Debts;
      - Revenue from Sales;
      - Sales Returns and Allowances.

3. Export the Balance Sheet as at October 31, 1991 to a spreadsheet application.

4. Calculate the following key ratios in your spreadsheet:
   - current ratio;
   - quick ratio.

Instructions for November

1. Using the Chart of Accounts and other information provided, enter the transactions for the month of November.

2. Print the following reports:

   a. the General Journal entries for the month of November;

   b. the Accounts Payable Detail Report for all vendors for the month of November;

   c. the Employee Summary report for all employees for the pay period ending November 30, 1991;

   d. the Inventory Synopsis Report (observe and report items that have not sold well over the two-month period).

3. Export the Balance Sheet as at November 30, 1991 to a spreadsheet application.

4. Enter October balances and compare performance over the two-month period.

Instructions for December

1. Using the Chart of Accounts and other information provided, enter the transactions for the month of December.

2. Using the Additional Information Memo provided, enter the adjustments into the computer using the General Journal. Because there are no source document numbers, use the corresponding letter for the adjustment (e.g., a, b, c, etc.). The using date is December 31, 1991.

3. Print the following reports:

   a. the General Journal entries for the month of December;

   b. a Trial Balance, Balance Sheet and Income Statement on the last day of business operations (pre-adjustment phase);

   c. an Adjusted Trial Balance, Income Statement and Balance Sheet (post-adjustment phase).

4. Export the Balance Sheet and Income Statement to a spreadsheet application. Compare first and second quarter figures to assess the performance of Artistic Interiors.

5. Print T4 slips and the cumulative year-to-date 1991 payroll information for each employee.

6. Perform end-of-period closing routines. Remember to make a backup copy of your Data Disk before you proceed with these closing routines. You may wish to refer to your ACCPAC Simply Accounting user's guide for more information on closing routines.

Source Documents

Oct. 7 ☐ Purchase Invoice #AP-3401
Dated: Oct. 2/91
From Ayre Office Supplies, $60 for stationery and
other office supplies plus GST paid $4.20. Purchase
Invoice total $64.20. Terms: cash on receipt.

☐ Cheque Copy #833
Dated: Oct. 2/91
To Ayre Office Supplies, $64.20 in full payment of
account. Reference invoice #AP-3401.

☐ Purchase Invoice #DC-311
Dated: Oct. 2/91
From Direct Connections, $200 for delivery of
furniture and other goods to customers plus GST
paid $14. Purchase Invoice total $214. Terms: net
30 days.

☐ Cheque Copy #834
Dated: Oct. 3/91
To Persia Carpets, $5 600 for payment of invoices
#PC-279 and #PC-287 on account.

☐ Purchase Invoice #CCW-99
Dated: Oct. 4/91
From Custom Craft Woodworks;

two Wall Units:Office-mhg	$2 000.00
two Wall Units:Office-oak	1 800.00
Freight Expense	100.00
Goods & Services Tax (7%) Paid	273.00
Total	$4 173.00

Terms: 1/10 net 30 days.

☐ Credit Invoice #AI-C5
Dated: Oct. 4/91
To Dubhei Consulate, $100 allowance for damaged
Persian carpet.

☐ Cash Receipt #1
Dated: Oct. 5/91
From Faigaux Insurance Co., cheque #122, $2 000
in full payment of account. Reference invoice
#AI-84.

Sales Invoice #AI-100
Dated: Oct. 5/91
To Faigaux Insurance Co;

one Carpet:Kashan	$2 200.00
one Chair:Prof-lounger	250.00
one Table:7 m -oak	2 500.00
one Sofa:2 seater-leather	1 000.00
Goods and Services Tax	7%
Provincial Sales Tax	8%

Terms: 1/10 net 30 days.

Memo #1
Dated: Oct. 6/91
From owner to manager: Adjust inventory records for one Lamp:Table-brass, valued at $40, unaccounted for and considered lost or stolen. Open and charge to a new expense account called Lost Inventory (5200).

Purchase Invoice #TS-347
Dated: Oct. 6/91
From the Toronto Star, $600 for weekly advertisement to be prepaid for four months plus GST paid $42. Purchase Invoice total $642. Terms: cash on receipt. Open and charge to a new current asset account called Prepaid Advertising (1290).

Cheque Copy #835
Dated: Oct. 6/91
To the Toronto Star, $642 in full payment of account. Reference invoice #TS-347.

Oct. 14

Sales Invoice #AI-101
Dated: Oct. 8/91
To Bremner Architects Inc. (new customer);

one Carpet:Chinese Floral	$1 200.00	
one Chair:Classic-armchair	350.00	
one Wall Unit:Office-mhg	1 800.00	
one Accessory:Vase	150.00	
two Accessories:Prints	450.00	each
two Lamps:Floor-brass	120.00	each
Goods and Services Tax	7%	
Provincial Sales Tax	8%	

Terms: 1/10 net 30 days.

Memo #2
Dated Oct. 8/91
From owner to manager: All new customers will be assigned an initial credit limit of $10 000.

NOTES:

Bremner Architects Inc. (contact: Dee Sign) is located at
31 Safdie Rd.
Toronto, Ontario
M3F 1X1
Tel: 651-0987
(Fax: 651-0999)

☐ Cash Receipt #2
Dated: Oct. 9/91
From Baihai & Cello Investment Group, cheque #995, $500 in full payment of account. Reference invoice #AI-67.

Memo #3
Dated: Oct. 10/91
From owner to manager: For audit and internal control purposes:

☐ Record GST Owing (Refund) as a liability owing to the Receiver General of Canada.

☐ Record UI, CPP and Income Tax Payable accounts as a liability owing to the Receiver General of Canada.

☐ Record the EHT Payable account as a liability owing to the Treasurer of Ontario.

☐ Record the PST Payable account as a liability owing to the Treasurer of Ontario.

☐ Record the RRS-Plan and CSB-Plan as liabilities owing to the Fairchild Insurance and Equity Investment Corporations respectively.

☐ Record the WCB Payable as a liability owing to the Workers' Compensation Board.

☐ Cheque Copy #836
Dated: Oct. 10/91
To the Receiver General of Canada, $1 050 for the payment of GST for the previous month.

☐ Cheque Copy #837
Dated: Oct. 10/91
To the Receiver General of Canada, $3 125.23 for the payment of UI, CPP and Income Tax for the previous month.

☐ Cheque Copy #838
Dated: Oct. 10/91
To the Treasurer of Ontario, $274.12 for payment of EHT Payable for the previous quarter.

HINT:
Refer to the previous end-of-the-month balance for these accounts for the actual amount of each liability.

NOTES:
The liability to the provincial treasurer must be reduced by the sales tax commission earned for prompt payment of 4 % of the PST Payable account balance (4% of $3 600 = $144).

□ Cheque Copy #839
Dated: Oct. 10/91
To the Treasurer of Ontario, $3 456 for the payment of PST Payable for the previous month.

□ Cheque Copy #840
Dated: Oct. 11/91
To the Fairchild Insurance Corporation, $175 for RRS-Plan deductions withheld in previous month.

□ Cheque Copy #841
Dated: Oct. 11/91
To the Equity Investment Corp. $175 for CSB-Plan deductions withheld in previous month.

□ Cheque Copy #842
Dated: Oct. 12/91
To the Workers' Compensation Board, $255.28 for quarterly payment of WCB Payable.

□ Bank Debit Memo #TB-751
Dated: Oct. 12/91
From the Tutorial Bank, $500 for NSF cheque from Baihai & Cello Investment Group. Reference invoice #AI-67 and Cash Receipt #2.

□ Memo #4
Dated: Oct. 13/91
From the owner to manager: Write off the Baihai & Cello Investment Group account because of bankruptcy declaration by customer. Reduce this customer's credit limit to $0.00 in the Receivables Ledger. Please read NOTES on this page and Accounting Procedures on page 227.

□ Cash Receipt #3
Dated: Oct. 14/91
From Faigaux Insurance Co., cheque #231, $6 774.08 in full payment of account. Reference invoice #AI-100.

□ Negative Invoice #AI-100D
Dated: Oct. 14/91
To Faigaux Insurance Co., $68.42, discount for early payment of account. Reference invoice #AI-100 and Cash Receipt #3. Open and charge to a new expense account called Sales Discount (5240).

NOTES:
$30.50 of this amount should be charged to ITC Adjustments as the GST portion.

Oct. 21   ☐   Cheque Copy #844
Dated: Oct. 16/91
To Direct Connections, $250 in payment of invoice #DC-271.

☐   Credit Invoice #AI-C6
Dated: Oct. 16/91
To Bremner Architect Inc., $138 for the return of one Lamp:Floor-brass valued at $120, plus GST (7%) of $8.40 and PST (8%) of $9.60.

☐   Purchase Invoice #FFD-87
Dated: Oct. 16/91
From Fine Furniture Designers;

two Sofas:2 seater-leather	$1 200.00
two Sofas:3 seater-leather	2 000.00
Goods & Services Tax (7%) Paid	224.00
Total	$3 424.00

Terms: 2/10 net 30 days.

☐   Sales Invoice #AI-102
Dated: Oct. 16/91
To Axiom Real Estate;

two Carpets:Tabriz	$2 400.00	each
two Chairs:Exec-highback	550.00	each
two Lamps:Table-brass	80.00	each
two Lamps:Wall-brass	100.00	each
two Tables: 7 m -mahogany	2 800.00	each
one Wall Unit:Office-mhg.	1 800.00	
one Sofa:3 seater-leather	1 500.00	
Goods and Services Tax	7%	
Provincial Sales Tax	8%	

Terms: 1/10 net 30 days.

☐ Cheque Copy #845
Dated: Oct. 16/91
To Artworks Inc., $1 000 in full payment of account.
Reference invoices #AW-121 and #AW-130.

☐ Sales Invoice #AI-103
Dated: Oct. 17/91
To Dr. Denise Schultz (new customer);

one Sofa:3 seater-leather	$1 500.00
one Sofa:2 seater-leather	1 000.00
one Chair:Classic-highback	400.00
Goods and Services Tax	7%
Provincial Sales Tax	8%

Terms: 1/10 net 30 days.

☐ Cash Receipt #4
Dated: Oct. 17/91
From Axiom Real Estate, cheque #231, $3 200 in
payment of account. Reference invoice #AI-95.

☐ Utility Statement #BC-1211
Dated: Oct. 19/91
From Bell Canada, $50 for service charges plus
GST paid $3.50. Statement total $53.50. Terms:
cash on receipt.

☐ Cheque Copy #846
Dated: Oct. 19/91
To Bell Canada, $53.50 in full payment of account.
Reference invoice #BC-1211.

☐ Sales Invoice #AI-104
Dated: Oct. 19/91
To Dyle & Groen, Lawyers;

one Carpet:Qum	$2 100.00	
one Table:5 m-oak	1 500.00	
one Chair:Prof-swivel	300.00	
two Lamps:Table-brass	80.00	each
Goods and Services Tax	7%	
Provincial Sales Tax	8%	

Terms: 1/10 net 30 days.

Oct. 28 ☐ Realty Tax Bill #1991-3
Dated: Oct. 22/91
From the City Treasurer, $425 for quarterly property
tax assessment. Terms: EOM.

☐ Cheque Copy #847
Dated: Oct. 22/91
To City Treasurer, $425 in full payment of account.
Reference invoice #1991-3.

☐ Sales Invoice #AI-105
Dated: Oct. 23/91
To Shanti Employment Agency (new customer);
one Carpet:Kashan	$2 200.00
one Wall Unit:Office-oak	1 500.00
one Accessory:Sculpture	200.00
one Sofa:2 seater-leather	1 000.00
Goods and Services Tax	7%
Provincial Sales Tax	8%
Terms: 1/10 net 30 days.

☐ Bank Debit Memo #TB-778
Dated: Oct. 23/91
From Tutorial Bank, for $2 500. This amount
includes the reduction of principal on Mortgage
Payable of $250 and Interest on Mortgage of
$2 250.

☐ Cheque Copy #848
Dated: Oct. 25/91
To Fine Furniture Designers, $3 355.52 in payment
of account. Reference invoice #FFD-87.

☐ Negative Invoice #FFD-87D
Dated: Oct. 25/91
From Fine Furniture Designers, $68.48 discount
taken for early payment of account. Reference
invoice #FFD-87 and Cheque Copy #848.

☐ Utility Statement #TH-1080
Dated: Oct. 26/91
From Toronto Hydro, $120 for hydro services plus
GST paid $8.40. Statement total $128.40. Terms:
cash on receipt.

☐ Cheque Copy #849
Dated: Oct. 26/91
To Toronto Hydro, $128.40 in full payment of
account. Reference invoice #TH-1080.

Sales Invoice #AI-106
Dated: Oct. 26/91
To Unity Bank (new customer);

one Carpet:Isfahan	$1 400.00	
three Lamps:Spotlight-enamel	80.00	each
one Chair:Exec-armchair	500.00	
one Sofa:3 seater-fabric	750.00	
Goods and Services Tax	7%	
Provincial Sales Tax	8%	

Terms: 1/10 net 30 days.

Sales Invoice #AI-107
Dated: Oct. 28/91
To Dubhei Consulate;

one Table:5 m -oak	$1 500.00	
one Carpet:Indian Floral	1 100.00	
one Wall Unit:Office-oak	1 500.00	
two Accessories:Vases	150.00	each
Goods and Services Tax	7%	
Provincial Sales Tax	8%	

Terms: 1/10 net 30 days.

TIME SUMMARY SHEET #2
(pay period ending October 28)

Name of Employee	Week 3 Hours	Week 4 Hours	Reg. Hours	O/T Hours
Marcos Zarkos	41	41	80	2

1. Using Time Summary Sheet #2 and the Employee Information Sheet, complete payroll for the hourly employee.
2. Issue cheque #850

Purchase Invoice #EC-111
Dated: Oct. 28/91
From Excel Computer Store, $250 for computer supplies plus GST paid $17.50. Purchase Invoice total $267.50. Terms: net 30 days.

Oct. 31

Cash Receipt #5
Dated: Oct. 29/91
From Dubhei Consulate, cheque #376, $4 400 in payment of account. Reference invoices #AI-99 and #AI-C5.

☐ Bank Debit Memo #TB-879
Dated: Oct. 30/91
From Tutorial Bank for $2 400. This includes $2 100 reduction of principal on Bank Loan and $300 for Interest on Bank Loan. Insert new expense account, Interest:Bank Loan (5180).

☐ Sales Invoice #AI-108
Dated: Oct. 30/91
To Rudd Manpower Consultants (new customer);

one Table:3 m -mahogany	$1 000.00
two Carpets:Mashad	800.00 each
one Chair:Classic-highback	400.00
one Sofa:2 seater-fabric	500.00
two Accessories:Sculptures	200.00 each
Goods and Services Tax	7%
Provincial Sales Tax	8%

Terms: 1/10 net 30 days.

NOTES:
☐ Rudd Manpower Consultants (contact: Red E. Plasement) are located at
4510 Yonge Street
North York, Ontario
M8L 1P9
Tel: 619-1234
(Fax: 619-1239)

☐ ☐ Memo #5
Dated: Oct. 30/91
From manager: Using the Employee Information Sheet, prepare payroll for the salaried employees, Sweeney and Young. Issue cheques #851 and #852.

Nov. 4 ☐ Cheque Copy #853
Dated: Nov. 1/91
To Direct Connections, $214 in full payment of account. Reference invoice #DC-311.

☐ Cheque Copy #854
Dated: Nov. 2/91
To Custom Craft Woodworks, $4 173 in full payment of account. Reference invoice #CCW-99.

☐ Sales Invoice #AI-109
Dated: Nov. 3/91
To Molnar Engineers Inc. (new customer);

two Wall Units:Office-mhg	$1 800.00 each
three Chairs:Exec-highback	550.00 each
two Chairs:Exec-armchair	500.00 each
five Accessories:Prints	450.00 each
Goods and Services Tax	7%
Provincial Sales Tax	8%

Terms: 1/10 net 30 days.

NOTES:
☐ Molnar Engineers Inc. (contact: Inge Nir) is located at
367 Davisville Ave.
East York, Ontario
M6Y 1M2
Tel: 461-7651
(Fax: 461-7650)

☐ Memo #6
Dated: Nov. 3/91
From manager: Adjust inventory records for recovery of one Lamp:Table-brass valued at $40, which was shipped by mistake to a customer. This item was considered lost or stolen earlier (see Memo #1).

Nov. 11 ☐ Bank Debit Memo #TB-981
Dated: Nov. 5/91
From Tutorial Bank, $30 for bank service charges.

☐ Cash Receipt #6
Dated: Nov. 5/91
From Bremner Architect Inc., cheque #98, $5 198 in full payment of account. Reference invoices #AI-101 and #AI-C6.

☐ Sales Invoice #AI-110
Dated: Nov. 8/91
To LeFarge Realty (new customer);

one Sofa:2 seater-leather	$1 000.00	
one Sofa:3 seater-leather	1 500.00	
two Carpets:Tabriz	2 400.00	each
five Lamps:Floor-brass	120.00	each
Goods and Services Tax	7%	
Provincial Sales Tax	8%	

Terms: 1/10 net 30 days.

☐ Purchase Invoice #DC-401
Dated: Nov. 9/91
From Direct Connections, $225 for delivery of furniture and other goods to customers plus GST paid $15.75. Purchase Invoice total $240.75. Terms: net 30 days.

☐ Purchase Invoice #PC-358
Dated: Nov. 10/91
From Persia Carpets;

two Carpets:Tabriz	$3 600.00
two Carpets:Mashad	1 000.00
one Carpet:Qum	1 600.00
Freight Expense	50.00
Goods & Services Tax (7%) Paid	437.50
Total	$6 687.50

Terms: 2/10 net 30 days.

☐ Purchase Invoice #AW-229
Dated: Nov. 10/91
From Artworks Inc.;

five Accessories:Prints	$1 000.00
Goods & Services Tax (7%) Paid	70.00
Total	$1 070.00

Terms: net 30 days.

Memo #7
Dated: Nov. 11/91
Refer to the previous end-of-the-month General
Ledger account balances to:

☐☐☐☐☐ Record liabilities owing to the following agencies:
the Receiver General - GST only;
the Receiver General - UI, CPP and Income Tax
the Treasurer Of Ontario - PST only;
Fairchild Insurance Corporation - RRS-Plan only;
Equity Investment Corporation - CSB-Plan only.

☐☐☐☐☐ Remit payment to the above agencies and issue
cheques #855 to #859.

TIME SUMMARY SHEET #3
(pay period ending November 11)

Name of Employee	Week 5 Hours	Week 6 Hours	Reg. Hours	O/T Hours
☐ Marcos Zarkos*	41	41	80	2

*1. Marcos Zarkos will receive an additional $200 advance for personal reasons.
His next four paycheques will have $50 recovered each time.
2. Using Time Summary Sheet #3 and the Employee Information Sheet, complete
payroll for the hourly employee.
3. Issue Cheque #860.

NOTES:
☐ Martinez Advertising Inc.
(contact: Colm R. Shill) is
located at
345 Pape Avenue
Toronto, Ontario
M9O 1Q9
Tel: 383-1232
(Fax: 383-1235)

☐ Sales Invoice #AI-111
Dated: Nov. 11/91
To Martinez Advertising Inc. (new customer);

one Chair:Prof-swivel	$ 300.00
one Table:3 m-mahogany	1 000.00
one Carpet:Chinese Floral	1 200.00
Goods and Services Tax	7%
Provincial Sales Tax	8%

Terms: 1/10 net 30 days.

Nov. 18   ☐   Credit Invoice #AW-C13
Dated: Nov. 13/91
From Artworks Inc., $214 for return of a damaged
Accessory:Print valued at $200 plus GST (7%) of
$14. Reference invoice #AW-229.

☐   Purchase Invoice #VL-777
Dated: Nov. 14/91
From Vision Lighting Co.;

three Lamps:Floor-brass	$210.00
three Lamps:Wall-brass	180.00
three Lamps:Table-brass	120.00
Goods & Services Tax (7%) Paid	35.70
Total	$545.70

Terms: 1/10 net 30 days.

☐   Sales Invoice #AI-112
Dated: Nov. 14/91
To J. Ilyich, Accountant (new customer);

one Wall Unit:Office-oak	$1 500.00
one Carpet:Kashan	2 200.00
Goods and Services Tax	7%
Provincial Sales Tax	8%

Terms: 1/10 net 30 days.

☐   Cash Receipt #7
Dated: Nov. 15/91
From Axiom Real Estate, cheque #33, $17 434 in full
payment of account. Reference invoice #AI-102.

☐   Cash Receipt #8
Dated: Nov. 16/91
From Dr. Denise Schultz, cheque #45, $3 335 in full
payment of account. Reference invoice #AI-103.

☐   Sales Invoice #AI-113
Dated: Nov. 18/91
To Unity Bank;

two Carpets:Qum	$2 100.00	each
one Sofa:2 seater-leather	1 000.00	
one Table:5 m-oak	1 500.00	
one Chair:Classic-armchair	350.00	
two Accessories:Vases	150.00	each
Goods and Services Tax	7%	
Provincial Sales Tax	8%	

Terms: 1/10 net 30 days.

Nov. 25 ☐ Purchase Invoice #KA-901
Dated: Nov. 19/91
From Kwik-Air Inc., $220 for repairs to heating system for the building plus GST paid $15.40. Purchase Invoice total $235.40. Terms: cash on receipt.

☐ Cheque Copy #861
Dated: Nov. 19/91
To Kwik-Air Inc., $235.40 in full payment of account. Reference invoice #KA-901.

☐ Cash Receipt #9
Dated: Nov. 19/91
From Dyle & Groen, Lawyers, cheque #87, $4 669 in full payment of account. Reference invoice #AI-104.

☐ Cash Receipt #10
Dated: Nov. 20/91
From Shanti Employment Agency, cheque #123, $5 635 in full payment of account. Reference invoice #AI-105.

☐ Sales Invoice #AI-114
Dated: Nov. 21/91
To Shanti Employment Agency;

one Carpet:Isfahan	$1 400.00
one Table:7 m-oak	2 500.00
one Chair:Classic-highback	400.00
Goods and Services Tax	7%
Provincial Sales Tax	8%

Terms: 1/10 net 30 days.

☐ Bank Debit Memo #TB-1101
Dated: Nov. 23/91
From Tutorial Bank, for $2 500. This includes the reduction of principal on Mortgage Payable of $275 and Interest on Mortgage of $2 225.

☐ Sales Invoice #AI-115
Dated: Nov. 24/91
To Axiom Real Estate;

one Carpet:Indian Floral	$1 100.00
one Sofa:3 seater-fabric	750.00
one Wall Unit:Office-mhg.	1 800.00
three Accessories:Sculptures	200.00 each
Goods and Services Tax	7%
Provincial Sales Tax	8%

Terms: 1/10 net 30 days.

☐ **Utility Statement #BC-3012**
Dated: Nov. 24/91
From Bell Canada, $50 for telephone services plus GST paid $3.50. Statement total $53.50. Terms: cash on receipt.

☐ **Cheque Copy #862**
Dated: Nov. 24/91
To Bell Canada, $53.50 in full payment of account. Reference invoice #BC-3012.

☐ **Cash Receipt #11**
Dated: Nov. 24/91
From Unity Bank, cheque #1352, $3 323.50 payment of account. Reference invoice #AI-106.

☐ **Utility Statement #TH-2109**
Dated: Nov. 25/91
From Toronto Hydro, $130 for hydro services plus GST paid $9.10. Statement total $139.10. Terms: cash on receipt.

☐ **Cheque Copy #863**
Dated: Nov. 25/91
To Toronto Hydro, $139.10 in full payment of account. Reference invoice #TH-2109.

☐ **Cheque Copy #864**
Dated: Nov. 25/91
To Excel Computer Store, $267.50 in full payment of account. Reference invoice #EC-111.

TIME SUMMARY SHEET #4
(pay period ending November 25)

Name of Employee	Week 7 Hours	Week 8 Hours	Reg. Hours	O/T Hours
☐ Marcos Zarkos	40	42	80	2

1. Using Time Summary Sheet #4, and the Employee Information Sheet, complete payroll for the hourly employee. Recover $50 advanced to Marcos.
2. Issue cheque #865.

Memo #8
Dated: Nov. 25/91
From owner to manager:
Add two new employees to the employee records:
Shaina Sokol and Wendy Papierre.

□ Shaina Sokol lives at
155 Sherwood Rd.
Toronto, Ontario
M4J 1H5
Telephone: 488-2333
Social Insurance Number: 237 986 234
Date of Birth (mm-dd-yy): 08-12-57

Shaina Sokol is an experienced interior decorator. She is single and self-supporting. Shaina will work for the company on a straight commission of 40% on decorating contracts negotiated. She will not receive any company benefits. Shaina has opted out of the Registered Retirement Savings and Canada Savings Bond plans. She will be paid monthly at the same time salaried employees are paid. Vacation pay of 4% will be retained. The company will contribute a WCB rate of 1.01 for this employee.

□ Wendy Papierre lives at
439 Broadway Lanes
Toronto, Ontario
M4K 1S3
Telephone: 391-0342
Social Insurance Number: 342 123 678
Date of Birth (mm-dd-yy): 09-06-67

Wendy Papierre is a recent graduate of the Metropolitan School of Interior Design and Decorating. She will assist Shaina Sokol in completing the interior decorating contracts. She is single and self-supporting. Wendy will earn $12 per hour for regular work and $18 per hour for overtime work. Wendy has opted out of the Registered Retirement Savings and Canada Savings Bond plans. There are 26 pay periods for this employee. Vacation pay of 4% is retained. The company will contribute a WCB rate of 1.01 for this employee.

NOTES:

☐ Drigo Ristorante (contact: Derek Rigo) is located at 187 Cumberland Street Toronto, Ontario M6E 1A2 Tel: 383-1234 (Fax: 383-1239)

Nov. 30 ☐ Sales Invoice #AI-116
Dated: Nov. 27/91
To Drigo Ristorante (new customer);

one Carpet:Kashan	$2 200.00	
two: Chairs:Prof-lounger	250.00	each
three Accessories:Prints	450.00	each
Goods and Services Tax	7%	
Provincial Sales Tax	8%	

Terms: 1/10 net 30 days.

☐ Cash Receipt #12
Dated: Nov. 27/91
From Dubhei Consulate, cheque #411, $5 060 in full payment of account. Reference invoice #AI-107.

☐ Cash Receipt #13
Dated: Nov. 29/91
From Rudd Manpower Consultants, cheque #39, $4 485 in full payment of account. Reference invoice #AI-108.

☐ Bank Debit Memo #TB-1379
Dated: Nov. 30/91
From Tutorial Bank for $2 400. This includes $2 108 reduction of principal on Bank Loan and $292 for Interest on Bank Loan.

☐ ☐ Memo #9
Dated: Nov. 30/91
From manager: Using the Employee Information Sheet, prepare payroll for the salaried employees, Sweeney and Young. Issue cheques #866 and #867. Sweeney is leaving the company.

NOTES:

☐ Since Sweeney, Sales Rep. #1, is leaving the business, his paycheque should include the vacation pay withheld. Remember to modify the Payroll Ledger for this employee by turning the *Retain* option off so that vacation pay is no longer retained. Do not delete his employee records because you need them to produce T4 slips.

Dec. 2 ☐ Cash Receipt #14
Dated: Dec. 1/91
From Drigo Ristorante, cheque #151, $1 000 for 40% advance on interior decorating contract. Work to start immediately. Balance of contract due upon completion of contract estimated to last 10 days. Insert new account, Revenue from Decorating (4080).

☐ Cash Receipt #15
Dated: Dec. 2/91
From Molnar Engineers Inc., cheque #87, $9 775 in full payment of account. Reference invoice #AI-109.

NOTES:

☐ Classic Decor Inc.
(contact: Klaas Icor) is
located at
3 Berber Drive
Etobicoke, Ontario
M7U 9P3
Tel: 279-6534
(Fax: 279-3569)

☐ **Purchase Invoice #CD-111**
Dated: Dec. 2/91
From Classic Decor Inc. (new vendor), $900 for interior decorating supplies plus GST paid $63. Purchase Invoice total $963. Terms: net 30 days. Insert new account, Supplies: Decorating (1340).

Dec. 9 ☐ **Sales Invoice #AI-117**
Dated Dec. 3/91
To Dubhei Consulate;

one Wall Unit:Office-oak	$1 500.00
one Sofa:2 seater fabric	500.00
one Table:5 m-oak	1 500.00
one Carpet:Tabriz	2 400.00
Goods and Services Tax	7%
Provincial Sales Tax	8%

Terms: 1/10 net 30 days.

☐ **Cash Receipt #16**
Dated: Dec. 6/91
From Dyle & Groen, Lawyers, cheque #52, $1 600 for 40% advance on interior decorating contract. Work to start immediately upon completion of the Drigo Ristorante contract. Estimated completion time is 12 days.

☐ **Cash Receipt #17**
Dated: Dec. 7/91
From LeFarge Realty, cheque #45, $9 085 in full payment of account. Reference invoice #AI-110.

NOTES:

☐ A. Geddis (contact:
Antonia Geddis) is located
at
24 Bay Street
Toronto, Ontario
M6R 1S2
Tel: 455-0987
(Fax: 455-0988)

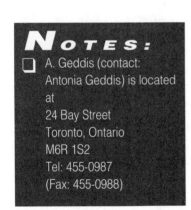

☐ **Sales Invoice #AI-118**
Dated: Dec. 7/91
To A. Geddis, Psychologist (new customer);

one Carpet:Chinese Floral	$1 200.00
one Chair:Prof-lounger	250.00
three Accessories:Prints	450.00 each
Goods and Services Tax	7%
Provincial Sales Tax	8%

Terms: 1/10 net 30 days.

☐ **Cheque Copy #868**
Dated: Dec. 8/91
To Direct Connections, $240.75 in full payment of account. Reference invoice #DC-401.

☐ Cheque Copy #869
Dated: Dec. 9/91
To Persia Carpets, $6 687.50 in full payment of
account. Reference invoice #PC-358.

☐ Cheque Copy #870
Dated: Dec. 9/91
To Artworks Inc., $856 in full payment of account.
Reference invoices #AW-229 and #AW-C13.

TIME SUMMARY SHEET #5
(pay period ending December 9)

Name of Employee	Week 9 Hours	Week 10 Hours	Reg. Hours	O/T Hours
☐ Marcos Zarkos	42	40	80	2
☐ Wendy Papierre	5	35	40	-

1. Using Time Summary Sheet #5 and the Employee Information Sheet, complete payroll for the hourly employees. Recover $50 advance from Marcos.
2. Issue cheques #871 and #872.

Dec. 16 ☐ Service Contract #1
Dated: Dec. 10/91
To Drigo Ristorante, $2 500 for interior decorating
contract completed plus GST charged $175.
Service Contract total $2 675. Terms: cash on
receipt.

☐ Cash Receipt #18
Dated: Dec. 10/91
From Drigo Ristorante, cheque #156, $1 675 for
balance owing on contract. Reference Service
Contract #1, Cash Receipt #14 or Cheque #151.

☐ Sales Invoice #AI-119
Dated Dec. 10/91
To Faigaux Insurance Co;

one Carpet:Tabriz	$2 400.00	
two Chairs:Classic-highback	400.00	each
three Accessories:Prints	450.00	each
one Table:5 m-mahogany	1 800.00	
Goods and Services Tax	7%	
Provincial Sales Tax	8%	

Terms: 1/10 net 30 days.

☐ Cash Receipt #19
Dated: Dec. 10/91
From Martinez Advertising Inc., cheque #142,
$2 875 in full payment of account. Reference
invoice #AI-111.

Memo #10
Dated: Dec. 11/91
Refer to the previous end-of-the-month General
Ledger account balances to:

☐☐☐☐☐ Record liabilities owing to the following agencies:
the Receiver General - GST only;
the Receiver General - UI, CPP and Income Tax;
the Treasurer Of Ontario - PST only;
Fairchild Insurance Corporation - RRS-Plan only;
Equity Investment Corporation - CSB-Plan only.

☐☐☐☐☐ Remit payment to the above agencies and issue
cheques #873 to #877.

☐ Purchase Invoice #DC-554
Dated: Dec. 12/91
From Direct Connections, $270 for delivery of
furniture and other goods to customers plus GST
paid $18.90. Purchase Invoice total $288.90. Terms:
net 30 days.

☐ Cheque Copy #878
Dated: Dec. 13/91
To Vision Lighting Co., $545.70 in full payment of
account. Reference invoice #VL-777.

☐ Cash Receipt #20
Dated: Dec. 16/91
From J. Ilyich, Accountant, cheque #86, $4 255 in
full payment of account. Reference invoice #AI-112.

☐ Cash Receipt #21
Dated: Dec. 16/91
From Dubhei Consulate, cheque #424, $1 200 for
40% advance on interior decorating contract. Work
to start immediately upon completion of the Dyle &
Groen, Lawyers contract. Estimated completion
time is 12 days.

Dec. 23 ☐ Sales Invoice #AI-120
Dated Dec. 17/91
To LeFarge Realty;

one Carpet:Kashan	$2 200.00	
two Sofas:3 seater leather	1 500.00	each
two Chairs:Exec-armchair	500.00	each
one Wall Unit:Office-oak	1 500.00	
three Accessories:Vases	150.00	each
Goods and Services Tax	7%	
Provincial Sales Tax	8%	

Terms: 1/10 net 30 days.

☐ Cash Receipt #22
Dated: Dec. 17/91
From Unity Bank, cheque #1512, $8 452.50 in full
payment of account. Reference invoice #AI-113.

☐ Cash Receipt #23
Dated: Dec. 18/91
From Shanti Employment Agency, cheque #156,
$4 945 in full payment of account. Reference
invoice #AI-114.

☐ Cash Receipt #24
Dated: Dec. 22/91
From Axiom Real Estate, cheque #47, $4 887.50 in
full payment of account. Reference invoice #AI-115.

☐ Service Contract #2
Dated: Dec. 22/91
To Dyle & Groen, Lawyers, $4 000 for interior
decorating contract completed plus GST charged
$280. Service Contract total $4 280. Terms: cash on
receipt.

☐ Cash Receipt #25
Dated: Dec. 22/91
From Dyle and Groen, Lawyers, cheque #56, $2 680
for balance owing on contract. Reference Service
Contract #2, Cash Receipt #16 or Cheque #52.

☐ Bank Debit Memo #TB-1509
Dated: Dec. 23/91
From Tutorial Bank, $28 for bank service charges.

☐ Bank Debit Memo #TB-1511
Dated: Dec. 23/91
From Tutorial Bank for $2 500. This includes $300 reduction of principal on Mortgage Payable and $2 200 for Interest on Mortgage.

TIME SUMMARY SHEET #6
(pay period ending December 23)

Name of Employee	Week 11 Hours	Week 12 Hours	Reg. Hours	O/T Hours
☐ Marcos Zarkos	40	42	80	2
☐ Wendy Papierre	25	25	50	-

1. Using Time Summary Sheet #6 and the Employee Information Sheet, complete payroll for the hourly employees. Recover $50 advanced to Marcos.
2. Issue cheques #879 and #880.

Dec. 30 ☐ Utility Statement #BC-5611
Dated: Dec. 24/91
From Bell Canada, $50 for service charges plus GST paid $3.50. Statement total $53.50. Terms: cash on receipt.

☐ Cheque Copy #881
Dated: Dec. 24/91
To Bell Canada, $53.50 in full payment of account. Reference invoice #BC-5611.

☐ Purchase Invoice #CD-133
Dated: Dec. 24/91
From Classic Decor Inc., $900 for interior decorating supplies plus GST paid $63. Purchase invoice total $963. Terms: net 30 days.

☐ Utility Statement #TH-2345
Dated: Dec. 24/91
From Toronto Hydro, $140 for hydro services plus GST paid $9.80. Statement total $149.80. Terms: cash on receipt.

☐ Cheque Copy #882
Dated: Dec. 24/91
To Toronto Hydro, $149.80 in full payment of account. Reference invoice #TH-2345.

☐ Sales Invoice #AI-121
Dated Dec. 29/91
To Bremner Architect Inc.;
   one Carpet:Qum $2 100.00
   one Sofa:2 seater fabric   500.00
   two Accessories:Sculptures   200.00 each
   Goods and Services Tax   7%
   Provincial Sales Tax   8%
Terms: 1/10 net 30 days.

☐ Bank Debit Memo #TB-1609
Dated: Dec. 30/91
From Tutorial Bank for $2 400. This amount includes
$2 150 reduction of principal on Bank Loan and
$250 for Interest on Bank Loan.

HINT:
Remember Interest Receivable.

☐ Bank Credit Memo #TB-1610
Dated: Dec. 30/91
From Tutorial Bank, $540 for semi-annual interest on
bank account.

☐☐ Memo #11
Dated: Dec. 30/91
From manager: Using the Employee Information
sheet, prepare payroll for salaried and
commissioned employees, Sokol and Young. Issue
cheques #883 and #884.

Additional Information Memo - Adjustments

USING DATE: December 31, 1991

1. The portion of the prepaid advertising that has expired is two months. Advertising was prepaid for four months. $150 of the prepaid insurance has expired.

2. The amount of supplies of hand based on a physical count is:

Supplies: Computer	$410.00
Supplies: Decorating	$250.00*
Supplies: Office	$396.00

   * A new account is required, 5270 Supplies Used: Decorating

3. The Dubhei Consulate contract is 50 percent complete at the end of December 31, 1991.

4. Depreciation for the fiscal period ending December 31, 1991 is:

Buildings	$1 000.00
Computers	$ 150.00
Van	$ 750.00

5. Artistic Interiors' accumulated unpaid interest on the mortgage is $555.00.

6. Estimated Allowance for Bad Debts should be increased to $1 500.00.

7. Payroll liability accrued for hourly wage employees on December 31, 1991 follows:

Marcos Zarkos	$240.00
Wendy Papierre	$150.00

   A new account is required, 2140 Accrued Payroll

Case Problems

1. Vivian Young, the senior salesperson and accountant for Artistic Interiors, made the following suggestions to Joyce Klassen, the owner, at the beginning of March, 1992:

   • Artistic Interiors should consider accepting art works on consignment from artists.
   • It should consider leasing office furniture and accessories to businesses.
   • It should include computer office furniture in inventory.
   • It should consider expanding by buying an adjoining property, which is being sold by the retiring owner. The building has an additional 500 square metres of space.

   a. How would you evaluate each of her suggestions?
   b. Present and discuss arguments in favour of her suggestions.
   c. Present and discuss arguments to discredit her suggestions.

2. The Tutorial Bank sent a bank statement to Artistic Interiors in December. The bank statement balance did not match the balance in the Cash in Bank account in the General Ledger. How would you go about preparing a bank reconciliation statement for Artistic Interiors? Explain.

3. Artistic Interiors uses the perpetual inventory method in its inventory control system. It maintains current inventory records and the accounting software flags low inventory levels. Discuss other methods of internal control that are essential for Artistic Interiors to implement for receiving, replenishing, issuing and paying for inventory.

4. Over the holiday period, one of the data disks with Artistic Interiors' accounting files was misplaced. A thorough search of the premises revealed nothing. Fortunately, Vivian Young kept a backup copy of the data disk at her home. What is the rationale for keeping file backups? Explain.

5. Suggest reasons why you might wish to incorporate the Project module for the Artistic Interiors' files. Explain the procedure you would follow in implementing the Project module.

CHAPTER ELEVEN

Manga Corporation

OBJECTIVES

Upon completion of this chapter, you will be able to:

1. *enter* corporation-related transactions in the General Journal;
2. *edit* and *review* General Journal transactions;
3. *post* transactions;
4. *display* and *print* reports.

Company Information

Company Profile

Michael Manga, an intelligent and hard-working entrepreneur, has run a very succesful business as a sole proprietor for several years. His business, Michaels, sells a line of high-quality leather goods catering mainly to an upscale female clientele. Most of the leather goods are handmade in Canada. The remainder of his inventory is imported largely from Italy and Spain. Michaels is located in the exclusive high-fashion district of Yorkville in Toronto. Having established himself, Michael was eager to operate his business on a much larger scale. His store was well known, and, according to a report from a management consultant, he could quite easily expand his present business to include leather goods for men, as well as open new locations.

In order to raise capital, Michael organized the **Manga Corporation**, which was authorized to issue 75 000 shares of no-par value common stock and 10 000 shares of $25 par value cumulative preferred stock. On January 1, 1991, Michael was issued 12 500 no-par value common stock, valued at $125 000, and 2 000 cumulative preferred stock, par value $25 for $50 000, in exchange for his business assets.

The following information is provided:

1. Chart of Accounts;
2. Share Register to record shares issued;
3. Trial Balance dated December 31, 1991;
4. Additional Information Memo.

**MANGA CORPORATION
CHART OF ACCOUNTS**

Assets
1080 Cash in Bank
1100 Visa
1200 Accounts Receivable
1220 Subscrip Rec: Common
1240 Subscrip Rec: Preferred
1300 Merchandise Inventory
1540 Building
1560 Computers & Peripherals
1580 Furniture & Fixtures
1600 Land
1620 Van
1920 Organization Costs

Liabilities
2100 Bank Loan
2200 Accounts Payable
2220 Dividends Payable
2840 Mortgage Payable

Shareholders' Equity
3020 Common Stock
3040 Preferred Stock
3100 Common Stock:Subscribed
3120 Preferred Stock:Subscribed
3180 Stk Div to be Distributed
3560 Retained Earnings
3580 Reserve for Contingencies

Revenue
4020 Revenue from Sales

Expense
5020 Cost of Goods Sold
5040 Payroll
5060 Other Expenses & Taxes

**MANGA CORPORATION
SHARE REGISTER**

| Date | Common | | Preferred | |
	Issued & Outstanding	Value	Issued & Outstanding	Value
Jan, 1	12 500	$125 000.00	2 000	$50 000.00

```
MANGA CORPORATION
TRIAL BALANCE

December 31, 1991

1080 Cash in Bank              $  15 000.00
1100 Visa                         25 000.00
1200 Accounts Receivable          25 000.00
1300 Merchandise Inventory        75 000.00
1540 Building                    125 000.00
1560 Computers & Peripherals      15 000.00
1580 Furniture & Fixtures         40 000.00
1600 Land                        275 000.00
1620 Van                          20 000.00
2100 Bank Loan                                    $  10 000.00
2200 Accounts Payable                                30 000.00
2840 Mortgage Payable                               200 000.00
3020 Common Stock                                   125 000.00
3040 Preferred Stock                                 50 000.00
3560 Retained Earnings                              150 000.00
4020 Revenue from Sales                             200 000.00
5020 Cost of Goods Sold           50 000.00
5040 Payroll                      50 000.00
5060 Other Expenses & Taxes       50 000.00
                              _____        _____
                              $ 765 000.00        $ 765 000.00
                              ============        ============
```

Additional Information Memo

The following are some of the transactions that occurred during 1991:

Jan. 8   Issued for cash 1 500 shares of common stock to investors at $10 per share.

Jan. 9   Paid $8 000 to Finn & Barr, lawyers, for legal services relating to forming the corporation.

Jan. 21   Issued to investors 500 preferred stock for cash at $25 per share.

Feb. 1   Received subscriptions for 5 000 no-par value common shares at $12 per share. Received subscriptions for 500 cumulative preferred shares at $25 per share.

Feb. 3   Received first instalment of $30 000 from common stock subscribers. Received first instalment of $6 250 from preferred stock subscribers.

Feb. 10   Collected full amount owing for subscriptions from common and preferred stock subscribers. Issued stock certificates.

Mar. 11   Acquired adjoining land for expansion of store in exchange for $50 000 cash, 20 000 no-par value common shares at $12 per share and 2 000 cumulative preferred shares at $25 per share. Work on expansion to start at the end of the month. Project estimated to last five months.

June 10   Declared a cash dividend of $5 per share on preferred stock still outstanding, payable on July 15 to shareholders of record June 30.

July 15   Paid the dividend declared on June 10.

Aug. 15   Issued for cash 16 000 common stock to investors for $12 per share. Issued for cash 1 000 preferred stock to investors at $25 per share.

Sep. 12   Paid $175 000 for completed building expansion .

Dec. 10   Declared a cash dividend of $5 per share on preferred stock still outstanding, payable on January 15, 1992 to shareholders of record December 31, 1991.

Dec. 10   Declared a 5% stock dividend on the outstanding common shares, consisting of 2 750 shares of no-par value common stock to be distributed on January 15, 1992 to common shareholders of record on December 31, 1991. Market price $12 per share.

Dec. 28   Appropriated $10 000 reserve for contingencies.

Instructions

NOTES:

You will enter transactions involving capital stock and related transactions that were omitted during 1991. All other transactions relating to this company are already included in the year-end balances provided. The Retained Earnings account is provided so that you can enter transactions involving cash dividends, stock dividends and reserves.

1. Using the Chart of Accounts and additional information provided, record the transactions for 1991 in the General Journal. There are 14 transactions for this accounting simulation.

2. The **using date** is December 31, 1991. Use the letters a, b, c, etc. as the source document number.

3. Print the following reports:
   a. the General Journal entries from January 8 to December 28, 1991;
   b. the Balance Sheet as at December 31, 1991.

Case Problem

Harold Hynes owns 1 000 shares of no-par value common stock of Caprice Corporation. He has been receiving a cash dividend on his investment over the past two years. In the current year, the corporation has declared a stock dividend.

1. What effect does a cash dividend have on the assets and shareholders' equity of a corporation?

2. What are the reasons for issuing a stock dividend instead of a cash dividend?

3. What effect does a stock dividend have on the assets and shareholders' equity of a corporation?

4. What effect will the stock dividend have on Harold Hynes' portfolio?

5. What effect will the stock dividend have on the market value of the shares?

CHAPTER TWELVE

Carefree Carpets

OBJECTIVE

Upon completion of this chapter, you will be able to:
- *enter* depreciation on plant- and equipment-related transactions in the General Journal.

Company Information

Company Profile

Carefree Carpets, a wholesale and retail carpet business, is located in Winnipeg, Manitoba. The business is owned and operated by Amos Scallato. The company earns its income as a wholesaler and distributor of industrial carpets to various retailers; it also sells directly to businesses that install industrial carpets in office buildings and department stores. The company started operations on April 1, 1990 and has just completed its first year of operations.

At the end of the fiscal year, the company wishes to calculate depreciation on plant and equipment. It prefers to use the **straight-line** method of calculating depreciation, but it knows that for tax purposes it must use the **capital cost allowance** method. The following information allows you to calculate and record depreciation on plant and equipment using ACCPAC Simply Accounting:

1. Chart of Accounts;
2. Trial Balance dated March 30, 1991;
3. Additional Information Memo.

**CAREFREE CARPETS
CHART OF ACCOUNTS**

Assets
1080 Cash in Bank
1200 Accounts Receivable
1260 Inventory
1550 Delivery Trucks
1560 Accum Deprec: Trucks
1600 Escalator Belt
1610 Accum Deprec: Belt
1630 Land
1650 Loading Platform
1660 Accum Deprec: Platform
1700 Forklift Vehicles
1710 Accum Deprec: Vehicles
1750 Strapping Machine
1760 Accum Deprec: Machine
1800 Warehouse
1810 Accum Deprec: Warehouse

Liabilities
2100 Bank Loan
2200 Accounts Payable
2450 Mortgage Payable

Owner's Equity
3560 A. Scallato, Capital
3600 Net Income

Revenue
4020 Revenue from Sales

Expense
5020 Cost of Goods Sold
5040 Depreciation: Trucks
5060 Depreciation: Belt
5080 Depreciation: Platform
5100 Depreciation: Vehicles
5120 Depreciation: Machine
5140 Depreciation: Warehouse
5160 General Expense
5180 Interest Expense
5200 Wages & Salaries
5220 Utilities

**CAREFREE CARPETS
TRIAL BALANCE**

March 30, 1991

Account	Debit	Credit
1080 Cash in Bank	$ 15 000.00	
1200 Accounts Receivable	20 000.00	
1260 Inventory	120 000.00	
1550 Delivery Trucks	48 000.00	
1600 Escaltor Belt	10 000.00	
1630 Land	50 000.00	
1650 Loading Platform	3 500.00	
1700 Forklift Vehicles	22 000.00	
1750 Strapping Machine	5 500.00	
1800 Warehouse	250 000.00	
2100 Bank Loan		$ 25 000.00
2200 Accounts Payable		50 000.00
2450 Mortgage Payable		220 000.00
3560 A. Scallato, Capital		160 000.00
4020 Revenue from Sales		420 000.00
5020 Cost of Goods Sold	170 000.00	
5160 General Expense	1 000.00	
5180 Interest Expense	25 000.00	
5200 Wages & Salaries	130 000.00	
5220 Utilities	5 000.00	
	$ 875 000.00	$ 875 000.00

Additional Information Memo

1. Carefree Carpets purchased the delivery trucks at a cost of $24 000 each on April 1, 1990. It is estimated that the trucks will have a useful life of five years and a disposal value of $8 000. The capital cost allowance rate for this class of fixed assets for tax purposes is 30 percent.

2. The escalator belt was installed on July 1, 1990 at a cost of $10 000. It was intended to improve shipping and receiving in the warehouse. The escalator belt is estimated to last for six years with an expected disposal value of $1 000. The capital cost allowance rate for this class of fixed assets for tax purposes is 20 percent.

3. The hydraulic loading platform was valued at $3 500 when the plant and equipment were purchased on April 1, 1990. It was estimated to have two years of useful life, with a scrap value of $500. Installation of a new, technologically advanced platform to improve work capacity has been considered for the new year. The capital cost allowance rate for this class of fixed assets for tax purposes is 20 percent.

4. Carefree Carpets purchased the forklift vehicles at a cost of $11 000 each on April 1, 1990. It is estimated that the vehicles will have a useful life of five years and a disposal value of $2 000. The capital cost allowance rate for this class of fixed assets for tax purposes is 30 percent.

5. The electronic strapping machine, valued at $5 500, was purchased on October 1, 1990 to replace hand-held manual machines. It is estimated that the strapping machine will have a useful life of five years and a disposal value of $500. The capital cost allowance rate for this class of fixed assets for tax purposes is 20 percent.

6. The warehouse purchased on April 1, 1990 is estimated to have a useful life of 30 years and a salvage value of $10 000. The capital cost allowance rate for this class of fixed assets for tax purposes is five percent.

Instructions

1. You will need two copies of your ACCPAC Simply Accounting data files for Carefree Carpets to complete transactions using two methods of depreciation. You should make an extra copy of the Carefree Carpets accounting files before you enter any transactions. Use the **Save As** command from the pull-down menu under **File** and rename the copy of the data files (e.g., **carecca.asc**).

2. Using the Chart of Accounts, Trial Balance and Additional Information Memo provided, calculate the accumulated depreciation and depreciation expense on the plant and equipment. Record the necessary General Journal entries. The using date is March 31, 1991. Use the following two methods of depreciation:

   - the straight-line method;
   - the capital cost allowance method for income tax purposes.

3. Print the following reports for each method used:
   a. the General Journal for the depreciation entries;
   b. a Trial Balance dated March 31, 1991;
   c. an Income Statement for the period ending March 31, 1991;
   d. a Balance Sheet as at March 31, 1991.

Case Problems

1. Carefree Carpets intends to purchase batteries for the forklift vehicles. Will this purchase increase the value of the fixed asset? Explain your answer.

2. At the end of June 1991, Carefree Carpets decides to install a new loading platform costing $10 000, estimated to last for six years with a scrap value of $1 000. If the company uses the straight-line method of depreciation, what accounting procedures would you follow:

   a. to dispose of the old loading platform at scrap value?
   b. to insert the new loading platform in the records?

3. Show the depreciation in chart form for the fixed assets at the end of Year 2 and Year 3, using the straight-line and capital cost allowance methods. Take into consideration case problem #2 above in your calculations.

CHAPTER THIRTEEN

Frame-Around Manufacturing Company

Company Information

Company Profile

The Frame-Around Manufacturing Company is located in Montreal. It started operations on July 1, 1991 and will produce a single product — picture frames. The raw materials to manufacture the picture frames include frames made of wood and metal; glass; matting; and assembly parts, such as nails, screws and wire. These raw materials are purchased from various dealers throughout the province.

The manufacturing process involves three stages:

1. cutting frames, glass and matting into various sizes and shapes;
2. assembling all the parts into picture frame units;
3. packaging the units for shipment to wholesalers.

The company already has a cost accounting system in place. Employees gather data relating to the manufacturing process on a regular basis. For example, requisitions of materials and supplies for the production of picture frames are recorded on a Materials Issued and Returned form. At the end of a production cycle, the summary of all the materials used in the manufacturing process can be applied to the Work in Progress account (sometimes referred to as the Work in Process or the Goods in Process account).

The cost accounting system is also designed to gather information about labour costs — both direct and indirect labour involved in the production process. The Labour Cost Summary form is used to sort and summarize the direct labour costs involved so that these costs can also be applied to the Work in Progress account.

Finally, all factory overhead costs involved in the production process (such as indirect materials, indirect labour, depreciation and other occupancy costs) are summarized on the Factory Overhead Summary form to be applied to the Work in Progress account.

The business started operations on July 1, 1991 and has completed one week of production. The following information is provided:

1. Chart of Accounts;
2. Trial Balance dated July 7, 1991;
3. Special Information;
4. Additional Transaction Information.

FRAME-AROUND MANUFACTURING COMPANY
CHART OF ACCOUNTS

Assets
1080 Cash in Bank
1200 Accounts Receivable
1220 Factory Supplies
1320 Raw Materials
1340 Work in Progress
1360 Finished Goods
1500 Factory
1520 Accum Deprec:Factory
1600 Machinery
1620 Accum Deprec:Machinery

Liabilities
2100 Bank Loan
2200 Accounts Payable
2840 Mortgage Payable

Shareholders' Equity
3200 Capital Stock
3600 Current Earnings

Revenue
4020 General Revenue

Expense

Manufacturing Costs
5020 Direct Labour
5040 Factory Overhead

Operating Expenses
5100 Cost of Goods Sold

Admin & Selling Expenses
5200 Admin - Salaries
5220 Selling - Salaries
5240 General Expenses

FRAME-AROUND MANUFACTURING COMPANY
TRIAL BALANCE

July 7, 1991

1080 Cash in Bank	$ 15 000.00	
1220 Factory Supplies	2 000.00	
1320 Raw Materials	50 000.00	
1500 Factory	420 000.00	
1520 Accum Deprec:Factory		$ 300.00
1600 Machinery	40 000.00	
1620 Accum Deprec:Machinery		200.00
2100 Bank Loan		4 500.00
2200 Accounts Payable		20 000.00
2840 Mortgage Payable		375 000.00
3200 Capital Stock		180 000.00
5020 Direct Labour	25 000.00	
5040 Factory Overhead	25 000.00	
5200 Admin-Salaries	1 400.00	
5220 Selling-Salaries	1 400.00	
5240 General Expenses	200.00	
	$580 000.00	$580 000.00

Special Information

The Chart of Accounts for Frame-Around include accounts that will allow you to enter end-of-production transactions using the basic cost accounting principles you have learned. Specifically you will be able to:

1. apply or charge the raw materials inventory used to the Work in Progress inventory account;
2. apply or charge direct labour costs to the Work in Progress inventory account;
3. apply or charge factory overhead to the Work in Progress inventory account;
4. transfer the value of the completed product to the Finished Goods inventory account from the Work in Progress inventory account;
5. calculate the cost price per unit of the Finished Goods inventory;
6. record the sale of finished goods;
7. calculate the cost of goods sold.

The two accounts provided under Manufacturing Costs are:

- Direct Labour, obtained from the Labour Cost Summary Form;
- Factory Overhead, obtained from the Factory Overhead Summary Form.

NOTES:
Please read the Special Information carefully before proceeding.

When you display your Income Statement or Balance Sheet prior to recording your transactions, notice that the Current Earnings account will initially have a negative balance. This negative balance reflects the nature of most manufacturing businesses - they must incur costs to produce finished goods before they can make a profit by selling those goods.

Additional Transaction Information

NOTES:
The using date and source document date is July 7, 1991.

1. The Materials Issued and Returned Summary form MIR-1 for this week indicated that $25 000 worth of raw materials were requested, issued and used in production. Apply these material costs to the Work in Progress account.

2. The Labour Cost Summary form LC-1 for this week indicated that $25 000 in direct labour costs are to be applied to the Work in Progress account.

3. The Factory Overhead Summary form FO-1 for this week indicated that $25 000 in factory overhead costs are to be applied to the Work in Progress account.

4. Finished goods valued at $60 000 were completed. The Cost of Production Summary form PC-1 indicates that 20 000 units were produced and ready for shipment.

5. Sales invoice #1 shows that 10 000 units were sold on account for $60 000. Cash receipt #1 indicates that 5 000 units were sold for $30 000 cash. Calculate and charge the units sold to the Cost of Goods Sold account, and reduce the Finished Goods inventory account.

6. Additional raw materials for $30 000 were purchased on account for the next stage of production (purchase invoice #1239).

Instructions

1. Enter transactions using the General Journal in ACCPAC Simply Accounting.

2. After completing your entries, print the following reports:
   a. General Journal (July 7/1991 - July 7/1991);
   b. the Income Statement for the week ending July 7, 1991;
   c. the Balance Sheet as at July 7, 1991;
   d. the Trial Balance on July 7, 1991.

Case Problem

The Refit Parts Manufacturing Company manufactures parts for automobiles. It uses hundreds of different parts and tools as raw materials in the manufacturing of component parts for automobiles. The company has observed the following illegal activities during the manufacturing process:

1. employees requesting materials that are not used in the production process with the Materials Requisition Form;

2. employees adding additional hours to the Labour Cost Summary by getting their coworkers to punch time cards for them when they haven't performed the work;

3. a clerk in the raw materials storeroom inflating the quantities issued;

4. employees deliberately entering the wrong quantities issued on the computer terminal.

What controls are necessary to protect against each of these illegal activities in the manufacturing process?

CHAPTER FOURTEEN

Pacific Chalet

OBJECTIVES

Upon completion of this chapter, you will be able to:

1. *plan* and *design* an accounting system for a small business;
2. *prepare* a conversion procedure from manual records;
3. *understand* the objectives of a computerized accounting system;
4. *create* company files;
5. *set up* company accounts using set-up input forms;
6. *make* the accounting system ready for operation;
7. *enter* accounting transactions from realistic source documents;
8. *display* and *print* reports;
9. *analyse* and *interpret* case studies;
10. *develop* further group interpersonal skills;
11. *develop* further oral and written skills.

Company Information

Company Profile

Pacific Chalet is a 33-room winter resort hotel owned and operated by Aldo Morson. The resort is located at 23 Mountainside Drive, Prince Rupert, British Columbia. The employer number issued to it by Revenue Canada is PCA369875, and its GST registration number is R345234556.

The business earns its revenue by renting out its double rooms to individuals, families, ski clubs and other groups. Most of the guests who stay at the Chalet ski at one of the many nearby ski sites. Because it is so convenient, ski clubs often choose to stay at Pacific Chalet. Three clubs, Harbour, Nordic and CanSki, have already made reservations for their members. Pacific Chalet offers group rates to these clubs and has set up accounts for them. They are expected to settle their accounts within ten days. Individuals who rent the rooms pay in cash at the end of their stay.

The Chalet does not have a restaurant, but it does have several vending machines that serve hot and cold food. These vending machines are owned by Quality Caterers, which maintains the machines and stocks them regularly with fresh food. Quality Caterers pays a commission to Pacific Chalet for the use of its premises.

Other services required by the Chalet are contracted out to local firms. FreshKleen Room Services does the housekeeping, changes and launders the linen and cleans the rooms, hallways and lobby. It bills the Chalet weekly for this work. Snow removal and general outdoor winter maintenance are provided by Ski-Mountain Services, which bills the Chalet biweekly according to their annually contracted rate.

Morson purchased the Chalet on December 1, 1990 and will be welcoming his first guests on January 1, 1991. He has assumed the assets and liabilities of the previous owner. Most of the assets were in good condition and could be used without any major changes, but he needed to purchase some additional linen and furniture.

During December, Morson hired Tanya Mishibata and Gregory Tyndal to work at the desk. They will take turns working the day and evening shifts. Both employees have previous hotel management experience and will begin work on January 1, 1991. Aldo Morson and his family live at Pacific Chalet and are therefore available to handle emergencies and to fill in when neither Greg nor Tanya is at work.

Morson, a graduate of Eastern High School of Commerce's accounting program, is planning to use the ACCPAC Simply Accounting program. He saw it demonstrated by Mary Watson at a business conference workshop in Vancouver. On December 31, 1990, he plans to convert and set up his accounts on the computer so that he can begin to use them on Janaury 1, 1991. The Trial Balance reflects the state of his business on December 31, 1990. Because of his accounting expertise, he has also prepared the additional information he will need to set up the computer accounts. This information includes a complete chart of the accounts that he will need for his daily business operation, as well as a list of customers (ski clubs) and vendors with whom he has contracts. He has also gathered the necessary employee information to enter into ACCPAC Simply Accounting.

PACIFIC CHALET
CHART OF ACCOUNTS

Assets
Cash in Bank
Accounts Receivable
Bedding & Towels
Supplies: Computer
Supplies: Office
Supplies: Washroom
Chalet
Accum Deprec: Chalet
Computers & Peripherals
Accum Deprec: Comp & Peri
Furniture & Fixtures
Accum Deprec: Furn & Fix
Land

Liabilities
Bank Loan
Accounts Payable
Vacation Payable
UI Payable
CPP Payable
Income Tax Payable
Medical Payable
WCB Payable
GST Charged on Services
GST Paid on Purchases
PST Payable
Mortgage Payable

Owner's Equity
A. Morson, Capital
A. Morson, Drawings

Revenue
Revenue from Accomodation
Commission from Caterers

Expense
Depreciation: Chalet
Depreciation: Comp & Peri
Depreciation: Furn & Fix
General Expense
Hydro Expense
Interest: Bank Loan
Maintenance: Chalet
Maintenance: Grounds
Postage
Telephone Expense
Wages Expense
UI Expense
CPP Expense
WCB Expense

```
PACIFIC CHALET
TRIAL BALANCE

December 31, 1990

Cash in Bank                $  25 300.00
Bedding & Towels               3 200.00
Supplies: Computer               160.00
Supplies: Office                 240.00
Supplies: Washroom               300.00
Chalet                       225 000.00
Computers & Peripherals        5 000.00
Furniture & Fixtures          10 000.00
Land                          75 000.00
Bank Loan                                   $  12 000.00
Accounts Payable                               2 200.00
Mortgage Payable                             200 000.00
A. Morson, Capital                           130 000.00

                             $ 344 200.00   $ 344 200.00
```

PACIFIC CHALET
CUSTOMER INFORMATION

Customer Name (Contact)	Address	Telephone
CanSki School (John Wood)	500 Sloping Way Burnaby British Columbia V5T 5H8	(604)659-3489
Harbour Ski Club (Jane Martin)	155 High Street Vancouver British Columbia V6Y 4R5	(604)477-7421
Nordic Alpine Ski Club (Freda Karlson)	888 Ridge Road Prince George British Columbia V9E 2N2	(604)774-7410

PACIFIC CHALET
VENDOR INFORMATION

Vendor Name (Contact)	Address & Telephone	Invoice Date	Invoice Number	Outstanding Balance
Blue Mountain Furniture Co. (Cherri Pine)	65 Maple Blvd. Penticton British Columbia V3P 9J9 Tel: 452-8866	Dec. 15/90	BF-106	$1 450.00
FreshKleen Room Services (Mr. Kleen)	150 Bleech Ave. Prince Rupert British Columbia V8T 4B3 Tel: 692-3348			
LinenHouse Wholesalers (Tau El)	444 Sheeting Rd. Prince Rupert British Columbia V8A 1C3 Tel: 693-4291	Dec. 21/90	LW-321	$ 750.00
Ski-Mountain Services (N. O. Snow)	290 Ploughing Cr. Prince Rupert British Columbia V8I 7G1 Tel: 692-6111			

PACIFIC CHALET
EMPLOYEE INFORMATION

Employee Number:	1	2
Position:	Assistant	Assistant
Social Insurance Number:	139 988 661	404 622 233
Employee Name:	Tanya Mishibata	Gregory Tyndal
Address & Telephone:	34 Clark Street Prince Rupert British Columbia V8Y 5R5 604-493-6245	551 Manual Dr. Prince Rupert British Columbia V8F 1E3 604-886-8810
Date of Birth (dd-mm-yy):	21-2-65	1-2-66
Tax Exemptions: **(TD1-1991)** Basic Personal	$6 280.00	$6 280.00
Total Exemptions	$6 280.00	$6 280.00
Net Claim	$6 280.00	$6 280.00
Employee Earnings: Regular Wage Rate Overtime Wage Rate Vacation Pay	$18.00/hour $27.00/hour 4% (retained)	$18.00/hour $27.00/hour 4% (retained)
Employee Deductions: Medical CPP UI Income Tax	$13.50/period * * *	$13.50/period * * *
Pay Periods	26	26

* Calculations built into ACCPAC Simply Accounting Program

Additional Payroll Information

The employer's contributions include:

- CPP contributions equal to employee contributions;
- UI factor of 1.4;
- WCB rate of 1.02.

Instructions

1. Using the set-up input forms provided in Appendix A and all of the information presented in this application, set up the company accounts for Pacific Chalet in ACCPAC Simply Accounting using the following steps:

   a. Create company files on your data directory or disk for storing the company records using the Integration Plus starter files.
   b. Enter the company information.
   c. Enter names and printer information.
   d. Prepare the settings by changing the default settings as necessary.
   e. Organize the Balance Sheet and Income Statement accounts.
   f. Turn off the integration function for accounts not required.
   g. Modify, create and remove accounts to correspond to your Balance Sheet and Income Statement.
   h. Enter customer, vendor and employee information.
   i. Enter historical balances in all ledgers.
   j. Back up your files.
   k. Set ledgers to ready.
   l. Finish your session.

2. Using the Chart of Accounts and other information provided, record entries for the source documents using ACCPAC Simply Accounting.

3. After you have completed your entries, print the following reports:

   - General Journal entries from January 1 to January 15, 1991;
   - the Accounts Payable Detail Report for all vendors on January 15, 1991;
   - the Accounts Receivable Detail Report for all customers on January 15, 1991;
   - the Payroll Report for all employees for the pay period ending January 14, 1991;
   - the Income Statement for the period ending January 15, 1991;
   - the Balance Sheet as at January 15, 1991.

Source Documents

British Columbia Hydro
23 Power Avenue
Prince Rupert, B.C.
V7N 3T3

No: ___2013 09567___1_

Invoice No : ___121456___

BC HYDRO

Months	Reading	Description	Net Amount	
1	63538	Commercial consumption 5000 KWH	300	00
1		Flat Rate Energy Charge – Water Heaters	100	00
1		Water Heater Rental 5 Tank (s)	50	00
			$450	00

AVERAGE DAILY K.W.h. CONSUMPTION

Same period Last Year	203	This Bill	167

DUE DATE

Jan.10/91

Invoice Date: ___01-01-91___

CUSTOMER COPY

SERVICE NAME AND ADDRESS
Pacific Chalet
23 Mountainside Drive
Prince Rupert, B.C.
V8J 1N3

LinenHouse Wholesalers
444 Sheeting Road Prince Rupert, B.C. V8A 1C3   693-4291
"WHERE STYLE AND QUALITY COUNT"

NOM NAME:	Pacific Chalet		DATE:	January 1, 19 91

ADRESSE ADDRESS: 23 Mountainside Drive, Prince Rupert

LIVREZ À DELIVER TO: as above   PAR VIA: Truck

Qte Qty	Stock #	Description	Prix Price		Montant Amount	
36	762	poly/cotton sheets 81 x 108	20	00	720	00
72	863	poly/cotton pillow covers	3	00	216	00
					936	00
		Taxe Tax TPS GST			65	52
		Taxe Tax PST			56	16
		TOTAL			1057	68

Terms : net 15 days

Clerk A.J.	Payment Method	Cash	Cheque	On Account ✓

Customer Copy	N0. LW-407	Signature *A. Morson*

Pacific Chalet

23 Mountainside Drive
Prince Rupert, B.C.
V8J 1N3
1-800-693-1121 (604) 693-1233

Aldo Morson		No : 010

January 2,   19 91

Pay to the order of   Canada Post $ 42.80

----------Forty-two----------   80 /100 Dollars

Bank of British Columbia
95 Bankers road
Prince Rupert, B.C.
V8R 3S4

A. Morson

⑆ 50948⑈2 ⑆010⑉

Postage stamps $40. GST Paid $2.80   No : 010
Canada Post   Jan. 2, 19 91

Pacific Chalet
23 Mountainside Drive
Prince Rupert, B.C.
V8J 1N3
1-800-693-1121   (604) 693-1233

NO. PC - 0001

GUEST STATEMENT

CaSki School
500 Sloping Way
Burnaby, B.C.
V5T 5H8

CHECK IN _____ January 1 _____

CHECK OUT _____ January 3 _____

ROOM(S) _____ 8 _____

DATE	TRANSACTION	DAILY ROOM RATE		CHARGES	
01-03-91	Room Charges Room # 1, 2, 3, 4, 5, 6, 7, 8 2 nights Less: Group discount (10%)	30	00	480	00
				48	00
				432	00

Signature:	*J. Wood*		TERMS : Net 10 Days		GST	30	24
Clerk	Payment Method	Cash	Cheque	On Account	PST	34	56
T.M.				✓	BALANCE	496	80

FILE COPY

Pacific Chalet
23 Mountainside Drive
Prince Rupert, B.C.
V8J 1N3
1-800-693-1121 (604) 693-1233

NO. PC - 0002

GUEST STATEMENT

Henry Groen
68 Grover Road,
Vancouver, B.C.
V5J 1Q3

CHECK IN   January 1

CHECK OUT   January 4

ROOM(S)   2

DATE	TRANSACTION	DAILY ROOM RATE		CHARGES	
01-04-91	Room Charges Room # 30, 31 3 nights	30	00	180	00
				48	00
				180	00

Signature:	*H. Groen*		TERMS : Net 10 Days		GST	12	60
Clerk	Payment	Cash	Cheque	On Account	PST	14	40
G.T.	Method	✓			BALANCE	207	00

FILE COPY

Pacific Chalet
23 Mountainside Drive
Prince Rupert, B.C.
V8J 1N3
1-800-693-1121   (604) 693-1233

| NO. PC - 0003 |

GUEST STATEMENT

Harbour Ski Club
155 High Street
Vancouver, B.C.
V6Y 4R5

CHECK IN   January 1

CHECK OUT   January 4

ROOM(S)   9

DATE	TRANSACTION	DAILY ROOM RATE		CHARGES	
01-04-91	Room Charges Room # 21, 22, 23, 24, 25, 26, 27, 28, 29 3 nights Less: (Group discount (10%)	30	00	810 81	00 00
				729	00

Signature:	*J Martin*		TERMS : Net 10 Days	GST	51	03
Clerk	Payment Method	Cash	Cheque	On Account	PST	58	32
T.M.				✓	BALANCE	838	35

FILE COPY

Pacific Chalet
23 Mountainside Drive
Prince Rupert, B.C.
V8J 1N3
1-800-693-1121   (604) 693-1233

| Aldo Morson | | No : 011 |

January 4,   19 91

Pay to the order of ___ LinenHouse Wholesalers ___ $ 750.00

--------- Seven hundred and fifty ---------   00 /100 Dollars

Bank of British Columbia
95 Bankers road
Prince Rupert, B.C.
V8R 3S4

A. Morson

⑈ 50948⑈⑈2 ⏤ 011⑈⑈

| Reference invoice #LW-321 | $750.00 | No : 011 |
| LinenHouse Wholesalers | | Jan. 4, 19 91 |

Pacific Chalet
23 Mountainside Drive
Prince Rupert, B.C.
V8J 1N3
1-800-693-1121 (604) 693-1233

NO. PC - 0004

GUEST STATEMENT

Nordic Alpine Ski Club
888 Ridge Road
Prince George, B.C.
V9E 2N2

CHECK IN ___January 1___

CHECK OUT ___January 5___

ROOM(S) ___8___

DATE	TRANSACTION	DAILY ROOM RATE		CHARGES	
01-05-91	Room Charges Room # 9, 10, 11, 12, 13, 14, 15, 16 4 nights Less: (Group discount (10%)	30	00	960 96	00 00
				864	00

Signature: *F. Karlson*		TERMS : Net 10 Days		GST	60	48
Clerk	Payment Method	Cash	Cheque	On Account	PST	69	12
G.T.				✓	BALANCE	993	60

FILE COPY

Pacific Chalet
23 Mountainside Drive
Prince Rupert, B.C.
V8J 1N3
1-800-693-1121 (604) 693-1233

Aldo Morson

No : 012

January 5,   19 __91__

Pay to the order of ___Blue Mountain Furniture Co.___ $ __1450.00__

----------One thousand four hundred and fifty ---------00 /100 Dollars

Bank of British Columbia
95 Bankers road
Prince Rupert, B.C.
V8R 3S4

A. Morson.

⑆ 50948 ⑆ 2 ⁃ 012 ⑆

Reference Invoice #BF-106 $1450.00   No : 012
Blue Mountain Furniture Co.   Jan. 5, 19 __91__

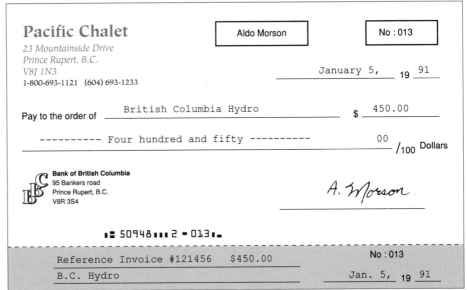

Pacific Chalet

23 Mountainside Drive
Prince Rupert, B.C.
V8J 1N3
1-800-693-1121 (604) 693-1233

Aldo Morson

No : 013

January 5, 19 91

Pay to the order of ___British Columbia Hydro___ $ __450.00__

---------- Four hundred and fifty ---------- 00 /100 Dollars

BC
B**B** Bank of British Columbia
95 Bankers road
Prince Rupert, B.C.
V8R 3S4

A. Morson

⑈ 50948⑈⑈2 ⑈013⑈

Reference Invoice #121456 $450.00

B.C. Hydro

No : 013

Jan. 5, 19 91

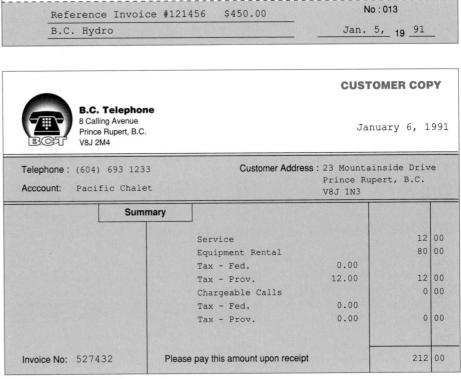

CUSTOMER COPY

B.C. Telephone
8 Calling Avenue
Prince Rupert, B.C.
V8J 2M4

January 6, 1991

Telephone : (604) 693 1233

Acccount: Pacific Chalet

Customer Address : 23 Mountainside Drive
Prince Rupert, B.C.
V8J 1N3

Summary			
Service		12	00
Equipment Rental		80	00
Tax - Fed.	0.00		
Tax - Prov.	12.00	12	00
Chargeable Calls		0	00
Tax - Fed.	0.00		
Tax - Prov.	0.00	0	00

Invoice No: 527432

Please pay this amount upon receipt

212 | 00

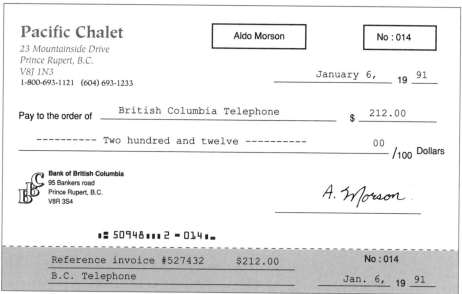

Pacific Chalet

23 Mountainside Drive
Prince Rupert, B.C.
V8J 1N3
1-800-693-1121   (604) 693-1233

| Aldo Morson | | No : 014 |

January 6, 19 91

Pay to the order of ___British Columbia Telephone___ $ __212.00__

---------- Two hundred and twelve ----------   00 /100 Dollars

Bank of British Columbia
95 Bankers road
Prince Rupert, B.C.
V8R 3S4

A. Morson

⑈ 50948 ⑈⑈ 2 ⑆ 014 ⑈⑈

Reference invoice #527432 $212.00   No : 014

B.C. Telephone   Jan. 6, 19 91

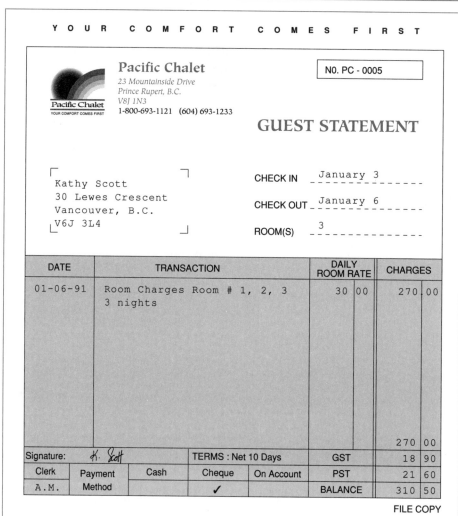

Y O U R   C O M F O R T   C O M E S   F I R S T

Pacific Chalet

23 Mountainside Drive
Prince Rupert, B.C.
V8J 1N3
1-800-693-1121   (604) 693-1233

NO. PC - 0005

GUEST STATEMENT

Kathy Scott
30 Lewes Crescent
Vancouver, B.C.
V6J 3L4

CHECK IN   January 3

CHECK OUT   January 6

ROOM(S)   3

DATE	TRANSACTION	DAILY ROOM RATE		CHARGES	
01-06-91	Room Charges Room # 1, 2, 3	30	00	270	00
	3 nights				
				270	00

Signature: *K. Scott*			TERMS : Net 10 Days	GST	18	90
Clerk	Payment Method	Cash	Cheque ✓	On Account	PST	21	60
A.M.				BALANCE	310	50

FILE COPY

Ski-Mountain Services
290 Ploughing Crescent
Prince Rupert, B.C.
V8I 7G1   692-6111

"Depend on us"

No:	SMS-69

Pacific Chalet
23 Mountainside Drive
Prince Rupert, B.C.
V8J 1N3

January 7, 19 91

Date	Description	Fee
01-07-91	Snow removal from private road and walkways	$150.00
	GST	10.50
Terms: Payment due upon receipt of invoice	TOTAL	$160.50

Pacific Chalet
23 Mountainside Drive
Prince Rupert, B.C.
V8J 1N3
1-800-693-1121 (604) 693-1233

NO. PC - 0006

GUEST STATEMENT

Julia Gordon
37 Clark Street
Kelowna, B.C.
V3T 1P6

CHECK IN   January 3

CHECK OUT   January 7

ROOM(S)   2

DATE	TRANSACTION	DAILY ROOM RATE		CHARGES	
01-07-91	Room Charges Room # 4, 5 4 nights	30	00	240	00
				240	00

Signature:	*J Gordon*		TERMS : Net 10 Days		GST	16	80
Clerk	Payment Method	Cash	Cheque	On Account	PST	19	20
T.M.		✓			BALANCE	276	00

FILE COPY

CUSTOMER COPY

FS-1163

FRESH CLEAN ROOM SERVICE

FreshKleen Room Services
150 Bleech Avenue
Prince Rupert, B.C. V8T 4B3
692-3348

"BETTER HOUSKEEPING"

STATEMENT

To:
Pacific Chalet
23 Mountainside Drive
Prince Rupert, B.C.
V8J 1N3

Billing Date ___01-07-91_____

Customer No ___1167_____

Previous Balance __0.00_____

Date	Description	Charges		Payments		Amount	
01-07-91	Room Cleaning Services	350	00			350	00
	Laundry Services	150	00			150	00
					GST	35	00
	Terms : net 10 days				**Subtotal**	535	00
	Overdue Accounts are subject to interest at 16.9% per year				**Pay this amount**	535	00

□

Quality Caterers
55 Gourmet Avenue
Prince Rupert, B.C.
V8M 3Z6

No : 55

January 8, 19 91

Pay to the order of ___Pacific Chalet_____ $ __220.00__

---------- Two hundred and twenty ---------- 85/100 Dollars

W TRUST Western Trust
453 Richmond Road
Prince Rupert, B.C.
V8j 3K1

Johnathan Kwan

J. Kwan

⑈1053 ⑈⑈087 ▪ 55⑈▪

Commission on Vending Machines   No : 55

Pacific Chalet $220.00   Jan. 8, 19 91

Invoice

Invoice No.

SW-121

SUPERIOR SIUPPLIES SINCE 1951

Sanitation Wholesalers
34 Refreshing Road,
Prince Rupert, B.C.
V7R 2G4   698-8026

To:

Pacific Chalet
23 Mountainside Drive
Prince Rupert, B.C.
V8J 1N3

Date: _January 8, 1991_____

Phone: _693-1233_____

Stock Code	Qty	Description	Price		Amount	
YX-37	6	Cases - Toilet Paper	15	00	90	00
ZY-43	3	Cases - Industrial cleaner/disinfectant	10	00	30	00
AC-12	2	Cases - Soap	15	00	30	00
					150	00

CUSTOMER COPY		Authorized by: *L. Sialtas*		Federal GST	10	50
Method of Payment	On account	C.O.D.	Credit Card	Provincial Sales Tax	9	00
		✓		**TOTAL**	169	50

Pacific Chalet

23 Mountainside Drive
Prince Rupert, B.C.
V8J 1N3
1-800-693-1121 (604) 693-1233

Aldo Morson

No : 015

January 8,   19 91

Pay to the order of   Sanitation Wholesalers $ 169.50

---------- One hundred and sixty-nine ----------   50 /100 Dollars

Bank of British Columbia
95 Bankers road
Prince Rupert, B.C.
V8R 3S4

A. Morson

ı⫶ 50948ııı2 ⫶015ı⫶

Reference Invoice #SW-121	$169.50	No : 015
Sanitation Wholesalerss		Jan. 8, 19 91

Pacific Chalet

Aldo Morson

No : 016

23 Mountainside Drive
Prince Rupert, B.C.
V8J 1N3
1-800-693-1121 (604) 693-1233

January 9, 19 91

Pay to the order of ___ Ski-Mountain Services ___ $ ___ 160.50 ___

---------- One hundred and sixty ---------- 50 /100 Dollars

Bank of British Columbia
95 Bankers road
Prince Rupert, B.C.
V8R 3S4

A. Morson

⑊ 50948⑊⑊2 ⑊ 016⑊

Reference Invoice #SMS-69	$160.50	No : 016
Ski-Mountain Services		Jan. 9, 19 91

Pacific Chalet

23 Mountainside Drive
Prince Rupert, B.C.
V8J 1N3
1-800-693-1121 (604) 693-1233

NO. PC - 0007

GUEST STATEMENT

Sven Munsen
331 Scandian Avenue,
Prince George, B.C.
V9E 1S8

CHECK IN January 3

CHECK OUT January 9

ROOM(S) 1

DATE	TRANSACTION	DAILY ROOM RATE		CHARGES	
01-09-91	Room Charges Room # 6 6 nights	30	00	180	00
				180	00

Signature: *S Munsen*		TERMS : Net 10 Days		GST	12	60
Clerk	Payment	Cash	Cheque	On Account	PST	14	40
G.T.	Method		✓		BALANCE	207	00

FILE COPY

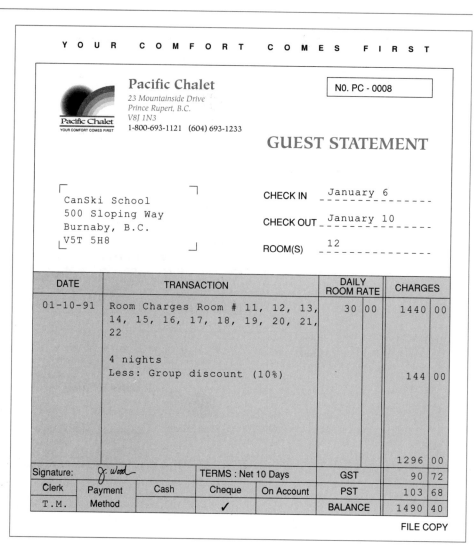

YOUR COMFORT COMES FIRST

Pacific Chalet
23 Mountainside Drive
Prince Rupert, B.C.
V8J 1N3
1-800-693-1121   (604) 693-1233

NO. PC - 0008

GUEST STATEMENT

CanSki School
500 Sloping Way
Burnaby, B.C.
V5T 5H8

CHECK IN   January 6

CHECK OUT   January 10

ROOM(S)   12

DATE	TRANSACTION	DAILY ROOM RATE		CHARGES	
01-10-91	Room Charges Room # 11, 12, 13, 14, 15, 16, 17, 18, 19, 20, 21, 22	30	00	1440	00
	4 nights Less: Group discount (10%)			144	00
				1296	00

Signature:	_J. Wood_		TERMS : Net 10 Days		GST	90	72
Clerk	Payment Method	Cash	Cheque	On Account	PST	103	68
T.M.			✓		BALANCE	1490	40

FILE COPY

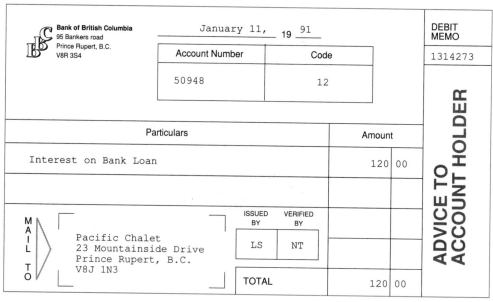

Bank of British Columbia
95 Bankers road
Prince Rupert, B.C.
V8R 3S4

January 11, 19 91

DEBIT MEMO

1314273

Account Number	Code
50948	12

Particulars	Amount	
Interest on Bank Loan	120	00

MAIL TO

Pacific Chalet
23 Mountainside Drive
Prince Rupert, B.C.
V8J 1N3

	ISSUED BY	VERIFIED BY	
	LS	NT	
	TOTAL	120	00

ADVICE TO ACCOUNT HOLDER

Pacific Chalet

23 Mountainside Drive
Prince Rupert, B.C.
V8J 1N3
1-800-693-1121 (604) 693-1233

NO. PC - 0009

GUEST STATEMENT

Harbour Ski Club
155 High Street
Vancouver, B.C.
V6Y 4R5

CHECK IN _____ January 8 _____

CHECK OUT _____ January 12 _____

ROOM(S) _____ 12 _____

DATE	TRANSACTION	DAILY ROOM RATE		CHARGES	
01-12-91	Room Charges Room # 1, 2, 3, 4, 5, 6, 7, 8, 9, 10, 23, 24	30	00	1440	00
	4 nights Less: (Group discount (10%)			144	00
				1296	00

Signature: *J. Martin*			TERMS : Net 10 Days	GST	90	72
Clerk	Payment Method	Cash	Cheque	On Account	PST	103	68
G.T.				✓	BALANCE	1490	40

FILE COPY

CanSki School

500 Sloping Way
Burnaby, B.C.
V5T 5H8

No : 016

January 13, 19 91

Pay to the order of _____ Pacific Chalet _____ $ 496.80

---------- Four hundred and ninety-six ---------- 80 /100 **Dollars**

Western Trust
100 Silver Street
Burnaby, B.C.
V6K 2P3

John Wood, Manager

J. Wood

⑈2153 ⑈ 1⫶016⑈

Reference Invoice #PC-0001 $496.80   No : 016

Pacific Chalet   Jan.13, 19 91

Pacific Chalet

23 Mountainside Drive
Prince Rupert, B.C.
V8J 1N3
1-800-693-1121 (604) 693-1233

NO. PC - 0010

GUEST STATEMENT

Nordic Alpine Ski Club
888 Ridge Road
Prince George, B.C.
V9E 2N2

CHECK IN __January 11__

CHECK OUT __January 14__

ROOM(S) __14__

DATE	TRANSACTION	DAILY ROOM RATE		CHARGES	
01-14-91	Room Charges Room # 11, 12, 13, 14, 15, 16, 17, 18, 19, 26, 27, 28, 29, 30	30	00	1260	00
	3 nights Less: (Group discount (10%)			126	00
				1134	00

Signature:	*F. Karlsson*		TERMS : Net 10 Days		GST	79	38
Clerk	Payment	Cash	Cheque	On Account	PST	90	72
G.T.	Method			✓	BALANCE	1304	10

FILE COPY

Pacific Chalet
23 Mountainside Drive
Prince Rupert, B.C.
V8J 1N3
1-800-693-1121   (604) 693-1233

N0. PC - 0011

GUEST STATEMENT

Julie Rooke
396 Castlefield Rd.
Burnaby, B.C.
V7N 1J4

CHECK IN ___January 9___

CHECK OUT ___January 14___

ROOM(S) ___3___

DATE	TRANSACTION	DAILY ROOM RATE		CHARGES	
01-14-91	Room Charges Room #31, 32, 33 5 nights	30	00	450	00
	Telephone Charges-long distance			15	00
				465	00

Signature:	*J. Rooke*		TERMS : Net 10 Days	GST	32	55
Clerk	Payment Method	Cash	Cheque	On Account	PST	37	20
T.M.		✓			BALANCE	534	75

FILE COPY

Harbour Ski Club
155 High Street
Vancouver, B.C.
V6Y 4R5

No : 023

January 14, 19 91

Pay to the order of ___Pacific Chalet___ $ ___838.35___

---------- Eight hundred and thirty-eight ---------- 35/100 Dollars

Vancouver Trust
392 Billing Avenue
Vancouver, B.C.
V4M 9A2

J Marten

⑈4117⑈023 ⑆87⑈

Reference Invoice #PC-0003 $838.35
Pacific Chalet

No : 023
Jan. 14, 19 91

Nordic Alpine Ski Club

888 Ridge Road
Prince George, B.C.
V9E 2N2

No : 035

January 14, 19 91

Pay to the order of _____ Pacific Chalet _____ $ 993.60

---------- Nine hundred and ninety-three ---------- 60 /100 Dollars

B Pacific Bank
53 Golding Blvd.
Prince George, B.C.
V9J 1E5

F. Karlson

⑆5025⑈035⑇87⑉

---

reference invoice #PC-0004 $993.60   No : 035

Pacific Chalet   Jan. 14, 19 91

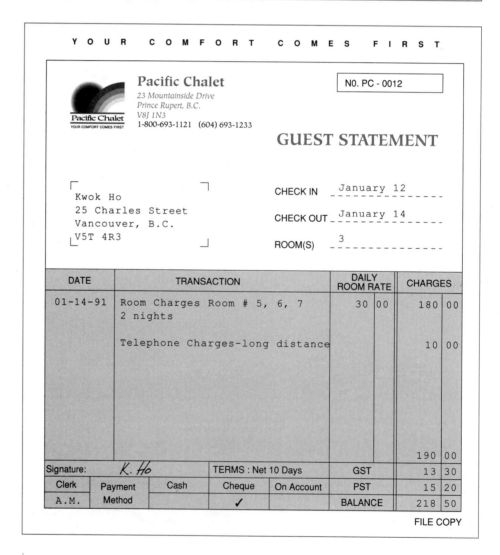

Pacific Chalet

23 Mountainside Drive
Prince Rupert, B.C.
V8J 1N3
1-800-693-1121 (604) 693-1233

NO. PC - 0012

GUEST STATEMENT

Kwok Ho
25 Charles Street
Vancouver, B.C.
V5T 4R3

CHECK IN   January 12

CHECK OUT   January 14

ROOM(S)   3

DATE	TRANSACTION	DAILY ROOM RATE		CHARGES	
01-14-91	Room Charges Room # 5, 6, 7 2 nights	30	00	180	00
	Telephone Charges-long distance			10	00
				190	00

Signature:	*K. Ho*		TERMS : Net 10 Days		GST	13	30
Clerk	Payment Method	Cash	Cheque	On Account	PST	15	20
A.M.			✓		BALANCE	218	50

FILE COPY

FreshKleen Room Services
150 Bleech Avenue
Prince Rupert, B.C. V8T 4B3
692-3348

"BETTER HOUSEKEEPING"

STATEMENT

To:

Pacific Chalet
23 Mountainside Drive
Prince Rupert, B.C.
V8J 1N3

Billing Date ___01-14-91___

Customer No ___1167___

Previous Balance ___535.00___

Date	Description	Charges		Payments		Amount	
01-14-91	Room Cleaning Services	350	00			350	00
	Laundry Services	150	00			150	00
					GST	35	00
	Terms : net 10 days				**Subtotal**	535	00
	Overdue Accounts are subject to interest at 16.9% per year				**Pay this amount**	1070	00

Pacific Chalet
*23 Mountainside Drive
Prince Rupert, B.C.
V8J 1N3*

Pacific Chalet
YOUR COMFORT COMES FIRST

EMPLOYEE TIME SHEET

Name ___Tanya Mishibata___ Employee Number ___1___

Social Insurance Number ___139 988 661___ Pay Period Ending ___01-14-91___

Day	Week 2 Jan.1–Jan.7		Week 2 Jan.8–Jan.14	
	Hours		Hours	
	Regular	Overtime	Regular	Overtime
Mon	8			
Tues			8	
Wed	8		8	
Thur			8	
Fri	8		8	
Sat	8		8	2
Sun	8	2		
TOTAL HOURS	40	2	40	2

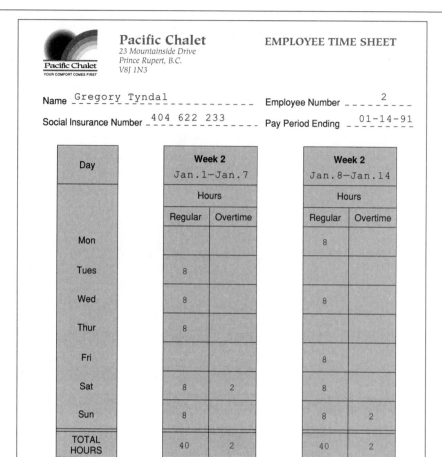

Pacific Chalet
23 Mountainside Drive
Prince Rupert, B.C.
V8J 1N3

YOUR COMFORT COMES FIRST

EMPLOYEE TIME SHEET

Name __Gregory Tyndal__   Employee Number __2__

Social Insurance Number __404 622 233__   Pay Period Ending __01-14-91__

Day	Week 2 Jan.1–Jan.7 Hours Regular	Overtime	Week 2 Jan.8–Jan.14 Hours Regular	Overtime
Mon			8	
Tues	8			
Wed	8		8	
Thur	8			
Fri			8	
Sat	8	2	8	
Sun	8		8	2
TOTAL HOURS	40	2	40	2

Pacific Chalet

23 Mountainside Drive
Prince Rupert, B.C.
V8J 1N3
1-800-693-1121 (604) 693-1233

Aldo Morson

No : 019

January 15, 19 __91__

Pay to the order of __DanceWear Unlimited__ $ __58.85__

---------- Fifty-eight ----------   85 /100 Dollars

B C B Bank of British Columbia
95 Bankers road
Prince Rupert, B.C.
V8R 3S4

A. Morson

⑈50948⑈2 - 019⑈

For personal use	$58.85	No : 019
DanceWear Unlimited		Jan. 15, 19 91

Case Study

The Soma brothers, Hira and Sapa, run an automobile service centre in Brandon, Manitoba. The service centre was owned and operated by their father until his retirement six months ago. When the brothers took over the business, they quickly realized that their father's manual accounting system, although accurate, was outdated for their present needs. They were particularly concerned about the adequacy of the record-keeping forms. Their father kept track mentally of a great deal of customer and vendor account information.

The full service centre sells oil, gasoline and automobile parts. Its regular inventory consists of about 500 different parts. Three full-time employees service and repair automobiles in the five bays, two of which are equipped with hydraulic lifts. Hira, an experienced licensed mechanic, assumes the responsibility of head mechanic. His brother Sapa performs most of the clerical and administrative duties, including ordering parts and maintaining all business and accounting records. In addition, three part-time student employees serve gas and perform general maintenance at the service centre.

1. Both Hira and Sapa want to adopt a more efficient, computerized accounting system. They have hired you as a consultant to advise them on the conversion and the implementation of a new system. Prepare a report for them including the following:

   (a) a description of the tasks involved in converting their accounting records and implementing the new system for the service centre;

   (b) a time frame for completing each of these tasks;

   (c) your rationale or decision-making criteria for each of the tasks and time estimates;

   (d) an estimate of the training required to familiarize Sapa with the new methods (Sapa has no previous experience with computers);

   (e) a description of the problems they can expect to encounter in using the new system and any limitations of the new system.

2. To prepare your answer, you could visit a local service centre to investigate its methods of operation. Use this information to guide your discussion of the conversion process for the Soma Brothers Service Centre. (Your instructor will tell you whether you should investigate an actual service centre as part of the case problem.)

3. You may wish to work in groups. If so, suggest a plan by which members within your group could be given specific duties in helping to assess the needs of the Soma brothers and to implement the computerized accounting system. Your group should decide the following questions in advance.

    (a) What information will you gather?

    (b) Who will gather information?

    (c) How much time will you allow for each stage?

    (d) How will you coordinate the work of the different team members?

    (e) How will you implement the conversion for the Soma Brothers?

    (f) How will the group members be accountable to one another?

PART THREE

Appendices

APPENDIX A
Input Forms

SYSTEM PREPARATION

COMPANY INFORMATION

Name:

Street:

City:

Province:

Postal Code:

Employer #:

GST Reg. #:

Fiscal Start: (mm-dd-yy)

Fiscal End: (mm-dd-yy)

Conversion: (mm-dd-yy)

PAYROLL NAMES

Income A: Deduction B:

Income B: Deduction C:

Deduction A: Project Title:

PRINTER NAMES

| | Margins | |
| | TOP | LEFT |

Reports:

Cheques:

Invoices:

Other Forms:

| | Number across page | Height | Width |

Labels:

SYSTEM PREPARATION

SETTINGS

Receivables

Aging: ⌴⌴ , ⌴⌴ , ⌴⌴

Interest Charges: ⌴⌴⌴⌴⌴⌴⌴⌴ %   Y ___ , N ___

GST Rate 1:   ⌴⌴⌴⌴⌴⌴⌴ %

GST Rate 2:   ⌴⌴⌴⌴⌴⌴⌴ %

PST Rate: ⌴⌴⌴⌴⌴⌴⌴ %

Apply PST to Freight: Y ___ , N ___

Apply PST to GST: Y ___ , N ___

Payables

Aging: ⌴⌴ , ⌴⌴ , ⌴⌴

Payroll

Auto Payroll Deduction : Y ___ , N ___

Deduction A after Tax   : Y ___ , N ___

Deduction B after Tax   : Y ___ , N ___

Deduction C after Tax   : Y ___ , N ___

UI Factor   : ⌴⌴⌴⌴⌴⌴⌴

EHT Factor   : ⌴⌴⌴⌴⌴⌴⌴

Payroll WCB

Province : ⌴⌴⌴⌴⌴⌴⌴⌴⌴⌴⌴⌴⌴⌴⌴

WCB Maximum Assessable Earnings: ⌴⌴⌴⌴⌴⌴⌴⌴⌴⌴

Forms

Next invoice number : ⌊_⌊_⌊_⌊_⌊_⌊_⌊_⌋

Next payables cheque number : ⌊_⌊_⌊_⌊_⌊_⌊_⌊_⌋

Next payroll cheque number : ⌊_⌊_⌊_⌊_⌊_⌊_⌊_⌋

Confirm printing   for invoices : Y __ , N __

                     for cheques : Y __ , N __

Print company address on invoices : Y __ , N __

                     on statements : Y __ , N __

                     on cheques : Y __ , N __

Default invoice comment : ⌊_⌋

⌊_⌋

Inventory

Markup _____   Margin _____   (Choose one only)

Distributions

Distribute General Journal by: Distribute Payroll Journal by:

(Choose one only)   (Choose one only)

         Amount : _____   Amount : _____

         Percent : _____   Percent : _____

                                             Hours   : _____

Warn if distribution is not complete: Y __ , N __

Report Font

Display Font : ⌊_⌊_⌊_⌊_⌊_⌊_⌊_⌊_⌊_⌊_⌊_⌊_⌊_⌊_⌊_⌊_⌋   Size : ⌊_⌊_⌊_⌋

ORGANIZATION: BALANCE SHEET ACCOUNTS

ASSETS – [section heading]

Account Description	Amount	Amount
	Left	Right

Account Description	Amount	Amount
	Left	Right

Account Description	Amount	Amount
	Left	Right

TOTAL ASSETS – [section total]

LIABILITIES – [section heading]

Account Description	Amount	Amount
	Left	Right

Account Description	Amount	Amount
	Left	Right

TOTAL LIABILITIES – [section total]

EQUITY – [section heading]

Account Description	Amount	Amount
	Left	Right

TOTAL EQUITY – [section total]
LIABILITIES AND EQUITY

ORGANIZATION: INCOME STATEMENT ACCOUNTS

REVENUE – [section heading]

Account Description

Amount | Amount

Left | Right

TOTAL REVENUE – [section total]

EXPENSE – [section heading]

Account Description

Amount | Amount

Left | Right

TOTAL EXPENSE – [section total]
INCOME

INTEGRATION PLUS ACCOUNTS - MAINTENANCE

SECTION:
A = ASSETS
L = LIABILITIES
E = EQUITY
R = REVENUE
X = EXPENSE

TYPE:
H = Heading
R = Right
L = Left
S = Subtotal
X = Current Earnings
T - Total

MODULE:
GL = GENERAL
AP = PAYABLE
AR = RECEIVABLE
PR = PAYROLL
IN = INVENTORY

CODE:
R = Remove
M = Modify
* = no change

Account Title [Initial]	SECTION	TYPE	Module [used by]	Initial Account Number	CODE	Account Title [New]	TYPE	New Account Number
CURRENT ASSETS	A	H	T	1 0 0 0				
Bank A - Payable	A	L	A P	1 0 6 0				
Bank B - Receivable	A	L	A R	1 0 8 0				
Bank C - Payroll	A	L	P R	1 1 0 0				
Cash - Total	A	S	T	1 1 2 0				
Accounts Receivable	A	R	A R	1 2 0 0				
Advances Receivable	A	R	A R	1 2 4 0				
Inventory	A	R	T	1 2 6 0				
TOTAL CURRENT ASSETS	A	T	T	1 3 9 0				
CURRENT LIABILITIES	L	H	T	2 0 0 0				
Accounts Payable	L	R	A P	2 2 0 0				
Vacation Payable	L	R	P R	2 3 0 0				
UI Payable	L	L	P R	2 3 1 0				
CPP Payable	L	L	P R	2 3 2 0				
Income Tax Payable	L	L	P R	2 3 3 0				
Receiver General Payable	L	S	T	2 3 4 0				

INTEGRATION PLUS ACCOUNTS - MAINTENANCE

SECTION:
A = ASSETS
L = LIABILITIES
E = EQUITY
R = REVENUE
X = EXPENSE

TYPE:
H = Heading
R = Right
L = Left
S = Subtotal
X = Current Earnings
T - Total

MODULE:
GL = GENERAL
AP = PAYABLE
AR = RECEIVABLE
PR = PAYROLL
IN = INVENTORY

CODE:
R = Remove
M = Modify
* = no change

Account Title [Initial]	SECTION	TYPE	Module [used by]	Initial Account Number	Account Title [New]	CODE	TYPE	New Account Number
QPP Payble	L	L	P R	2 3 5 0				
Que. Income Tax Payable	L	L	P R	2 3 6 0				
QHIP Payable	L	L	P R	2 3 7 0				
Que. Minister of Finance	L	S	—	2 3 8 0				
EHT Payable	L	R	P R	2 3 9 0				
Deduction A Payable	L	R	P R	2 4 0 0				
Deduction B Payable	L	R	P R	2 4 2 0				
Deduction C Payable	L	R	P R	2 4 4 0				
WCB Payable	L	R	P R	2 4 6 0				
PST Payable	L	R	A R	2 6 4 0				
GST Charged on Sales	L	L	A R	2 6 5 0				
GST Paid on Purchases	L	L	A P	2 6 7 0				
GST Payroll Deductions	L	L	—	2 6 9 0				
GST Adjustments	L	L	—	2 7 1 0				
ITC Adjustments	L	L	—	2 7 3 0				
GST Owing (Refund)	L	S	—	2 7 5 0				
TOTAL CURRENT LIABILITIES	L	T	—	2 8 0 0				
EARNINGS	E	H	—	3 0 0 0				
Retained Earnings	E	R	—	3 5 6 0				
Current Earnings	E	X	—	3 6 0 0				
TOTAL EARNINGS	E	T	—	3 6 9 0				

INTEGRATION PLUS ACCOUNTS - MAINTENANCE

Account Title [Initial]	SECTION	TYPE	Module [used by]	Initial Account Number	CODE	Account Title [New]	TYPE	New Account Number
REVENUE	R	H	T	4 0 0 0				
General Revenue	R	R	T	4 0 2 0				
Freight Revenue	R	R	A R	4 2 0 0				
TOTAL REVENUE	R	T	T	4 3 9 0				
ADMINISTRATION	X	H	T	5 0 0 0				
General Expense	X	R	T	5 0 2 0				
Adjustment Write-off	X	R	I N	5 0 3 0				
Transfer Costs	X	R	I N	5 0 4 0				
Freight Expense	X	R	A P	5 2 0 0				
Wages	X	R	P R	5 3 0 0				
UI Expense	X	R	P R	5 3 1 0				
CPP Expense	X	R	P R	5 3 2 0				
WCB Expense	X	R	P R	5 3 3 0				
QPP Expense	X	R	P R	5 3 4 0				
QHIP Expense	X	R	P R	5 3 5 0				
EHT Expense	X	R	P R	5 3 6 0				
TOTAL ADMINSTRATION	X	T		5 3 9 0				

SECTION:
A = ASSETS
L = LIABILITIES
E = EQUITY
R = REVENUE
X = EXPENSE

TYPE:
H = Heading
R = Right
L = Left
S = Subtotal
X = Current Earnings
T - Total

MODULE:
GL = GENERAL
AP = PAYABLE
AR = RECEIVABLE
PR = PAYROLL
IN = INVENTORY

CODE:
R = Remove
M = Modify
* = no change

CHART OF ACCOUNTS MAINTENANCE

Code: M = Modify   Type: H = Heading   S = Subtotal   Suppress: Y = Yes
       C = Create   R = Right   X = Current Earnings   N = No
       R = Remove   L = Left   T = Total

Code	Account Title (Maximum 26 Characters)	Account No.	Type	Sup-press

VENDOR MAINTENANCE

Code

Code : **M = Modify**   **C = Create**   **R = Remove**

Vendor Name

Contact

Street Address

City

Province

Postal Code

Phone Number

| Clear Invoices when paid |

Fax Number

| Include in GST Report |

Yes/No

Code

Code : **M = Modify**   **C = Create**   **R = Remove**

Vendor Name

Contact

Street Address

City

Province

Postal Code

Phone Number

| Clear Invoices when paid |

Fax Number

| Include in GST Report |

Yes/No

VENDOR TRANSACTIONS (HISTORICAL)

PAYABLES LEDGER
Form VEN-2
Page ___ of ___

Code: 1 = Purchase   2 = Payment

Code	Vendor	Invoice	Date (mm-dd-yy)	Amount	Cheque

CUSTOMER MAINTENANCE

Code		**Code : M = Modify C = Create R = Remove**

Code	
Customer Name	
Contact	
Street Address	
City	
Province	
Postal Code	
Phone Number	
Fax Number	
Credit Limit	

Yes/No

Clear Invoices when paid ☐

Include in GST Report ☐

Print Statement for Customer ☐

Code : M = Modify   C = Create   R = Remove

Code	
Customer Name	
Contact	
Street Address	
City	
Province	
Postal Code	
Phone Number	
Fax Number	
Credit Limit	

Yes/No

Clear Invoices when paid ☐

Include in GST Report ☐

Print Statement for Customer ☐

CUSTOMER TRANSACTIONS (HISTORICAL)

RECEIVABLES LEDGER
Form CUS-2
Page ___ of ___

Code: 1 = Sale   2 = Receipt

Code	Customer	Invoice	Date (mm-dd-yy)	Amount	Cheque

EMPLOYEE MAINTENANCE

Code

Code : **M = Modify   C = Create   R = Remove**

Employee Name

Street Address

City

Province

Postal Code

Phone Number

Soc. Ins. Number

Birth Date   (mm-dd-yy)

Tax Table

Federal Claim   dollar amount [TDI – TPD1]

Pay Periods per Year

WCB Rate   (%) WCB = Workers' Compensation Board

UI Eligibility   Y = Yes   N = No

UI Premium Factor   (normally 1.4)

Vacation Pay Rate   (%)

Retain Vacation Pay   Y = Yes   N = No

Regular Wage Rate   dollars / hour

Overtime Wage Rate   dollars / hour

Salary per Period   dollars

Hire Date   (mm-dd-yy)

EMPLOYEE RECORDS (HISTORICAL)

PAYROLL LEDGER
Form EMP-2
Page ___ of ___

Employee Number			
Regular Wages			
Overtime Wages			
Salary			
Commissions			
Taxable Benefits			
Vacation Pay Paid Out			
CPP Contributions			
QPP Contributions			
UI Ins. Earnings			
UI Premiums			
Income Tax			
Quebec Income Tax			
Deduction A			
Deduction B			
Deduction C			
Net Earnings			
Advances Paid			
Vacation Pay Owed			

INVENTORY MAINTENANCE

Code: **M = Modify   C = Create   R = Remove**

Code	Item No. Description	Asset Acct.	Rev. Acct.	Exp. Acct.	Unit of Sale	Price/ Unit (Sell)	Min. Stk. Lev.	Qty on hand	Total Value (Cost)

A P P E N D I X   B
Integration with Other Software

There may be times when you want to work with the financial data of your company in ways that cannot be accomodated by your accounting software. ACCPAC Simply Accounting allows both primary and secondary reports that are displayed to be exported to other kinds of software. Exporting is the ability to transfer information from one software application to another. These exported reports may then be used with a spreadsheet or word processing application.

ACCPAC Simply Accounting allows files to be exported to a drive and path specified. File formats available for export purposes include Text files for word processsor applications, Lotus version workfiles, Lotus Symphony files, Microsoft Excel files, SuperCalc files and Comma separated files. Exporting report files to other software applications will allow the user to manipulate and interpret these reports for management decision making. Integration is an important step in making the accounting process meaningful.

Integrated files can be used by businesses in a number of different ways. These include preparing invoices, creating a mailing list of customers or vendors, preparing comparative statements, preparing budgets, sales forecasting, determining implications of new taxes and tax increases. Ratio analysis of financial statements as a decision support tool is also possible. Reports gathered from ACCPAC Simply Accounting and spreadsheet applications can be brought together in a word processing or desktop publishing application to prepare comprehensive final documents.

Depending on the applications that you are using, there may be some loss of formatting when you transfer files from one application to another. You may need to reformat the document in the new application. Please refer to the manuals for the software you are using for complete information about transferring files.

The examples below were prepared using Lotus 1-2-3 and Wordperfect 5.0, with reports exported from the Melody Music Centre files in ACCPAC Simply Accounting.

In Example 1, the ending balance sheet has been exported to a Lotus 1-2-3 file. Using the calculating abilities of Lotus, several key ratios were calculated.

Example 1

MELODY MUSIC CENTRE
BALANCE SHEET AS AT 01-31-91

ASSETS

CURRENT ASSETS			
Cash in Bank		19657.43	KEY RATIOS
Accounts Receivable		47153.00	
Musical Parts Inventory		2085.00	Current Ratio:
Software Library		500.00	
Supplies		500.00	Current Assets
TOTAL CURRENT ASSETS		69895.43	Current Liabilities
INVENTORY ASSETS			3.25
Brass		4225.00	
Musical Sheets		775.00	
Percussion		31225.00	Quick Ratio:
Strings		19700.00	
Woodwind		5650.00	Current Assets-Inventory
TOTAL INVENTORY ASSETS		61575.00	Current Liabilities
PLANT & EQUIPMENT			1.73
Computers & Peripherals		4500.00	
Delivery Truck		10000.00	
Equipment		7000.00	Debt Ratio:
Furniture & Fixtures		2890.00	
TOTAL PLANT & EQUIPMENT		24390.00	Total Liabilities
			Total Assets
TOTAL ASSETS		**155860.43**	0.26

LIABILITIES

CURRENT LIABILITIES		
Bank Loan		19300.00
Accounts Payable		9945.65
Vacation Payable		577.26
UI Payable	496.80	
CPP Payable	504.16	
Income Tax Payable	2998.65	
Receiver General Payable		3999.61
EHT Payable		117.02
CSB-Plan Payable		150.00
WCB Payable		117.14
GST Charged on Sales	3926.30	
GST Paid on Purchases -	1854.65	
GST Owing (Refund)		2071.65
PST Payable		4203.20
TOTAL CURRENT LIABILITIES		40481.53
TOTAL LIABILITIES		**40481.53**

EQUITY

OWNER'S EQUITY

L. Segovia, Capital	104740.00	
L. Segovia, Drawings	- 1435.80	
Capital before Income		103304.20
Net Income		12074.70
UPDATED CAPITAL		115378.90

TOTAL EQUITY 115378.90

LIABILITIES AND EQUITY 155860.43

In Example 2, we show the relative amounts of assets and cost of goods sold for each inventory asset group in pie chart form.

Example 2

Share of Inventory Assets for each Asset Group

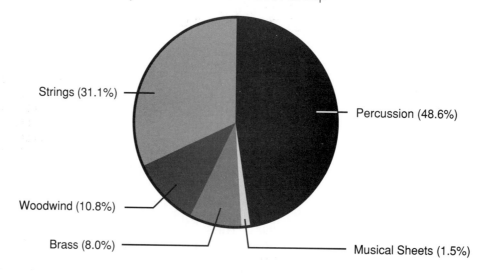

Share of Cost of Goods Sold for each Inventory Group

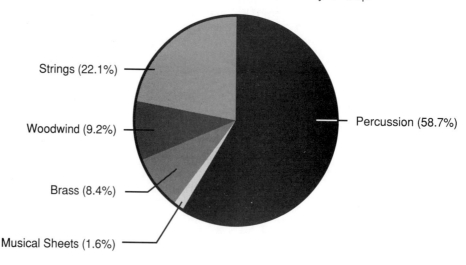

In Example 3, the Income Statement has been exported to a text file. Using Wordperfect 5.0, a word processing software application, it has been included as part of a memo to the owner.

Example 3

MEMO TO: L. Segovia
FROM: Valerie Chaikovsky
DATE: February 1, 1991

As requested, here is the copy of the Income Statement for January.

Melody Music Centre Income Statement Jan 1,1991 TO Jan 31,1991

REVENUE
GENERAL REVENUE

Revenue from Sales		48180.00
Revenue from Services		5360.00
Revenue from Instruction		3550.00
TOTAL GENERAL REVENUE		57090.00

TOTAL REVENUE   **57090.00**

EXPENSE
COST OF GOODS SOLD

Brass	2250.00	
Musical Sheets	425.00	
Percussion	15675.00	
Strings	5900.00	
Woodwind	2450.00	
Freight Expense	190.00	
TOTAL COST OF GOODS SOLD		26890.00

OPERATING EXPENSES

Advertising Expense	400.00	
Bank Charges	36.50	
Delivery Expense	1180.00	
Hydro Expense	160.00	
Legal Expense	300.00	
Musical Parts Used	415.00	
Rent Expense	2200.00	
Telephone Expense	80.00	
Truck Expense	60.00	
TOTAL OPERATING EXPENSES		4831.50

PAYROLL EXPENSES

Wages	12517.76	
UI Expense	289.80	
CPP Expense	252.08	
WCB Expense	117.14	
EHT Expense	117.02	
TOTAL PAYROLL EXPENSES		13293.80

TOTAL EXPENSE   **45015.30**

NET INCOME   **12074.70**

A P P E N D I X   C
Correcting Errors after Posting

Obviously, you should try to detect errors before posting. Reviewing the journal entry should become routine practice. To help you not make mistakes, the software has built in a number of safeguards which make errors less likely to occur. For example, outstanding invoices cannot be overpaid; inventory cannot be oversold, and employee wages are calculated automatically.

Furthermore, names of accounts, customers, vendors, employees, inventory items and jobcosting projects, departments and divisions appear in full, so that you can check your journal information easily.

Some errors also originate from outside sources. For example, purchase items may be incorrectly priced by the vendor.

For audit purposes, a memo should be prepared explaining the error and the correction procedure. There are alternatives ways of correcting some errors, and a complete reversing entry may not always be necessary. Under all circumstances, however, Generally Accepted Accounting Principles should be followed.

The errors below are listed according to the journal in which the transactions were entered. The list is not exhaustive, but it does deal with the more common kinds of mistakes.

JOURNAL	ERROR	CORRECTION
General	**• account**	Complete a reversing entry by debiting the accounts that were originally credited and by crediting the accounts that were originally debited. Add an appropriate comment and source document number. Post the transaction.
		Enter the correct transaction. Post the correct transaction.
Purchase Non-Inventory	**• vendor** **• account**	Complete a reversing entry, using a new invoice number, by entering negative amounts to replace positive amounts that were entered originally, and positive amounts to replace the original negative amounts. Post the transaction.
		Enter the correct transaction. Post the correct transaction.

	• amount	Complete an additional purchase invoice, using a new invoice number, for the amount of the difference, positive or negative. Enter the appropriate account number. Post the transaction.
	• gst	Complete an additional purchase invoice, using a new invoice number, for the amount of the difference, positive or negative. Enter the tax difference in the amount field and the account number for GST Paid on Purchases in the account field. Post the transaction.
Purchase Inventory	• **vendor** • **item** • **account** • **amount**	Complete a reversing entry, using a new invoice number, by entering a negative quantity to replace a previously entered positive quantity. Be sure that the amount appears as a negative amount. Post the transaction. Enter the correct transaction. Post the correct transaction. Errors for returns should be handled in the opposite way, by entering positive quantities to replace negative quantities and positive amounts for negative amounts. Post the transaction. Enter the correct transaction. Post the correct transaction.
	• **quantity**	Complete an additional purchase invoice, using a new invoice number, for the difference in quantity, either positive or negative. Post the transaction.
	• **freight** • **gst**	Complete an additional non-inventory purchase invoice for the amount of the difference in freight charges or Goods and Services Tax paid. Enter the appropriate account number. Post the transaction.
Payment	• **amount**	Make an additional payment for the amount of the underpayment. You cannot overpay an invoice. Post the transaction.
Sale Non-Inventory	• **customer** • **account**	Complete a reversing entry, using a new invoice number, by entering negative amounts to replace the positive amounts that were entered originally or by entering positive amounts to replace the original negative amounts. Post the transaction. Enter the correct transaction. Post the correct transaction.
	• **amount**	Complete an additional sales invoice, using a new invoice number, for the amount of the difference, positive or negative. Post the transaction.
	• **pst**	Complete an additional sales invoice, using a new invoice number for the amount of the sales tax, or the difference, positive or negative. Enter the sales tax in the amount field and the PST Payable account number in the account field. Post the transaction.
	• **gst**	Complete an additional sales invoice, using a new invoice number for the amount of the GST, or the difference, positive or negative. Enter the tax in the amount field and the GST Charged on Services account number in the account field. Post the transaction.
Sale Inventory	• **customer** • **account** • **item**	Complete a reversing entry, using a new invoice number, by entering negative quantities to replace previously entered positive quantities, or by entering positive quantities to replace negative quantities. Re-enter the unit price that was used in the incorrect entry. Enter appropriate tax codes. Post the transaction. Enter the correct transaction. Post the correct transaction.
	• **amount** • **unit price**	Complete an additional non-inventory sales invoice, using a new invoice number, for the amount of the difference. Be sure that the GST Charged on Sales and PST Payable amounts are correct and that the correct revenue account number is entered. Post the transaction.

	• pst	Complete an additional non-inventory sales invoice for the amount of the sales tax, or the difference, positive or negative. Enter the sales tax in the amount field and the PST Payable account number in the account field. Post the transaction.
	• gst	Complete an additional non-inventory sales invoice for the amount of the Goods and Services Tax, or the difference, positive or negative. Enter the tax in the amount field and the GST Charged on Sales account number in the account field. Post the transaction.
Receipt	• **amount**	Record an additional receipt for the amount of the difference. Overpayments will not be accepted by the software. Post the transaction.
Payroll	• **amount** • **underpayment**	Prepare an additional payroll cheque for the amount of the underpayment. Add a new cheque number. Post the transaction.
	• **employee** • **amount** • **overpayments** • **deductions**	Refer to your Payroll Registers in order to verify the amounts in the different payroll fields. You can also repeat the payroll entry as before - that is, incorrectly - and print the screen (press the Print Screen key on your keyboard) to use as a reference but DO NOT POST. Close the Payroll Journal and confirm that you want to discard the transaction.
		Turn off the Automatic payroll deductions option. Choose Settings from the pull-down menu under Setup. Click on Payroll to see the Automatic payroll deductions option. Click on the box for this option to turn automatic deductions off. Click on OK to save the setting. In the Payroll Journal, enter the employee name, cheque number and the date. Enter the amounts from your payroll registers or screen printout in the appropriate fields carefully, using negative amounts to replace positive amounts. Be sure all of the amounts correspond to your printout, with a change in sign. Review the journal entry. Make corrections if necessary. The review of the transaction should show the reverse of the original incorrect transaction that was posted. Post the transaction. Turn the Automatic payroll deductions option back on. Save the setting.
		Enter the correct transaction in the Payroll Journal. Post the correct transaction.
Inventory-Adjustment	• **item** • **account** • **amount**	Complete a reversing entry by entering negative quantities to replace previously positive quantities, or by entering positive quantities to replace negative quantities. Re-enter the amount and account that were used in the incorrect entry. Add an appropriate comment and a new source document number. Post the transaction.
		Enter the correct transaction. Post the correct transaction.
	• **quantity**	Complete an additional adjustment entry for the difference in quantity, either positive or negative. Add an appropriate comment and a new source document number. Post the transaction.
** Project Distribution**		Complete a reversing entry as described above for the relevant journal, including the distribution. Add an appropriate comment and new source document number if necessary. Post the transaction.
		Enter the transaction and distribution correctly. Post the correct transaction.

INDEX